The Expositor's Bible
The Epistles Of St. Peter

by

J. Rawson Lumby

The Expositor's Bible
The Epistles Of St. Peter
by J. Rawson Lumby

Copyright © 2024

All Rights reserved.

ISBN: 978-93-61154-96-6

Published by

DOUBLE 9 BOOKS
2/13-B, Ansari Road
Daryaganj, New Delhi – 110002
info@double9books.com
www.double9books.com
Tel. 011-40042856

This book is under public domain

ABOUT THE AUTHOR

Joseph Rawson Lumby was an English priest, scholar, author, and divine who was appointed Norrisian Professor of Divinity in 1879 and Lady Margaret's Professor of Divinity in 1892. He was the son of John Lumby of Stanningley, near Leeds, and was born on July 18, 1831. On August 2, 1841, he was admitted to Leeds Grammar School. In March 1848, he departed to become the master of a school in Meanwood, but was pushed to attend university. In October 1854, he enrolled at Magdalene College in Cambridge, and the following year was awarded a Milner Close scholarship. Lumby was appointed Dennis Fellow of his institution and began teaching students within a few months of graduating. In 1860, he received the Crosse scholarship and was ordained deacon and priest in the Diocese of Ely. He was assigned to the Magdalene chaplaincy and the Girton curacy for clerical duties. In 1861, he obtained the Tyrwhitt Hebrew scholarship and was appointed classical lecturer at Queens' College. He joined the Old Testament Revision Company in 1873 and worked on the Apocrypha revision as well (he only lived to see the revised edition published).

CONTENTS

PREFACE

The two letters which bear the name of St. Peter have from the earliest times met with very different degrees of acceptance. The genuineness of the First Epistle is attested by the unanimous voice of primitive Christendom. As it is addressed to Christians dwelling in different parts of Asia Minor, it is natural to look for a knowledge of it in those countries. And nowhere is it earlier noticed. Polycarp, Bishop of Smyrna, a contemporary of the last surviving Apostle, and whose martyrdom took place about the middle of the second century, has repeated quotations from this Epistle. It was known also to Papias († 163), Bishop of Hierapolis, and to Melito (170), Bishop of Sardis. That it was known to the Greeks is seen from the Epistle to Diognetus, which for a long time was attributed to Justin Martyr († 165), while the "Shepherd" of Hermas, written at Rome, testifies that it was known there also at about the same date. The inclusion of it in the Peschito-Syriac Version bears witness to its early circulation in the Eastern Church, as also does its quotation in the writings of Theophilus of Antioch (178). Heretics, no less than the faithful, regarded it as a portion of authoritative Christian literature. Basilides in Alexandria and the Marcosians and Theodotus in Syria all knew of and cited this Epistle. The Latin Church of Africa accepted it, as we can see from a few quotations in Tertullian († 218) and a greater number in the writings of Cyprian († 258). In the Alexandrian Church it is often quoted by both Clement († 218) and Origen († 254); while for Gaul we have the testimony of the Church of Vienne in the touching letter sent by the Christians there to their "brethren in Asia and Phrygia" (177), and of Irenæus, who was Bishop of Lyons shortly afterwards, and who, coming from Asia to fill that see, is a witness both for the East and the West. From the Christian Church of the early centuries it is hardly possible to produce stronger attestation.

But although so abundantly vouched for in ancient days, the Epistle has not been exempt from the assaults of modern criticism. Primitive Christendom regarded St. Peter, St. John, and St. Paul as heralds of one and the same Gospel, founded on the same promises, strengthened by the same faith. They were at one in what they taught and what they opposed. But some modern thinkers, taking as a thesis that the Gospel as set forth by the Apostle of the circumcision differed widely from the doctrines of St. Paul, have proceeded to make an eclectic Christian literature, out of which the First Epistle of St. Peter has been rejected. Its language is too much in harmony with accepted writings of St. Paul. It can only have been compiled by some later hand to promote the opinion that there was no discord between the teachings of the first Christian preachers. Moreover, it is inconceivable, they consider, that a letter should be addressed by St. Peter to the Christians in those very lands where the missionary labours of St. Paul had been specially exerted, where the converts were in a peculiar sense his "little children."

Now in this first letter of St. Peter there is unquestionably much that corresponds in tone with the Epistle to the Romans, especially with the twelfth and thirteenth chapters. In both letters Christians are exhorted to offer their bodies as spiritual sacrifices, to shun conformity with the world, to study to be sober in mind, and to use duly all the gifts which they possess; the same unfeigned love of the brethren is inculcated, the same patience under suffering. Christians are not to retaliate, but to overcome evil with good; they are to be in subjection to all lawful authority, and this for conscience' sake, to avoid all excesses, rioting, drunkenness, chambering, and wantonness, and to be ever looking forward to the coming of the Lord.

In like manner there will be found numerous passages in St. Paul's Epistle to the Ephesians which in spirit and tone greatly resemble the words of St. Peter. At the very outset St. Paul addresses his converts as "chosen of God in Christ before the foundation of the world, that they should be holy and without blemish before Him in love"; tells them that they were "foreordained unto adoption as sons through Jesus Christ, according to the good pleasure of His will, to the praise and glory of His grace, which He freely bestowed on them in the Beloved" (Eph. i. 3-6). Similarly St. Peter writes to "the elect ... according to the foreknowledge of God the Father, in sanctification of the Spirit, unto obedience and sprinkling of the blood of Jesus Christ," and presently he adds that "according to God's great mercy they were begotten again by the resurrection of Jesus Christ from the dead" (i. 1-3). In both epistles there is the same teaching, the same election in love, the same sonship, the same progress in holiness, the same free gift through Jesus Christ. But in neither is there a word that can be taken to militate against independent authorship. And the same remark applies to all the resemblances which exist between the two epistles in the exhortations to servants, wives, and husbands; in the commendations of humility, pity, courtesy; in the entreaties to the believers to gird up the loins of the mind and to lay aside all malice and hatred; in those passages which speak of them as strangers and pilgrims, as called from darkness to light, as being a spiritual house, built upon Christ as the head corner-stone. Of all these exhortations undoubted parallels are to be found; but they are only evidence of the common character which would pervade all the teaching of the apostolic missionaries where the people addressed were the same, the times not far apart, and the dangers and temptations known alike to all the writers. Hence parallels to St. Peter may be found in St. James too, but they are no proof that the one Apostle (or, as some critics say, some one writing under his name) copied from the other.

Nor is it easy to see reason why St. Peter might not be expected to write a letter to the congregations formed first by St. Paul. No Evangelist or Apostle could publish the message of the Gospel—that is, the life and works—of Christ without telling of His chosen followers; and amongst them, if our Gospels be a true picture, St. Peter must ever have filled a prominent place. The Churches in Asia assuredly had heard much of him, and in a time of persecution or impending trial nothing could be more fit than that the Apostle who had been most prominent amid Christ's companions should write from Babylon or from Rome, it may be, where the signs of the times would proclaim most clearly the sufferings for which the Christian inhabitants of the provinces should be prepared, to encourage the believers in Asia to steadfastness and to remind them that the same afflictions were being accomplished in their brethren that were elsewhere in the world.

This was likely enough even had St. Peter never visited the districts to which his letter was addressed. But we seem to find traces of him in Corinth (1 Cor. ix. 5; cf. also xv. 5), and he certainly was not unknown by name to the Christians of that city. And if so, why need we question his journeying through Asia Minor? And he was aware of the labours of his fellow-apostle. From personal intercourse and discussion, especially in connexion with the council at Jerusalem, he would be sure that they were of one mind. It may be that he had learnt something of St. Paul's letters to the Churches. Under such circumstances it is not foreign to St. Peter's character, nay rather quite in harmony with it, that he should fulfil the Lord's command to "strengthen the brethren"; that he should send them an earnest assurance that, spite of sufferings and trials, this was the true grace of God, in which they should rejoice to stand.

But there are internal tokens in the Epistle which seem more powerful evidence of its genuineness than anything else. The writer calls himself "Peter, an Apostle of Jesus Christ"; and he declares his personality by touches and allusions which a forger would never have fabricated. Thus he says, "All of you *gird yourselves* with humility, to serve one another" (v. 5). The verb which he employs here indicates a sort of girding about with some towel or apron, which a slave put on for doing some menial service. It is almost impossible that the writer had not in his thoughts the act of Christ when He gave His great lesson of humility: "If I have washed your feet, ye ought also to wash one another's feet."

So, too, the Master's exhortation, "Feed My sheep," "Feed My lambs," comes to mind as we read, "Tend the flock of God which is among you, exercising the oversight, not of constraint, but willingly" (v. 2). And St. Peter's own words spoken in the house of Cornelius are reproduced when the Father is declared to be One "who, without respect of persons, judgeth according to each man's work" (i. 17).

But it is in the allusions to Christ's passion and resurrection, those events which marked the deep fall and the rising again of St. Peter, that the personality of the Apostle becomes most manifest. He has been himself "a witness of the sufferings of Christ" (v. 1). He can speak as an eye-witness of the Lord's death in the flesh (iii. 18; iv. 1) and His quickening in the spirit; can exhort men to courage because they are partakers of the sufferings of Christ (iv. 13). Who does not feel that the writer of the words, "Let them also that suffer according to the will of God commit their souls in well-doing unto a faithful Creator" (iv. 19), is thinking of the scene on the cross, of the Saviour's finished work, of the dying cry, "Father, into Thy hands I commend My spirit"?

Perhaps the most striking instance of this peculiarity, this tendency to dwell on the events of the Passion, is found in ii. 19-24. Speaking to servants, he argues, "What glory is it if when ye sin and *are buffeted* for it ye shall take it patiently?" And having used the word by which the Evangelists describe (Matt. xxvi. 67; Mark xiv. 65) the insults heaped upon the Lord at His trial, the writer is carried away in mind to the whole scene: "He did no sin, neither was guile found in His mouth; when He was reviled, He reviled not again; when He suffered, He threatened not, but committed Himself to Him that judgeth righteously; in His own self He bare our sins in His own body upon the tree, that we, having died unto sins, might live unto righteousness, by whose stripes ye were healed." And in the last clause especially we see traces of one who had been present through the painful history. The word rendered "stripes" means "bruises" or "weals," such as come from savage blows, and is just the word which would occur to one who had seen the bruised body taken down from the cross, but hardly to any one else.

Again, the writer makes you feel without quoting that he has the words of Jesus constantly in his mind. Thus in the exhortation, "Cast all your anxiety upon God, for He careth for you" (v. 7); when he says, "If ye are reproached for the name of Christ, blessed are ye" (iv. 14), or "Be sober; be vigilant" (v. 8), or "Be sober unto prayer" (iv. 7), or commends "not rendering evil for evil, or reviling for reviling, but contrariwise blessing" (iii. 9), at each of the sentences—and the letter abounds with examples—there rise in the reader's mind some similar words of Christ, making him feel that he is perusing a writing of one to whom the Lord's language was abundantly familiar.

With the marks of personal character and associations meeting us constantly, and with the unbroken consensus of antiquity in favour of St. Peter's authorship, we shall not lightly allow speculations about hypothetical differences between the teaching of the Apostles of the Gentiles and of the circumcision to disturb our acceptance of this letter for what it proclaims itself to be: the work of the Apostle St. Peter, of one who was himself a witness of the sufferings of Christ.

Of the Second Epistle the whole history is very different. It appears to have been little known in the early Church, and is included by Eusebius (330) among the ἀντιλεγόμενα, "books to which objection was raised" as late as his day. It is true that in Clement of Rome there is a sentence (Ep. i., chap. xi.) which many have accepted as containing a clear allusion to the passage (2 Peter ii. 6, 7) which speaks of Lot and the destruction of Sodom. And if this could be demonstrated with certainty, it would be most valuable testimony. It would prove the Epistle to have been accepted at a very early date and by the important Church in Rome. But we have so far to go before we come upon any other notice that the silence makes us doubtful of the evidence from Clement. Moreover, such other witness as we do find is not of a very direct character. Firmilian, Bishop of Cæsarea, in Cappadocia, about 256 A.D., in a letter of which a Latin version is preserved among the writings of Cyprian, uses words which probably indicate that he knew both the epistles of St. Peter; but he gives no quotation. The Second Epistle was no doubt meant for the same readers as the First; and that is addressed, among others, to the Christians of Cappadocia, so that there is no improbability in supposing the letter to have been early known there. Theophilus of Antioch (170) uses the comparison of the word to a lamp shining in a dark place in such a way as to give the impression that he knew the Epistle, and a similar possible reference is found in the writings of Ephrem Syrus († 378). Palladius (400), who was a friend of Chrysostom, and wrote at Rome, makes a clear allusion to 2 Peter; and in the Apology of Melito, Bishop of Sardis, there is a passage concerning the destruction of the world by fire at the last day which is strikingly parallel to 2 Peter iii. 5-7, and can hardly have been written without a knowledge of the Epistle.

This is a very small amount of early evidence, and among the more voluminous writers of the first three centuries we find no mention of the Epistle. We cannot, therefore, be surprised that by Eusebius it is classed among the works of less acceptance. But the same fate befell larger and more important writings than this Epistle. The Apocalypse and the Epistle to the Hebrews stand in the same list in Eusebius. And St. Peter's second letter has not the same general interest as the first, and therefore is likely to have been less widely circulated; and this is all that Eusebius's classification means. The books were not generally received because there was a less general knowledge of their existence and history.

But when the Church entered on the settlement of the New Testament Canon at the Council of Laodicæa (366), the Second Epistle of St. Peter was accepted; and no doubt there was evidence then before the assembled Fathers which time has now destroyed. Yet in the letter itself there are points which no doubt weighed with them, and which are patent to us as they were then. The writer claims to be St. Peter, an Apostle and the writer of a previous epistle. He speaks solemnly of his death as near at hand; and still more solemn, when viewed as evidence, is the declaration that he had been one of the witnesses of Christ's transfiguration. It is almost inconceivable that a forger, writing to warn against false teachers, writing in the interest of truth, should have thus deliberately assumed a name and experience to which he had no claim. These statements must have influenced the opinion of the Laodicæan Council, and we know that they did not act on light evidence; they did not on the strength of a name accept into their canon, but excluded, works at the time widely circulated and passing for histories or letters of some of the Apostles.

Moreover, when we consider the kind of teaching against which St. Peter's epistle is directed, it is difficult to place it anywhere except at about the same date as St. Paul's epistles. It speaks of the "fables" (μῦθοι, i. 16), the groundless, baseless fancies, of the early heretics in the same manner which we find in St. Paul (cf. 1 Tim. i. 4; iv. 7). The same greed and covetousness (πλεονεξία) is noted by both the Apostles in the teachers against whom their voice is raised (cf. 2 Peter ii. 3; 1 Tim. vi. 5; Titus i. 11). There are the same beguiling promises of liberty (cf. 2 Peter ii. 19; 1 Cor. x. 29; Gal. v. 13), a perversion of the freedom of which St. Paul speaks so much to the Galatian converts; and just as he warns against "false brethren unawares brought in, who came in privily to spy out our liberty" (Gal. ii. 4), so does St. Peter condemn those "who privily bring in heresies of destruction" (2 Peter ii. 1). With so many common features in the two pictures, we can scarcely be wrong in referring them to the same times. No other period in early Church history suits the language of St. Peter so well as the few years before his martyrdom. The First Epistle may be dated eight or ten years earlier.

There is another morsel of evidence from the New Testament which is worth notice. St. Peter describes the heretics against whom he writes as following the error of Balaam the son of Beor, and notes this among the tokens of their covetousness. In the Apocalypse (ii. 14, 15) the same people are described, and in the same terms, but with an addition. They have received a definite name, and St. John terms them several times over "the Nicolaitanes." Such a distinctive title marks a later date than St. Peter's descriptive one, which is drawn from the Old Testament. The Apocalypse was assuredly written before the destruction of Jerusalem. If then we may take the mention of the Nicolaitanes by that designation as an indication of a later date than 2 Peter, we are again brought to the time to which we have already referred the Epistle: some time between 68 and 70 A.D.

Considerable discussion has arisen about the passages in 2 Peter which are like the language of St. Jude. There can be no doubt that either one Apostle copied the words of the other, or that both drew from a common original. But this point, in whatever way it be settled, need not militate against St. Peter's authorship. It is nothing unworthy of the Apostle, if he find to his hand the words of a fellow-teacher which will serve his need, to use what he finds. Nay, the letter itself tells us that he was prepared to do this. For he refers his readers (iii. 15) to the writings of St. Paul for support of his own exhortations. St. Peter's seems, however, to be the earlier of the two epistles, if we compare his words, "There *shall be* false teachers, who *shall bring* in heresies of destruction," etc. (ii. 1), with St. Jude, who speaks of these misleading teachers as already existent and active: "There *are certain men crept in* unawares"; "*These are* spots now existing in the feasts of charity"; "*They are feasting among the brethren* without fear." And St. Jude seems clearly to be alluding to St. Peter's words (2 Peter iii. 3) when he says, "Remember ye the words which were spoken before of the Apostles of our Lord Jesus Christ, how that they told you there should be *mockers*" (ἐμπαῖκται) "in the last time." This word for "mockers" is found only in St. Peter's epistle. It is nowhere else in the New Testament; and while St. Peter's words are a direct utterance, St. Jude's are a quotation.

But there are two or three features of resemblance between the style of St. Peter's first epistle and the second which support strongly the genuineness of the latter. The First Epistle has a large proportion of words found nowhere else in the New Testament. There are a score of such words in this short composition. Now the Second Epistle presents us with the same peculiarity in rather larger abundance. There are twenty-four words there which appear in no other New Testament writing. It seems to have been a peculiarity of the writer of both letters to use somewhat uncommon and striking words. Now take the Second Epistle to have been the work of an imitator. He would be sure to notice such a characteristic, and sure also to repeat, for the sake of connexion, some distinctive expressions of the first letter in the second. But the case is much otherwise. There is the same abundance of unusual words in both epistles, but not a single repetition; the same peculiarity is manifest, but displays itself in entirely new material. This is an index of authorship, not of imitation.

There are one or two differences between the two epistles which in their way are of equal interest. The first letter was one of encouragement and consolation; the second is full of warning. Hence, though the coming of the Lord is dwelt on alike in the two, in the former it is set forth as a *revelation* (1 Peter i. 5), as a day for which believers were looking, and in which their hopes would be realised, and their afflictions at an end; in the second letter the same event is called a coming (παρουσία), an appearing, a presence, but one which will usher in the great and terrible day of the Lord, and be the prelude of judgement to them that have fallen away.

Again, the sufferings of Christ are a theme much dwelt on in the First Epistle, where they are pointed to as the lot which Christians are to expect, and the Lord is the pattern which they are to imitate; in the Second they are hardly noticed. But was there not a cause for such reticence? Was it a time to urge on men the imitation of Christ when the danger was great that they would deny Him altogether?

No doubt many other points of evidence, which are lost to us, were presented to the Fathers of the Laodicæan Council, and with the result that the Second Epistle of St. Peter was received into the Canon side by side with the first. But the three centuries of want of acknowledgement have left their mark on its subsequent history, and many earnest minds have treated it as of less authority than other more accepted portions of the New Testament. Among these is Luther, who speaks of the First Epistle as one of the noblest in the New Testament, but is doubtful about the claims of the Second. Similar was the judgment of Erasmus and of Calvin.

We cannot, however, go back to the evidence produced at Laodicæa. Time has swept that away, but, while doing so, has left us the result thereof; and the acceptance of the Epistle by the Fathers there assembled will be judged by most men to stand in lieu of the evidence. No court of law would permit a decision so authenticated and of such standing to be disturbed or overruled.

And we ourselves can observe some points still which draw to the same conclusion. The letter harmonises in tone with the other New Testament writings, and some of its linguistic peculiarities are strikingly in accord with the universally accepted letter of St. Peter. We are therefore not unwilling, though we have not the early testimony which we could desire, and though the primitive Church held its genuineness for doubtful, to believe that ere this second letter was classed with the other New Testament writings these doubts were cleared away, and would be cleared away for us could we hear all the evidence tendered before those who fixed the contents of the Canon.

The discovery last year in Egypt of some fragments of the Gospel and Apocalypse once current under the name of St. Peter has drawn attention once more to the genuineness and authenticity of the Second Epistle in our canon. But the difference in character between it and these apocryphal documents is very great. The Gospel ascribed to Peter seems to have been written by some one who held the opinion, current among the early heretics, that the Incarnation was unreal, and that the Divine in Christ Jesus had no participation in the sufferings at the Crucifixion. Hence our Lord is represented as having no sense of pain at that time. He is said to have been deserted by His "power" in the moment of death. The stature of the angels at the Resurrection is represented as very great, but that of the risen Christ much greater. To these peculiar features may be added the response made by the cross to a voice which was heard from heaven, the cross having followed the risen Christ from the tomb. In the fragments of the Apocalypse we have a description of the torments of the wicked utterly foreign to the character of the New Testament writings, in which the veil of the unseen world is rarely withdrawn. The circumstance and detail given in the apocryphal fragment to the punishments of sinners mark it as the parent of those mediæval legends of which the "Visions of Furseus" and "St. Patrick's Purgatory" afford well-known examples.

The study of these fragments, of which the Gospel may be dated about 170 A.D., sends us back to the contemplation of the Second Epistle of St. Peter more conscious than before at what a very early date errors, both of history and doctrine, were promulgated among the Christian societies, while at the same time we are impressed more strongly with the sense that the accord of the Second Epistle with Gospel history, where it is alluded to, as well as the simplicity of Christian doctrine which it enforces, mark it as not unworthy of that place in the Canon which was accorded to it in the very earliest councils which dealt with the contents of New Testament Scripture.

I
THE WORK OF THE TRINITY IN MAN'S ELECTION AND SALVATION

"Peter, an Apostle of Jesus Christ, to the elect who are sojourners of the dispersion in Pontus, Galatia, Cappadocia, Asia, and Bithynia, according to the foreknowledge of God the Father, in sanctification of the Spirit, unto obedience and sprinkling of the blood of Jesus Christ: grace to you and peace be multiplied." —1 Peter i. 1, 2.

"When thou art converted, strengthen thy brethren" (Luke xxii. 32), was the Lord's injunction to St. Peter, of which this Epistle may be considered as a part fulfilment. So richly stored is it with counsel, warning, and consolation that Luther, the conflicts of whose life will bear some comparison with the trials of these Asian converts, calls it one of the most precious portions of the New Testament Scriptures. Its value is further enhanced because in so many places the Apostle reverts in thought or word to his own life-history, and draws his teaching from the rich stream of personal experience. Even the name which he sets at the head of the letter had its lesson in connexion with Jesus. Most Jews took a second name for profaner use in their commerce with the heathen; but to Simon, the son of Jonas, Peter must have been a specially sacred name, must have served as a watchword both to himself and to all others who had learnt the story of its bestowal and the meaning which was bound up with it.

That a letter by St. Peter should be, as this is, of a very practical character is no more than we might expect from what we know of the Apostle from the Gospels. Prompt in word and action, ever the spokesman of the twelve, he seems made for a guide and leader of men. What perhaps we should not have expected is the very definite doctrinal language with which the Epistle opens. Nowhere in the writings either of St. Paul or St. John do we find more full or more instructive teaching concerning the Holy Trinity. And herein St. Peter has been guided to choose the only order which tends to edification. Sound lessons for Christian life must be grounded upon a right faith, and a brother can afford no strength to his brethren unless first of all he point them clearly to the source whence both his strength and theirs must come.

Of the previous intercourse between St. Peter and those to whom he writes we can only judge from the Epistle itself. The Apostle's name disappears from New Testament history after the Council of Jerusalem (Acts xv.), but we feel sure his labours did not cease then; and though the first message of Christianity may have been brought to these Asiatic provinces by St. Paul, the allusions which St. Peter makes to the trials of the converts are such as seem impossible had he not himself laboured among them. The frequent reminders, the special warnings, could come only from one who knew their circumstances very intimately. Allusions to the former lusts indulged in in their days of ignorance, to the reproaches which they now have to suffer from their heathen neighbours, to their going astray like lost sheep, are a few of the unmistakable evidences of personal knowledge.

He writes to them as *sojourners of the dispersion*. In the minds of the Jews this name would wake up sad memories of their past history. It told of that great break in the national unity which was made by the tarrying in Babylon of so many of the people at the time of the return, then of those painful periods in later days when their nation, as the vassal now of Persia, now of Greece, of Egypt, of Syria, and of Rome, was made the sport of the world-powers as they rose and fell, times in which Israel could see few tokens of the Divine favour, could hear no voice of the prophet to encourage or to guide. But now to those who had accepted the Gospel of Christ those dark years would be seen to have been in no wise barren of blessing and of profit. The scattered Jews had carried much of their faith abroad among the nations; schools of religious teaching had arisen; the chosen people in their dispersion had adopted the language best known among the other nations; and thus the outcome of those sorrowful times had been a preparation for the Gospel. Proselytes had been made in the countries of their exile, and a wider field opened for the Christian harvest. The dispersion of Israel had been made, as it were, a bridge over which the grace of God passed for publishing the glad tidings of the Gospel, and to gather Jew and Gentile alike into the fold of Christ.

But it would be a mistake to restrict the word "dispersion" here to the Jewish converts. The Apostle speaks more than once in his letter to those who had never been Jews, to men who (i. 14) had been fashioned according to their former lusts in ignorance; who had in times past (ii. 10) no share with God's people; who (iv. 13) had wrought the will of the Gentiles, walking in lasciviousness, lusts, and abominable idolatries. To these too since their conversion the name "dispersion" might be fitly applied. They were but a few here and there among the multitudes of heathendom. And their acceptance of the faith of Jesus must have given to their lives a different aspect. It must often be so with the faithful. Their life is from the world apart. It must have been specially thus with these Christians in Asia. They could be verily only strangers and sojourners; their true home could never be made among their heathen surroundings. As the Jew in old days sighed for Jerusalem, so their hope was centred on a Jerusalem above.

Yet God had a mission for them in the world. This is a special portion of St. Peter's message. As the scattered Jews of old had opened a door for the spreading of the Gospel, so the Christians of the dispersion were to be its witnesses. Their election had made them a peculiar people; but it was that they might show forth the praises of Him who had called them out of darkness into His marvellous light, and that by their good works the heathen might be won to glorify God when in His own time He should visit them too with the day-star from on high.

But beside the words which speak of severance and pilgrimage, the Apostle uses one of a different character. With that large charity and hope which is stamped upon the whole of the New Testament, he calls these scattered Christian converts the *elect* of God. Just as St. Paul so often includes whole Churches, even though he find in them many things to blame and to reprove, under the title of "saints" or "called to be saints," so it is here. And the sense of their election is intended to be a mighty power. It is to bind them wherever they may be scattered into one communion in Christ Jesus. Through the world they are dispersed, but in Christ they constitute a great unity. And the sense of this is to lift their hearts above any sorrowing for their isolation in the world. For through Christ they have (i. 4) an inheritance, a home, a claim of sonship; and their salvation is ready to be revealed in the last time.

Later generations have witnessed much unprofitable controversy round this word "election." Some men have seen nothing else in the Bible, while others have hardly acknowledged it to be there at all. Then some have laboured to reconcile to their understandings the two truths of God's sovereignty and the freedom of the human will, not content to believe that in God's economy there may be things beyond their measure. St. Peter, like the other New Testament writers, enters on no such discussions. Whether amid the full assurance of newly quickened faith the first Christians found no room for intellectual difficulties, or whether the spirit within them led them to feel that such questions must ever be insoluble, we cannot know; but it is instructive to note that the Scripture does not raise them. They are the growth of later days, of times when Christianity was wide-spread, when men had lost the feeling that they were strangers and pilgrims of the dispersion, and were no longer prepared to welcome, with St. Peter and St. Paul, every Christian brother into the number of God's chosen ones, counting them as those who had been called to be saints.

Of the election of believers the Apostle here speaks in its origin, its progress, and its consummation. He views it as a process which must extend through the whole life, and connects its various stages with the Three Persons of the Trinity. But, with the same practical instinct which has already been noticed, he enters on no statements about the nature of the Godhead in itself; he neither discusses what may be known of God, nor how the knowledge is to be obtained. He says no word to intimate that the mention of three Persons may be difficult to understand in co-relation to the unity of the Godhead. Such inquiries exercise the mind, but can hardly further, what was St. Peter's special aim, the edification and comfort of the soul. That result comes from the inward experience of what each Person of the Godhead is to us, and on this the Apostle has a lesson. He makes plain for us the share which Father, Son, and Spirit bear in the work of human salvation. Christians, he teaches us, are elect, chosen to be saints, according to the foreknowledge of God the Father; the election is maintained when their lives are constantly hallowed by the influence of the Holy Ghost; while in Christ they have not only an example of perfect obedience after which they must strive, but a Redeemer whose blood can cleanse them from all the sins from which the most earnest strivings will not set them free. Of these things the Christian soul can have experience. It is thus that the life of the elect believer begins, grows, and is perfected.

It begins *according to the foreknowledge of God the Father*. Here St. Peter may be his own interpreter. In his sermon on the day of Pentecost he employs the same word, "foreknowledge," and he is the only one who uses it in the New Testament. There (Acts ii. 23) he says that Christ was delivered up to be crucified by the determinate counsel and foreknowledge of God. And on the same subject in this very chapter (i. 20) he speaks of Jesus as *foreknown*, as a Lamb without spot and blemish before the foundation of the world. In these passages we are carried back beyond the ages into the Divine council-chamber, and we find the whole course of human history naked and open before the eyes of the All-seeing. God knew even then what the history of the human race would be, saw that sin would find an entrance into the world, and that a sacrifice would be needed, if sinners were to be redeemed. Yet He called the world and its tenants into being, and provided the ransom in the person of His only Son. Why this was well-pleasing unto Him it is not ours to discuss; whether for the uplifting of humanity by providing an opportunity for moral obedience or for the greater manifestation of His infinite love. But whatever else is mysterious, one thing is plain: the counsel of the Holy One is seen to be a counsel of mercy and of love; and though its operation may not seldom be perplexing to our finite powers, the Apostle teaches us that this determination from all eternity was made with infinite tenderness. He tells us it was the ordinance of our Father. The beginning and the end thereof are hidden from us. We learn only a fragment of His dealings during the brief period of a human life. But men may rest content with the proof of their election in the sound of the Gospel message which they hear. They who are thus called may count themselves for chosen. This call is the Divine testimony that God is choosing them. Concerning His intention towards others who may seem to have passed away without hearing of His love, or who are living as though no loving message of glad tidings had ever been proclaimed, we must rest in ignorance, only assured that the Eternal God is as truly their Father as we know Him to be ours.

To limited human knowledge the course of the world has ever been, must ever be, full of darkness and perplexities. Men gaze upon it as they do upon the wrong side of a piece of tapestry as it is woven. To such observers the pattern is always obscure, many a time quite unintelligible. For full knowledge we have to wait to the end. Then the web will be reversed, God's designs and their working comprehended; we shall know even as we are known, and, with hearts and voices tuned to praise, shall cry, "He hath done all things well." Of such a revelation the poet (Shelley, *Adonais*, Stanza lii.) sings, a revelation of the all-seeing, unchanging Jehovah and of the glorious enlightenment that shall be in His presence:—

> "The one remains, the many change and pass;
> Heaven's light for ever shines, earth's shadows fly:
> Life, like a dome of many-coloured glass,
> Stains the white radiance of eternity,
> Until death tramples it to fragments."

In this wise would St. Peter have us think of the grace of election. It has its beginning from our Father; its fulfilment will also be with Him. The measure and the manner of its bestowal are according to His foreknowledge, according to the same foreknowledge which provided in Christ an atonement for sin, which appointed Him to die, and that not for some sinners only, but for the sins of the whole world.

But in the call according to God's foreknowledge the believer is not perfected. He must live worthily of his calling. And as his election at the first is of God, so the power to hold it fast is a Divine gift. He who would rejoice over God's election must feel and constantly foster within himself *the sanctification of the Spirit*. To be made holy is his great need. This demands a life of progress, of renewal, a daily endeavour to restore the image which was lost at the Fall. "Be ye holy, for I am holy," is a fundamental precept of both Old and New Testaments; and it is a continual admonition, speaking unto Christians that they go forward. Under the Law the lesson was enforced by external symbols. Holy ground, holy days, holy offices, kept men alive to the need of preparation, of purification, before they could be fit to draw near unto God or for God to draw near unto them.

For us there is opened a more excellent way: the inward, spiritual cleansing of the heart. Christ has gone away where He was before, and sends down to His servants the Holy Ghost, who bestows power that the election of the Father may be made sure. Hence we can understand those frequent exhortations in the epistles, "Walk in the Spirit"; "Live in the Spirit"; "Quench not the Spirit." The Christian life is a struggle. The flesh is ever striving for the mastery. This enemy the believer must do to death. And as aforetime, so now, sanctification begins with purification. Christ sanctifies His Church, those whom He has called to Him out of the world; and the manner is by cleansing them through the washing of water with the word. Here we gladly think of that sacrament which He ordained for admission into the Church as the beginning of this Divine operation, as the wonted entrance of the Holy Ghost for His work of purifying. But that work must be continued. He is called "holy" because He makes men holy by His abode with them. And Christ has described for us how this is brought to pass. "He shall take of Mine," says our Lord, "and shall show it unto you. All things that the Father hath are Mine" (John xvi. 14, 15). Every good gift, which the Father who calls men hath, the Spirit is sent to impart. The words speak of the gradual manner of its bestowal; all things may be given, but they are given little by little, as men can or are fit to receive them. He shall take a portion of what is Mine, is the literal meaning of the Evangelist's phrase (John xvi. 15). The plural phrase πάντα ὅσα ἔχει ὁ πατὴρ marks the boundless supply, the singular ἐκ τοῦ ἐμοῦ λήμψεται the Spirit's choice of such a portion therefrom as best suits the receiver's needs and powers. In this wise men may become gradually conformed to the image of Christ, grow more and more like Him day by day. More and more will they drink in of the whole truth, and more and more will they be sanctified.

In this daily enlightenment must God's faithful ones live, a life whose atmosphere is the hallowing influence of the Holy Ghost. But it is to be no mere life of receptivity, with no effort of their own. The Apostle makes this clear elsewhere, when he says, "Sanctify the Lord God in your hearts" (iii. 15)—make them fit abodes for His Spirit to dwell in; lead your lives in holy conversation, that the house may be swept and garnished, and you be vessels sanctified and meet for the Master's use.

Thus chosen by the Father and led onward by the Spirit, the Christian is brought ever nearer to the full purpose of his calling: *unto obedience and the sprinkling of the blood of Jesus Christ.* The Christ-pattern which the Spirit sets before men is in no feature more striking than in its perfect obedience. The prophetic announcement of this submission sounds down to us from the Psalms: "Lo, I come to do Thy will, O God"; and the incarnate Son declares of Himself, "My meat is to do the will of Him that sent Me, and to finish His work": and even in the hour of His supreme agony His word is still, "Father, not My will, but Thine, be done." Specially solemn, almost startling, is the language of the Apostle to the Hebrews when he says of Jesus that "He learned obedience by the things which He suffered," and that "it became the Father, in bringing many sons unto glory, to make Christ, the Captain of their salvation, perfect through suffering." With the Lord as an example, obedience is made the noblest, the New Testament form of sacrifice.

But when such obedience was connected with the sprinkling of the blood of Jesus, the Jews among St. Peter's converts must have been carried in thought to that scene described in Exod. xxiv. There, through Moses as a mediator, we read of God's law being made known to Israel, and the people with one voice promised obedience: "All the words which the Lord hath said will we do, and be obedient." Then followed a sacrifice; and Moses took the blood and sprinkled it on the people, saying, "Behold the blood of the covenant which the Lord hath made with you concerning all these words"; and the Lord drew nigh unto His people, and the sight of the glory of the Lord on Mount Sinai was like devouring fire in the eyes of the children of Israel.

For Christians there is a Mediator of a better covenant. We are not come unto the mount that burned with fire, but unto Mount Zion (Heb. xii. 18-22). In that other sacrament of His own institution, our Lord makes us partakers of the benefits of His passion. With His own blood He constantly maketh His people pure, fitting them to appear in the presence of the Father. There at length the purpose of their election shall be complete in fulness of joy in the sight of Him who chose them before the foundation of the world.

Thus does the Apostle set forth his practical, profitable lessons on the work of the Trinity in man's election and salvation; and he concludes them with a benediction part of which is very frequent in the letters of St. Paul: *Grace to you and peace.* The early preachers felt that these two blessings travelled hand in hand, and comprised everything which a believer could need: God's favour and the happiness which is its fruit. Grace is the nurture of the Christian life; peace is its character. These strangers of the dispersion had been made partakers of the Divine grace. This very letter was one gift more, the consolation of which we can well conceive. But St. Peter models his benediction to be a fitting sequel to his previous teaching. *Grace,* he says, *to you and peace be multiplied.* The verb "be multiplied" is only used by him here and in the Second Epistle, and by St. Jude, whose letter has so much in common with St. Peter's.

In this prayer the same thought is with him as when he spake of the stages of the Christian election. There must ever be growth as the sign of life. Let them hold fast the grace already received, and more would be bestowed. Grace for grace is God's rule of giving, new store for what has been rightly used. This one word of his prayer would say to them, Seek constantly greater sanctification, more holiness, from the Spirit; yield your will to God in imitation of Jesus, who sanctified Himself that His servants might be sanctified. Then, though you be strangers of the dispersion, though the world will have none of you, you shall be kept in perfect peace, and feel sure that you can trust His words who says to His warfaring servants, "Be of good cheer; I have overcome the world."

II
THE HEAVENLY INHERITANCE

"Blessed be the God and Father of our Lord Jesus Christ, who according to His great mercy begat us again unto a living hope by the resurrection of Jesus Christ from the dead, unto an inheritance incorruptible, and undefiled, and that fadeth not away, reserved in heaven for you, who by the power of God are guarded through faith unto a salvation ready to be revealed in the last time. Wherein ye greatly rejoice, though now for a little while, if need be, ye have been put to grief in manifold temptations, that the proof of your faith, being more precious than gold that perisheth, though it is proved by fire, might be found unto praise and glory and honour at the revelation of Jesus Christ: whom not having seen ye love; on whom, though now ye see Him not, yet believing, ye rejoice greatly with joy unspeakable and full of glory: receiving the end of your faith, even the salvation of your souls."—1 Peter i. 3-9.

"Out of the abundance of the heart the mouth speaketh," words true of all this letter, but of no part more true than of the thanksgiving with which it opens. The Apostle recalls those dark three days in which the life he bore was worse than death. His vaunted fidelity had been put to the proof, and had failed in the trial; his denial had barred the approach to the Master whom he had disowned. The crucifixion of Jesus had followed close upon His arrest, and Peter's bitter tears of penitence could avail nothing. He to whom they might have appealed was lying in the grave. The Apostle's repentant weeping saved him from a Judas-like despair, but dreary must have been the desolation of his soul until the Easter morning's message told him that Jesus was alive again.

We can understand the fervency of his thanksgiving: *Blessed be God, which hath begotten us again by the resurrection of Christ from the dead*. No better image than the gift of a new life could he find to describe the restoration that came with the words of the angel from the empty tomb, "He is risen; go your way: tell His disciples and Peter that He goeth before you into Galilee." The

Lord forgave His sinning, sorrowing servant, and through this forgiveness he lived again, and bears printed for ever on his heart the memory of that life-giving. The very form of his phrase in this verse is an echo from the resurrection morning: *Blessed be the God and Father of our Lord Jesus Christ.*

Only in a few passages resembling this in St. Paul's epistles[1] is God called "the God of our Lord Jesus Christ." But Peter is mindful of the Lord's own words to Mary, "Go unto My brethren and say unto them, I ascend unto My Father and your Father, and My God and your God" (John xx. 17); and now that he is made one of Christ's heralds, the feeder of His sheep, he publishes the same message which was the source of his own highest joy, and which he would make a joy for them likewise. That God is called theirs, even as He is Christ's, is an earnest that Jesus has made them His brethren indeed. To the doctrine of their election according to the foreknowledge of the Father he now adds the further grace which couples the Fatherhood of God with the brotherhood of Christ.

That these gifts are purely of God's grace he also implies: *He begat us again.* Just as in natural birth the child is utterly of the will of the parents, so is it in the spiritual new birth. *According to God's great mercy* we are born again and made heirs of all the consequent blessings. This passage from death unto life is rich, in the first place, in immediate comfort. Witness the rejoicing amidst his grief which St. Peter experienced when he could cry to the Master, "Lord, Thou knowest all things: Thou knowest that I love Thee." But the new life looks for ever onward. It will be unbroken through eternity. Here we may taste the joy of our calling, may learn something of the Father's love, of the Saviour's grace, of the Spirit's help; but our best expectations centre ever in the future. The Apostle terms these expectations a lively, or rather *a living, hope.* The Christian's hope is living because Christ is alive again from the dead. It springs with ever-renewed life from that rent tomb. The grave is no longer a terminus. Life and hope endure beyond it. And more than this, there is a fresh principle of vitality infused into the soul of the new-born child of God. The Spirit, the Life-giver, has made His abode there; and death is swallowed up of victory.

In continuing his description of the living hope of the believer, the Apostle keeps in mind his simile of Fatherhood and sonship, and gives to the hope the further title of *an inheritance.* As sons of Adam, men are heirs from their birth, but only to the sad consequences of the primal transgression. Slaves they are, and not free men, as that other law in their members gives them daily proof. But in the resurrection of Jesus the agonised cry of St. Paul, "Who shall deliver me?" (Rom. vii. 24), has found its answer. Christians are begotten again, not to defeat and despair, but to a hope which is eternal, to an inheritance which will endure beyond the grave. And as in their spiritual growth they are ever aspiring to an ideal above and beyond them, in respect of the saintly inheritance they have a like experience. They begin to grasp it now in part, and have even here a precious earnest of the larger blessedness; they are sealed by the Holy Spirit of promise and marked as the redeemed of God's own possession (Eph. i. 13, 14). But that which shall be is rich with an exceeding wealth of glory; Christ keeps the good wine of His grace to the last.

How beggared earthly speech appears when we essay by it to picture the glory that shall be revealed for us! The inheritance of the Christian's hope demands for its description those unspeakable words which St. Paul heard in paradise, but could not utter. The tongues of men are constrained to fall back upon negatives. What it will be we cannot express. We only know some evils from which it will be free. It shall be *incorruptible*, like the God and Father (Rom. i. 23) who bestows it. *Eternal*, it shall contain within it no seed of decay, nothing which can cause it to perish. Neither shall it be subject to injury from without. It shall be *undefiled*, for we are to share it with our elder Brother, our High-priest (Heb. vii. 26), who is now made higher than the heavens. Earthly possessions are often sullied, now by the way they are attained, now by the way they are used. Neither spot nor blemish shall tarnish the beauty of the heavenly inheritance. It shall *never fade away*. It is amaranthine, like the crown of glory (1 Peter v. 4) which the chief Shepherd shall bestow at His appearing; it is as the unwithering flowers of paradise.

Nor are these the only things which make the heavenly to differ from the earthly inheritance. In this life, ere a son can succeed to heirship, the parent through whom it is derived must have passed away; while the many heirs to an earthly estate diminish, as their number increases, the shares of all the rest. From such conditions the Christian's future is free. His Father is the Eternal God, his inheritance the inexhaustible bounty of heaven. Each and all who share therein will find an increase of joy as the number grows of those who claim this eternal Fatherhood, and with it a place in the Father's home.

St. Peter adds another feature which gives further assurance to the believer's hope. The inheritance is reserved. Concerning it there can be no thought of dwindling or decay. It is where neither rust nor moth can corrupt, and where not even the archthief Satan himself can break through to steal. There needs no preservation of the incorruptible and undefiled, but it is especially kept for those for whom it is prepared. He who has gone before to make it ready said, "I go to prepare it for you." The Apostle has made choice of his preposition advisedly. He says, ἐις ὑμᾶς[2]—on your behalf; for your own possession. The inheritance is where Christ has gone before us, in heaven, of which we can best think, as Himself hath taught us, as the place "where He was before" (John vi. 62), the Father's house, in which are many mansions. There it is in store, till we are made ready for it.

For the present life is only a preparation-time. Ere we are ready to depart we must pass through a probation. God suffers His beloved ones to be chastened, but He sends with the trial the means of rescue. They are *guarded*. The word which St. Peter here uses is one applicable to a military guard, such as would be needed in the country of an enemy. God sees what we stand in need of. For we are still in the territory of the prince of this world. But mark the abundant protection: *by the power of God through faith.* The Apostle's language sets our guardianship forth under a double aspect. The Christian is "in" (ἐν) "the power of God." Here is the strength of our wardship. Under such care the believer is enabled to walk amid the trials of the world unscathed. Yet the Divine shield around him is not made effective unless he do his part also. Through faith the shelter becomes impregnable. The Christian goes forward with full assurance, his eyes fixed on the goal of duty which his Master has set before him, and, heedless of assailants, perseveres in the struggles which beset him. Then, even in the fiercest fires of trial, he beholds by his side the Son of God, and hears the voice, "It is I; be not afraid."

Thus to the faithful warfarer the victory is sure. And to this certainty St. Peter points as he continues, and calls the heavenly inheritance a *salvation.* This will be the consummation. "Sursum corda" is the believer's constant watchword. The completed bliss will not be attained here. But when the veil is lifted which separates this life from the next, it is ready to be manifested and to ravish the sight with its glory. The sense of this salvation ready to be revealed nerves the heart for every conflict. By faith weakness grows mighty. Thus comes to pass the paradox of the Christian life, which none but the faithful can comprehend: "When I am weak, then I am strong"; "I can do all things through Christ, that giveth me power."

Hence comes the wondrous spectacle, which St. Peter was contemplating, and which amazed the heathen world, exceeding joy in the midst of sufferings. *Wherein ye greatly rejoice,* he says. Some have thought him to be referring to a mental realisation of the last time, about which he has just spoken, a realisation so vivid to the faith of these converts that they could exult in the prospect as though it had already arrived. And this exposition is countenanced in some degree by words which follow (ver. 9), where he describes them as now receiving the end of their faith, even the salvation of their souls.

But it seems less forced to consider the Apostle as speaking with some knowledge of the circumstances of these Asian Christians, a knowledge of the trials they had to undergo, and how hope was animating them to look onwards towards their inheritance, which was but a little while in reversion, towards the salvation which was so soon to be revealed. Full of this hope, he says, ye greatly rejoice, though ye have had many things to suffer. Then he proceeds to dwell on some of the grounds for their consolation. Their trials, they knew, were but for a little while, not a moment longer than the need should be. Their sorrow would have an end; their joy would last for evermore.

The form of St. Peter's words,[3] it is true, seems to imply that there must always be the need for our chastening. And what else can the children of Adam expect? But it is He, the Father in heaven, who fixes both the nature and the duration of His children's discipline. Some men have felt within themselves the need of chastisement so keenly that they have devised systems for themselves whereby they should mortify the flesh, and prepare themselves for the last time. But of self-appointed chastenings the Apostle does not speak. Of such the converts to whom he writes had no need. They *had been put to grief in manifold temptations.*

We can gather from the Epistle itself some notion of the troublous life these scattered Christians had amid the crowd of their heathen neighbours. They were regarded with contempt for refusing to mingle in the excesses which were so marked a feature of heathen life and heathen worship. They were railed upon as evil-doers. They suffered innocently, were constantly assailed with threatenings, and passed their time oft in such terror that St. Peter describes their life as a fiery trial.

Yet in the word (ποικίλος) which he here employs to picture the varied character of their sufferings we seem to have another hint that these did not fall out without the permission and watchful control of God Himself. It is a word which, while it tells of a countless variety, tells at the same time of fitness and order therein. The trials are meted out fitly, as men need and can profit by them. The Master's eye and hand are at work through them all; and the faithful God keeps always ready a way of deliverance. In this wise does St. Peter proclaim that the putting to grief may be made unto us a dispensation of mercy. Himself had been so put to grief by the thrice-repeated question, "Lovest thou Me?" (John xxi. 17). But a way was opened thereby for repentance of his triple denial, and that he might thrice over be entrusted with the feeding of Christ's flock. Such was the putting to grief of the Corinthian Church (2 Cor. vii. 9) by St. Paul's first letter, for it wrought in them repentance, so that they sorrowed after a godly sort. And such sorrow can exist side by side with, yea be the source of, exceeding joy. The Apostle of the Gentiles is a witness when he says that he and his fellow-labourers are "sorrowful, yet alway rejoicing" (2 Cor. vi. 10).

The Christian does not allow troubles to overwhelm him. The very comparison which St. Peter here institutes, speaking though it does of a furnace of trial, bears within it somewhat of consolation. Gold that is proved by the fire loses all the dross which clung about it and was mingled with it before the refining. It comes forth in all its purity, all its worth; and so shall it be with the believer after his probation. The things of earth will lose their value in his eyes; they will fall away from him, neither will he load himself with the thick clay of the world's honours or wealth. The ties of such things have been sundered by his trials, and his heart is free to rise above the anxieties of time. And better even than the most refined gold, which, be it never so excellent, will yet be worn away, the faith of the believer comes forth stronger for all trial, and he shall hear at the last the welcome of the Master, "Enter thou into the joy of thy Lord," the joy which He bestows, the joy which He shares with those that follow Him.

This is the revelation of Jesus Christ of which St. Peter speaks. This is the praise which through His atonement His servants shall find, and shall become sharers of the glory and honour which the Father has bestowed upon Him. To Christ then turns every affection. *Whom not having seen ye love.* This is the test since Christ's ascension, and has the promise of special blessing. To His doubting Apostle Christ vouchsafed the evidence he desired, for our teaching as well as for his; but He added therewith, "Blessed are they which have not seen and yet have believed." And their joy is such as no tongue can tell. Not for that are they silent in their rejoicing; their hearts overflow, and their voices go forth in constant songs of praise. But ever there remains with them the sense, "The half has not been told."

For faith anticipates the bliss which God hath prepared for them that love Him, and enters into the unseen. The Holy Spirit within the soul is ever making fuller revelation of the deep things of God. The believer's knowledge is ever increasing; the eye-salve of faith clears his spiritual vision. The thanksgivings of yesterday are poor when considered in the illumination of to-day. His joy also is glorified. As his aspirations soar heavenward, the glory from on high comes forth, as it were, to meet him. By gazing in faith on the coming Lord, the Christian progresses, through the power of the Spirit, from glory to glory; and the ever-growing radiance is a part of that grace which no words can tell. But so true, so real, is the sense of Christ's presence that the Apostle describes it as full fruition. Believers *receive even now the end of their faith, the salvation of their souls.* So assured does He make them of all which they have hoped for that they behold already the termination of their journey, the close of all trial, and are filled with the bliss which shall be fully theirs when Christ shall come to call His approved servants to their inheritance of salvation.

III
THE UNITY AND GLORIOUSNESS OF THE PLAN OF REDEMPTION

"Concerning which salvation the prophets sought and searched diligently, who prophesied of the grace that *should come* unto you: searching what *time* or what manner of time the Spirit of Christ which was in them did point unto, when it testified beforehand the sufferings of Christ and the glories that should follow them. To whom it was revealed, that not unto themselves, but unto you, did they minister these things, which now have been announced unto you through them that preached the Gospel unto you by the Holy Ghost sent forth from heaven; which things angels desire to look into." —1 Peter i. 10-12.

The message of the Gospel unlocks the treasures of Old Testament revelation. Evangelists and Apostles are the exponents of the prophets. The continuity of Divine revelation has never been broken. The Spirit which spake through Joel of the pentecostal outpouring had spoken to men in the earlier days, to Abraham, Jacob, Moses, and David, and was now shed forth upon the first preachers of the Gospel, and bestowed abundantly for the work of the newly founded Church of Christ. St. Peter, himself a chief recipient of the gift, here proclaims the oneness of the whole of revelation; and more than this, he bears witness to the oneness of the teaching of the whole body of Christian missionaries. St. Paul and his fellow-labourers had spread the glad tidings first of all among these Asian converts; but there is no thought in St. Peter's mind of a different gospel from his own. Those who preached the Gospel to them in the first instance were, even as himself, working in and by the same Holy Spirit.

In the preceding verses of the chapter the thoughts of the Apostle have been dwelling on the future, on the time when the hope of the believer shall attain its fruition, and faith shall be lost in sight. He now turns his glance backward to notice how the promise of salvation has been the subject of revelation through all time. To those among the converts who had studied the Jewish Scriptures such a retrospect would be fruitful in instruction. They would comprehend with him how the truths which they now heard preached had been gradually shadowed forth in the Divine economy. That first proclamation of the seed of the woman to be born for the overthrow of the tempter, but who yet must Himself be a Sufferer in the conflict, was now become luminous, and in outline presented the whole scheme of redemption. The study of the development of that scheme would beget a full trust in their hearts for the future as they contemplated the stages of its foreshadowing in the past.

Concerning which salvation, he says, *the prophets sought and searched diligently.* The Divine revelation could only be made as men were able to bear it, and the sentences of old must needs be dark. At first God's love was set forth by His covenants with the patriarchs. Then the wider scope of mercy was proclaimed in the promises given to Abraham and repeated to his posterity. In their seed, it was declared, not the chosen race alone, but all the nations of the earth, should be blessed. Here all through the history was ground enough for diligent searching among the faithful. How could these things be, Abraham solitary and aged, Isaac's sons at feud with each other, Jacob and his posterity in captivity? Even at their best estate these seemed little fitted for the destiny which had been foretold to them. But throughout the Mosaic history some clung to their faith, and their great leader foresaw that the promise would be fulfilled in its time through One of whom he was but a feeble representative. But to so wide a vision only a few attained.

In the evil days which followed, the hope of the people must often have dwindled down; but yet at times, as to Gideon's diminished army, it was made manifest that the Lord could do great things for His people: and the thought of the seed of the woman promised as a Deliverer lingered in many hearts, and enabled them to sing in thankfulness how the adversaries of the Lord should be broken in pieces, how out of heaven the Lord should thunder upon them, and prove Himself the Judge of all the ends of the earth, giving strength unto His king and exalting the horn of His anointed. In such wise the prophetic teaching, which had advanced from the blessing of an individual to the choice and exaltation of a chosen family, was expanded in the noblest spirits to the conception of a kingdom of God among all mankind, and assumed a more definite form when the promise was made to the Son of David that His throne should be established for ever.

But how imperfectly God's design was comprehended by the best among them we can see from the last words of David himself (2 Sam. xxiii. 1-7). In them we have an instance of the searching which must have occupied other hearts beside that of the king of Israel. The Spirit of the Lord had spoken by him, and a promise of future glory had been made, when all should be brightness, every cloud dispersed. But the vision tarried. The house of David was not so with God. Yet he still held firmly to the everlasting covenant, ordered in all things and sure, a covenant of salvation, though as yet God made it not to grow. David may be numbered among those *who prophesied of the grace that should come* hereafter; and his words are shaped by a power above his own, to suggest the advent of Him who was to be the "dayspring from on high."

He and the other enlightened Israelites who have left us their thoughts and aspirations in the Psalter felt that the history of the chosen people was from first to last a grand parable (Psalm lxxviii. 2), and that the present could always be learning from the leading and discipline of the past. The miracles and the chastisements which they recite were all tokens of the sure promise, tokens that the people were not forgotten, but constantly aided by instruction, warning, and reproof. So that another psalmist, though still searching for the fuller meaning of the parables and dark sayings through which he was conducted, could sing, "God shall redeem my soul from the hand of the grave, for He shall take me" (Psalm xlix. 15). There is a confidence in the words, a confidence enough to sustain amid many trials. To such a man the present was not all. There was a life to come where God should be and rule, and his heart had not seldom gone forth to the questioning *at what time and in what form* the promises should be fulfilled. Like Abraham, such men had seen the day of Christ in vision and rejoiced over it, and the *Spirit of Christ was within them* to sustain them. But the things which they had heard and known, and of which their fathers had told them, supplied cause for deep searchings as *to the time and the manner of time unto which the Spirit pointed*. The strength of the Lord and His wondrous works were to be rehearsed to the coming generations, that among them the hope might live, by them the searching be continued. And as time went on the vision was widened, for in no small number of the Psalms we find the promised blessedness described as the portion not of Israel only, but through Israel grace was to be extended to the ends of the earth. "Make a joyful noise unto the Lord, all ye lands," is no solitary invocation.

And when we turn to those prophets whose writings we possess, we recognise that in them the Spirit of Christ was working and pointing forward to the coming redemption. But long before the days of Isaiah and Micah the Spirit of the Lord had come mightily upon His servants, and that picture of a glorious future which both those seers have given to us was not improbably the utterance of some earlier servant of the Lord: "It shall come to pass in the last days that the mountain of the Lord's house shall be established in the top of the mountains and shall be exalted above the hills, and all nations shall flow unto it" (Isa. ii. 2; Micah iv. 1). Thus far had they attained, but the search was not ended. "The last days"! When these should come was known to God alone; and they spake only as they were moved by Him, standing on their towers of spiritual elevation, hearkening what the Lord would say to them, and delivering His message with all the fulness they could command. But they were sure of the final bliss.

Of the same character are those words of Joel, which St. Peter quoted in his sermon on the day of Pentecost, "It shall come to pass *afterward*" (ii. 28). Beyond this was not yet revealed. But it was the voice of God which spake through the prophet: "In those days I will pour out My Spirit." And the Divine voice spake of visitations of another kind. It *testified beforehand of the sufferings of Christ and the glories that should follow them*. We feel sure that here St. Peter had in mind Isa. liii., which the New Testament has taught us to apply in its fullest sense to our blessed Lord.

But the language of St. Peter in this clause deserves special notice. He does not use the ordinary words by which the personal sufferings of Christ would generally be expressed, but he says rather, "the sufferings which pertain unto Christ." And here we may well consider whether the variation of phrase be not designed. St. Paul uses the simple direct expression (2 Cor. i. 5), and so does St. Peter himself (1 Peter iv. 13); and in those passages the Apostles are speaking of the sufferings of Christ as shared by His people. It would almost seem as if St. Peter's phrase in the verse before us were intended to convey this sense more fully. The sufferings pertain unto Christ, were specially borne by Him; but they fall also upon those who are, and have been, His people, both before and after the Incarnation.

Those prophecies of Isaiah which speak of the sufferings of the servant of the Lord had long been expounded as meant of the Jewish nation, and with such interpretation St. Peter was doubtless familiar. Hence may have come his altered phrase, capable of being interpreted, not only of Christ Himself, but of the sufferings of those who, like these Asiatic converts, were for the Lord's sake exposed to manifold trials. This double application of the words, to Christ and to His servants also, explains, it may be, the unique use of the word "glories" in the clause which follows: the sufferings of Christ and the *glories* that should follow them. For the glories may be taken to signify not only that honour and glory which the Father has given unto Christ, but also the glory in which they shall share who have taken up their cross to follow Him. Nowhere else in the New Testament does this plural word occur. To draw a sense like this from it would minister no small comfort to the Christians in their trials; and just before St. Peter has described the joy which they should experience as "glorified," or "full of glory" (ver. 8). In like manner St. Paul speaks (Rom. viii. 18) of the sufferings of this present time as not worthy to be compared with the glory that shall be revealed in us in the resurrection.

It would also serve as consolation to the sufferers, who were thus pointed on to the future for Christ's best gifts, to know that a similar forward glance had been the lot of the prophets under the ancient dispensation. One here and there had felt, as Malachi (iii. 1), that the Lord whom they were seeking was soon to come; but we know of none before the aged Simeon to whom it had been made known that they should not die till they had seen the Lord's Christ. To the former generations *it was revealed*, says the Apostle, *that not unto themselves, but unto you, did they minister these things.* They beheld them, and greeted them, but it was afar off. They spake often one to another of a bliss that was to come; yet though praying, longing, and hoping for it, they saw it only with the eye of faith. The psalmists supply many illustrations of this forward projection of the thoughts which dwelt on the Messianic hope. Thus in Psalm xxii. 30, 31, while rejoicing over his own rescue from suffering, the speaker recognises that this is but a foreshadowing of another suffering and another deliverance, even the sufferings of Christ and the glories that should follow. "It shall be told of the Lord unto the next generation. They shall come; they shall declare His righteousness to a people that shall be born, that He hath done it," and again in another place, "This shall be written for the generation to come, and a people which shall be created shall praise the Lord" (Psalm cii. 18). And these anticipations are ever coupled with the thought of the wider extension of the kingdom of God, with the time when "all the ends of the world shall remember and turn unto the Lord," "when the nations shall fear the name of the Lord, and all the kings of the earth His glory."

But the things which prophets and psalmists ministered *have now been announced unto you through them that preached the Gospel unto you.* You, St. Peter would say, are now not heirs expectant, but possessors of the blessings which former ages of believers foresaw and foretold, just as in his pentecostal address he testifies, "This is that which was spoken by the prophet Joel." And those who have preached these glad tidings unto you, he continues, have not done so without warrant. They are joined by an unbroken link to the prophets who went before them. In those the Spirit of Christ wrought at such times as He found fit instruments for raising a little the veil that lay over the purposes of God. The preachers of the Gospel have the same Spirit, and speak unto you *by the Holy Ghost sent forth from heaven.* These (and of St. Peter is this specially true) had witnessed the sufferings of Christ, and been made partakers of the glories of the outpoured Spirit.

The promise of the Father had been fulfilled to them, and they had received a mouth and wisdom which their adversaries were not able to resist. The risen Lord, the assurance of a life to come, the guidance by the Spirit into all truth—these were now realities for them, and were to be made real for the rest of the world by their testimony.

And that he may further magnify that salvation which he has been describing as published in part under the Law and now assured by the message of the Gospel, he adds, *which things angels desire to look into*. Of the whole Divine plan for man's redemption the angels could hardly be cognisant. Of God's love for man they had been made conscious, had been employed as His agents in the exhibition of that love, both under the old and under the new covenant. Their ministry, we know, was exercised in the lives of Abraham and Lot; they watched over Jacob and over Elijah in their solitude and weariness. One of their host was sent to deliver Daniel and to instruct the prophet Zechariah. At a later day they, who stand above mankind in the order of creation, and are pure enough to behold the presence of the Most High, were made messengers to announce how the Son of God had deigned to assume, not their nature, but the nature of humanity, and would by His suffering lift up the race from its slavery to sin. They proclaimed the birth of the Baptist, and brought the message of the Annunciation to the Blessed Virgin. They heralded the birth of Christ to the shepherds of Bethlehem, and a multitude of their glorious company sang the song of glory to God in the highest. They tended the God-Man at His temptation, strengthened Him in His agony, were present at His sepulchre, and gave the news of the Resurrection to the early visitants. Nor were their services at an end with Christ's ascension, though they were present on that occasion also. To Cornelius and to Peter angels were made messengers, and our Lord has told us that their rejoicing is great over even one sinner that repenteth.

These immortal spirits whose home is before God's throne, and whose great office is to sing His praise, yet find in those ministrations to mankind in which they have been employed matter for admiration, matter which kindles in them fervent desire. They long to comprehend in all its fulness that grace which they are conscious God is shedding forth upon mankind. They would scan[4] all the workings of His love and His forbearance towards sinners. These things are to them a subject of admiration, even as was the empty tomb of Jesus to the disciples after the Resurrection; and from their high estate the angelic host would fain stoop down to gaze their fill upon what God's goodness has wrought and is working out for mankind. They feel that this knowledge would add a new theme to the songs around the throne, would give them still greater cause to extol that grace which manifests its noblest features in showing mercy and pity.

And if such be the aspiration of angels, sinless beings who feel not the need of rescue, shall the tongues of men be dumb, men who know, each from the experience of his own heart, how great is the evil of sin in which they are entangled, how hopeless without Christ's death was their deliverance from its thraldom; who know how constant and how undeserved is the mercy of which they are partakers, how true to Himself God has been in their case? "I am Jehovah; I change not: therefore ye children of men are not destroyed."

IV

THE CHRISTIAN'S IDEAL, AND
THE STEPS THEREUNTO

"Wherefore girding up the loins of your mind, be sober and set your hope perfectly on the grace that is to be brought unto you at the revelation of Jesus Christ; as children of obedience, not fashioning yourselves according to your former lusts *in the time of* your ignorance: but like as He which called you is holy, be ye yourselves also holy in all manner of living; because it is written, Ye shall be holy; for I am holy. And if ye call on Him as Father, who without respect of persons judgeth according to each man's work, pass the time of your sojourning in fear: knowing that ye were redeemed, not with corruptible things, with silver or gold, from your vain manner of life handed down from your fathers; but with precious blood, as of a lamb without blemish and without spot, *even the blood* of Christ: who was foreknown indeed before the foundation of the world, but was manifested at the end of the times for your sake, who through Him are believers in God, which raised Him from the dead, and gave Him glory; so that your faith and hope might be in God."—1 Peter i. 13-21.

The Apostle, who has set forth the character of the Christian's election, who has given to the converts large assurance for the hope which he exhorts them to hold, who has proclaimed the exceeding glory of their inheritance in the future and how its nature had been foreshadowed in type and prophecy, now turns to those practical lessons which he would enforce from the doctrines of election and of the future glory in heaven. Such glorious privileges cannot be looked forward to without awakening a sense of corresponding duties, and for these he would not have them unprepared. *Wherefore,* he says, because you have the assurance of what the best men of old only dimly foresaw, *girding up the loins of your mind, be sober.* The Apostle has in mind the words of his Master, "Let your loins be girded about, and your lamps burning; and be ye yourselves like unto men looking for their lord" (Luke xii. 35, 36). The advent of the bridegroom may be sudden; those who would be of his train must be prepared for their summons. To be girt in body is a token of readiness for coming duty. And St. Peter's figure would speak more forcibly to Eastern ears than it does to ours. Without such girding the Oriental is helpless for active work, the encumbrance of his flowing robes being fatal to exertion. The heart of the Christian must be untrammelled with the cares, the affections, the pleasures of the world. He must be free to run the race which lies before him, as was the well-girt prophet who ran before the royal chariot to the entrance of Jezreel.

And the Christian life is no light care, as St. Peter pictures it. First, he says, *Be sober*. To train the mind to exercise self-restraint is no easy duty at any time, but specially in a season of religious excitement. We know how converts in the very earliest days of Christianity were carried into excesses both in action and in word; and in every age of quickened activity some have been found with whom freedom degenerated into licence, and emotion took the place of true religious feeling. The Jewish converts in the provinces of Asia might be tempted to despise those who still clung to the ancient faith, while some of those who had been won from heathenism might by their conduct alienate rather than win their brethren in Christ. We gather what was the nature of the peril when we find the Apostle (iv. 7) urging this sobriety as a frame of mind to be cultivated even in their prayers, and St. Paul in his advice to Timothy combining the exhortation to sobriety with "Suffer hardship; do the work of an evangelist" (2 Tim. iv. 5). It is the frame of mind meet for the maintenance of sound doctrine, utterly opposed to those itching ears which are only satisfied with teaching according to their own lusts. Fitly therefore does our Apostle add to his first exhortation a second which will make the believers steadfast: *Set your hope perfectly on the grace that is to be brought unto you*. In those early days this counsel was not always easy to follow. There were many enticements to wavering, many trials which made the firm hold on strong faith difficult to maintain. And with the "perfectly" must be combined that other sense of the word "to the end." The hope must be perfect in its nature, unshaken in its firmness, persuaded of the certainty of the future grace, and strengthened in that persuasion by the experience of the present working of the Spirit. But the language of the Apostle almost anticipates the future. He says not so much that the grace is "to be brought," but rather that it is even now "being brought" near and coming ever nearer; for the revelation of Jesus Christ is progressive. Though we learn something, it is only so much as teaches us that there is more still to learn of the boundless stores of grace. But as in a former verse he spake of believers as having already by faith their salvation in possession, even such is his language here. And mark his lesson on the free gift of God s grace. It is not a blessing to which the believer can attain of his own power. He can hope for it; he can feel assured that God in His own time will bestow it. But whenever it comes, either as present grace to help in trial, or future grace which shall be revealed, it is given, brought, bestowed; and its full fruition will only be reached *at the revelation of Jesus Christ*. But assuredly these words may be applied to this life as well as to the next. He who said, "The Holy Spirit shall take of Mine and declare it unto you," designs to be ever more and more revealed in the hearts of His followers. His grace is being brought to them day by day, and trains continually unto obedience those who have been sprinkled with His blood.

And this obedience is the next precept for which they are to be made ready by the girding up of the loins of their minds, *as children of obedience*, the obedience not of slaves, but of sons. Children they are become by virtue of the new birth, and obedience it is which gives them a claim upon God's Fatherhood. They must seek for the docility and trustfulness of the childlike character; they must accept a law other than their own wills, having taken upon them the yoke of Christ and aiming, in the light of His example, to become worthy of being reckoned among His true followers.

When they contemplate their own lives, they must feel that a mighty change is needed from what they were aforetime. St. Peter's words mark the completeness of the needed change: *not fashioning yourselves according to your former lusts*. In time past they had sought no further for a guide and pattern than their own perverted desires; now they must school themselves to say, "Do with me as Thou wilt, for I am Thine." And He whose grace has begotten them again will help them to frame their lives by His rule, will have them learn of Him. But while the Apostle dwells on the difference which must come over the lives of these converts, mark the wondrous charity with which he alludes to their former life in error. *In the time of your ignorance*, he says. Even here he follows the example of the Lord, who prayed in His agony, "Father, forgive them, for they know not what they do." Sin blinds the moral and the mental vision too, and men so blinded sink deeper and deeper into the slough, while he who has learnt Christ has gained another source of light. But, to raise the ignorant, they must be taught; and tenderness makes teaching most effective, and charity dictates the apostolic words. So St. Paul at Athens to those who worshipped an unknown God offered instruction to win them from their ignorance, and pointed them to a God whose offspring they were, and to whose likeness they might be conformed.

Just so does St. Peter; *Like as He who called you is holy, be ye yourselves also holy in all manner of living*. This has been God's call from the first day until now, but what a hopeless height is this for the sinner to aim after, holy as

God is holy! Yet it is the standard which Christ sets before us in the Sermon on the Mount: "Be ye perfect, even as your Father which is in heaven is perfect." And why does He propose to us that which is impossible? Because with the command He is ready to supply the power. He knows our frailty; knows what is in man both of strength and weakness. At the same time He proclaims to us by this command what God intends to make of us. He will restore us again to His own likeness. That which was God's at first shall be made God's once more. The marred image, on which not even the superscription can be traced, shall again be revealed in full clearness, and the believer purged from all the defilements of sin by the grace and help of Him who says, "Be ye perfect," because He loves to make us so.

Because it is written, Ye shall be holy; for I am holy. This command comes down to us from the earliest days of the Law. But in those old times it could not be said, *in all manner of living.* These words betoken the loftier standard of the New Testament. The patriarchs and prophets and the people among whom they lived were trained, and could only be trained, little by little. Even in the best among them we cannot hope for holiness in all manner of living. It was only by the types and figures of external purification that their thoughts were directed to the inner cleansing of the heart, and long generations passed before the lessons were learnt. The full sense of the Fatherhood of God was not attained under the Law, nor did men under it learn fully to live as children of obedience, children of a Father who loves and will succour every effort which they make to walk according to His law. The Incarnation has brought God nearer to man, and on this relationship of love the Apostle grounds his further exhortation.

And if ye call on Him as Father, who without respect of persons judgeth according to each man's work, pass the time of your sojourning in fear. But the fear which St. Peter means is a fear which grows out of love, a fear to grieve One who is so abundant in mercy. Who can call on God as Father but the children of obedience? About the Father's will and His power to make you holy there need be no fear. He has called men and bidden them strive after holiness. The way is steep, but they will not be unattended. What fear then of failing to attain the goal? For the Father will also be the Judge. And here is the ground for eternal hope and thankfulness, which the Apostle expresses in words akin to those which he used in the house of Cornelius: "Now I see that God is no respecter of persons, but in every nation he that feareth God and worketh righteousness is accepted with Him." Yes, this is the fear which God looks for, not a paralysing dread which checks all effort and kills out all hope. Our Judge knows that our work will be full of faults, but fear of Him must nerve us to make the endeavour. It is not what men do, the feeble sum of their performance, that He regards. The way, the spirit, the motive, from which it is wrought—these will be the ground of our Father's judgement. Hence the Gospel is a message for all the world alike. The poor and lowly, to whom no great deeds are possible, may through it live a life of hope. It is not great gifts poured into the treasury from an abundant store that have value in His eyes, but the gifts which come with a heart's sacrifice—these are precious indications, and receive the blessing, "They have done what they could." And God's children are to look on their life as no more than a brief pilgrimage. It is a time of sojourning, in which the small occurrences are of little account.[5] Earth is to the Christian, what Egypt was of old to the Hebrews, no home, but a place of trial and oppression of the enemy. God will bring His children forth, even as He did of old. But the dread to be most entertained is lest the many attractions should, like the flesh-pots of the history, win the affection of the pilgrims, and make them not unwilling to linger in the house of bondage and to think lightly of peril which surrounds them there. The great preservative from this danger is to revive constantly the thought of the great things which have been done for us. Be in fear of the world and its beguilements, says St. Peter, *knowing that ye were redeemed, not with corruptible things, as silver and gold, from your vain manner of life handed down from your fathers.* The redemption price is paid, has been paid for all men. Shall any then be willing to tarry in their slavery? Ye were redeemed. The work is complete. "It is finished," was the last sigh of the dying Lord, who before had testified that His true disciples might be of good cheer, because He had overcome the world.

But in the hearts of men the world and its allurements die very hard. The men for whom St. Peter wrote would surely find this so. They had many of them lived long either under Judaism or in heathendom, and would be surrounded still by friends and kinsmen who clung to the ancient teaching and customs. Prejudices were sure to abound, and the ties of blood in such cases are very strong, as we know ourselves from mission experience in India. The Apostle speaks of their manner of life as handed down from their fathers. He may have had in his thought the corruption of the human race from the sin of our first parents. Generation after generation has been involved in the consequences of that primal transgression. But he probably thought rather of the converts from idolatry and the life which they had led in their days of ignorance. Of God's covenant with the chosen people, though now it was abolished, St. Peter would hardly speak as a *vain* manner of life. But to the worship of the heathen the word might fitly be applied. Paul and Barnabas entreat the crowd at Lystra, who would have done sacrifice to them as to their gods, to turn from these *vanities* to serve the living God (Acts xiv. 15); and to the Ephesians St. Paul writes that they should no longer walk, as the other Gentiles walk, in the *vanity* of their mind

(Eph. iv. 17). The parents of such men, having themselves no knowledge, could impart none to their children, could not lift them higher, could not make them purer; and yet the ties of natural affection would plead strongly for what had been held right by their fathers for generations.

But the price which has been paid for their ransom may convince them how precious they are in the eyes of a Father in heaven. They are redeemed *with precious blood, as of a lamb without blemish and without spot*, even the blood *of Christ*. For ages the offering of sacrifices had kept before the minds of Israel the need of a redemption, but they could do no more. The blood of bulls and goats and the ashes of a heifer suffice only to the purifying of the flesh, and can never take away sin. But now the true fountain is opened, and St. Peter has learnt, and bears witness, what was the meaning of the words of Jesus, "If I wash thee not, thou hast no part with Me" (John xiii. 8). The door of mercy is opened, that by the knowledge of such wondrous love the hearts of men may be opened also.

And this counsel of God has been from all eternity. Christ *was foreknown before the foundation of the world* as the Lamb to be offered for human redemption. The world and its history form but a tiny fragment of God's mighty works, and yet for mankind a plan so overflowing with love was included in the vision of Jehovah before man or his home had existence except in the Divine mind. Now by the Incarnation the secret counsel is brought to light, and the foretokenings of type and prophecy receive their interpretation. *He was manifested at the end of the times for your sake.* He was made flesh, and tabernacled among men; He showed by the signs which He wrought that He was the Saviour drawing near to them that they might draw near unto Him. His lifting up on the cross spake of the true healing of the souls of all who would look unto Him. And when death had done its work upon the human body, He was manifested more thoroughly as the beloved Son of God by His resurrection from the grave. The first Christians felt that God's work was now complete, salvation secured. It is not unnatural therefore that they should expect the drama of the world's history soon to be closed. For the Master had not seldom spoken of the coming of a speedy judgement. Hence the age in which they lived seemed to merit the name of "the end of the times." We now can see that the judgement of which Christ spake was wrought in great part by the overthrow of Jerusalem, though His words are still prospective, and will not find their entire fulfilment till the close of human history; and the whole Christian era may be intended and included in "the end of the times." This was the goal towards which God's counsel had been moving since the world was made. No new revelation is to be looked for, and we who live in the light of Christ's religion are those upon whom the ends of the world are come. In this sense the words may be applied in every age and to every generation of Christians. To them, as to St. Peter's converts, the preacher may testify, "For your sakes" all this was planned and wrought, and may offer the ransom of the Saviour to His people, assured that in this speck of time Christ is being manifested for their sake also. For *they through Him are believers in God*, as the Lord Himself hath testified. "No man cometh unto the Father but by Me"; "I am the Way, the Truth, and the Life." The words are as true to-day as when Christ was upon earth. Since the Fall the glory and majesty of Jehovah have been unapproachable. Sin rendered man both unfit and unable to have the pure communion of the days of innocence. It was the vision of Jesus by faith which brought Abraham near to God and filled him with joy. And so with all the saints and prophets of the first covenant. They beheld Him, but it was afar off. They greeted the maturing promises, but only as strangers and pilgrims upon earth. To the Asian converts and to us also the testimony of St. Peter and his fellows is from those who beheld the glory of God as it was manifested in Christ, who saw Him when raised from the dead, and watched His ascent into the glory of heaven. And by such witness faith in what God has wrought is confirmed. We are sure that He raised Christ from the dead; we are sure that He has received Him into glory: and thus through all generations the faith and hope of Christians are sustained and rest unshaken upon God.

V
CHRISTIAN BROTHERHOOD: ITS CHARACTER AND DUTIES

"Seeing ye have purified your souls in your obedience to the truth unto unfeigned love of the brethren, love one another from the heart fervently: having been begotten again, not of corruptible seed, but of incorruptible, through the word of God, which liveth and abideth. For all flesh is as grass, and all the glory thereof as the flower of grass. The grass withereth, and the flower falleth: but the word of the Lord abideth for ever. And this is the word of good tidings which was preached unto you. Putting away therefore all wickedness, and all guile, and hypocrisies, and envies, and all evil speakings, as new-born babes long for the spiritual milk which is without guile, that ye may grow thereby unto salvation; if ye have tasted that the Lord is gracious."—1 Peter i. 22-ii. 3.

That holy lives have been lived in solitude none would venture to dispute, and that devout Christians have found strength for themselves and given examples to the world by withdrawal from the society of their fellows is attested more than once in the history of Christendom. But with lives of such isolation and seclusion the New Testament exhibits little sympathy. To whatever preparation the Christian is exhorted, it is never with a view to himself. Though not of the world, he is to be in the world, that men may profit by his example. The prayer of the Lord for His disciples ere He left them was, not that they might be taken out of the world, but protected from its evils.

Christ's intention was to found a Church, a communion, a brotherhood, and all His language looks that way: "One is your Master, and all ye are brethren"; "So let your light shine before men that they may see your good works and glorify your Father which is in heaven." And of like character is the teaching of the Epistles: "Be kindly affectioned in love of the brethren" (Rom. xii. 10); "Let brotherly love continue" (Heb. xiii. 1). We are in no way surprised therefore when St. Peter turns from his exhortations to personal sobriety, obedience, and holiness, and addresses the converts on the application of these virtues, that through them they may bind in closer bonds the brotherhood of Christ: *Seeing ye have purified your souls in your obedience to the truth unto unfeigned love of the brethren, love one another from the heart fervently*. Obedience is the sole evidence by which the believer can show that God's call has wrought in him effectually. His election is of the Father's foreknowledge, his sanctification is the gift of the Holy Spirit, and it is the sprinkling of the blood of Christ which makes him fit for entry into the house of the Father. In the Christian, so called and so aided, there must be a surrender of himself to the guidance of that Spirit which deigns to guide him. The law in his members must be mortified, and another and purer law accepted as the rule of his life. This law St. Peter calls "the truth" because it has been made manifest in its perfection in the life of Jesus, who is the Way, the Truth, and the Life. Of this example St. Paul testifies as "the truth which is in Jesus." He therefore who would cherish the Christian hope will purify himself even as Christ is pure. The way and means unto such purification is obedience.

This first and most needful step the Apostle believes, from his knowledge of their lives, that these Asian converts have taken in earnest, and thus have attained to a love of their brethren which differs utterly from the love which the world exhibits, which is true, sincere, unfeigned. But the believer's life is a life of constant progress. Daily advance is the evidence of vitality. All the language which Scripture applies to it proclaims this to be its character. It is called a walk, a race, a pilgrimage, a warfare. The Christian all his life through will find himself so far from what Christ intends to make him that he must ever be pressing forward. Hence, though they have attained to a stage of purification, have put off in some degree the old man, the Apostle's exhortation is, "Press forward"; "Love one another from the heart fervently." The English word describes a warmth and earnestness of love which is deep-seated and true, but the original expresses more than this, more of the sustained effort to which St. Peter is urging them. It points to incessant striving, to a constancy like that of the prayers of the Church for the Apostle himself when he was in prison, a prayer made unto God without ceasing. So steadfast must be the Christian love; and such love the purified, undistracted heart alone can manifest, a heart which has been released from the entanglements of earthly ambitions and strivings, whose affections are fully set on the things above.

Such souls must be filled with the Spirit; a steadfastness like this comes only of the new birth. And of this the converts are reminded in the words which follow: *having been begotten again, not of corruptible seed, but of incorruptible, through the word of God*. It is true they are but at the outset of their Christian course; but if any man be in Christ, he is made a new creature. And in this connexion the word of God might be taken in a twofold sense. First, the Word who was made flesh, in whom was light; and the light was the life of men. Through His resurrection God has begotten men again to a life which shall know no corruption. But the figure which the Apostle presently employs of the withering grass and the falling flower carries our mind rather to Christ's explanation of His own parable. The seed is the word of God, *which liveth and abideth*. And throughout the New Testament the life-possessing and life-giving power of the Gospel is made everywhere conspicuous. When it was first proclaimed, we read again and again, "The word of God grew mightily and prevailed" (Acts xii. 24, xix. 20); and the figurative language used to describe its character shows how potent is its might. It is the sword of the Spirit (Eph. vi. 16); "It is quick and powerful" (Heb. iv. 12). By it Christ foiled the tempter. It makes those strong in whom it abides (1 John ii. 14). It is free, and not bound (2 Tim. ii. 9). St. Paul calls it "the power of God unto salvation" (Rom. i. 16), "the word of truth, the gospel of salvation" (Eph. i. 13), and says, "It comes, not in word only, but in power" (1 Thess. i. 5). This is the incorruptible seed of which St. Peter speaks. And his words force on our thoughts that for such a seed a fitting ground must be prepared, if the new life of which it is the source is to bear its due fruit. This preparation it is which the Apostle is anxious to enforce, the purifying and cleansing of the seed-plot of men's hearts. They must not be hardened so as to forbid it access, and leave it for every chance enemy to trample on or carry away; they must not be choked with alien thoughts and purposes: the cares of life, the pleasures of the world. Such things perish in the using, and can have no affinity with the living and abiding word of God, which, even as He, is eternal and unchanging.

And herewith is bound up a very solemn thought. The word may be neglected, may be choked, in individual hearts; but still it liveth and abideth, and will appear to testify against the scorners: "He that rejecteth Me and receiveth not My words hath one that judgeth him; the word that I have spoken, the same shall judge him in the last day. For I have not spoken of Myself" (John xii. 48). But for those who accept the message of the word and live thereby St. Peter's language is full of comfort, especially to those who are in like affliction with these Asian Christians. For them the acceptance of the faith of Jesus must have meant the rending asunder of earthly ties; the natural brotherhood would be theirs no longer. But they are enrolled in a new family, a family which cannot perish, whose seed is incorruptible, whose kinship shall stretch forward and be ever enlarging through all time and into eternity. For they, like the word by which they are begotten again, will live and abide for evermore.

And confirming this lesson by the prophecy of Isaiah (xl. 6-8), the Apostle thus links together the ancient Scriptures and the New Testament. But in so doing he shows by his language how he regards the latter as more excellent and a mighty advance upon the former. The margin of the Revised Version helpfully indicates the difference of the words. In Isaiah the teaching is styled a *saying*. It was the word whereby God, through some intermediary, made known His will to the children of men. But under the Gospel the word is that living, spiritual power which is used as synonymous with the Lord Himself. The word of good tidings has now been spoken unto men by a Son, the very image of the Divine substance, the effulgence of God's glory, and now possesses a might quick even to discern the thoughts and intents of the heart. This is verily the living word of God (Heb. iv. 12).

And we of to-day can see what ground there was for the Apostle's faith and for his teaching, how true the prophetic word has been found in the events of history. "All flesh is as grass, and all the glory thereof as the flower of grass. The grass withereth, and the flower falleth: but the word of the Lord abideth for ever." When we cast our thoughts back to the time when St. Peter wrote, we see the converts who had accepted the word of God a mere handful of people amid the throngs of heathendom, the religion which they professed the scorn of all about them, to the Jews a stumbling-block, to the Greeks foolishness, and its preachers in the main a few poor, untrained, uninfluential men, of no rank or conspicuous ability. On the other hand, worshipping crowds proclaimed the greatness of Diana of the Ephesians; and the power of the Roman empire was at its height, or seemed so, with the whole of the civilised world owning its sway. And now that world's wonder, the temple at Ephesus, is a pile of ruins, and over the Roman power such changes have passed that it has utterly faded out of existence; but the doctrines of the Galilean, who claimed to be the Incarnate Word of God, are daily extending their influence, proving their vitality to be Divine.

But though in his language he has seemed to mark the superiority of the Gospel message, the Apostle is deeply conscious that the office of the preacher has much, nay its chief character, in common with that of the prophet. Hence he proceeds to call the Gospel message, now that it is left to lips of Evangelists and Apostles to proclaim, a *saying* like that of Isaiah. In this way he links the New Testament to the Old, the prophet to the preacher. Both spake the same word of God; both were moved by the same spirit; both proclaimed the same deliverance, the one looking onward in hope to the coming Redeemer, the other proclaiming that the redemption had been accomplished. "This is the telling" (the saying) "of good tidings which was preached unto you."

Here St. Peter seems to allude to a preaching earlier than his own, and to none can we attribute the evangelisation of these parts of Asia with more probability than to St. Paul and his missionary colleagues. But there was no note of disagreement between these early ambassadors of Christ. They could all say of their work, "Whether it were I or they, so we preached, and so ye believed."

Having spoken of the seed, the Apostle now turns to the seed-plot which needs its special preparation. It must be cleared and broken up, or the seed, though scattered, will have small chance of roothold.

But here St. Peter recurs to his former metaphor. He has spoken (i. 13) of the Christian's equipment, how with girded loins he should prepare himself for the coming struggle. He now speaks of what he must lay aside. He has been purified, or made to long after purification, through his obedience to the truth, so that he can with earnest desire seek to make known his love to the brethren; and the word of God is powerful to overcome such dispositions as are destructive of brotherly love. Hence it is to no hopeless, unaided conflict that the Apostle urges his converts when he writes of their *putting away therefore all wickedness, and all guile, and hypocrisies, and envies, and all evil speakings.* It is a formidable list of evils, but St. Peter's words treat them as forming no part of the true man. These are overgrowths, which can be stripped away, though the operation will many a time be painful enough; they have enveloped and enclosed the sinner, and cling close about him, but the sanctification of the Spirit can help him to be unclothed of them all. They are the forces which make for discord. The word of good tidings began with "peace on earth, goodwill towards men." Hence those who hearken to the message must put away everything contrary thereto. First in the Apostle's enumeration stands a general term, *wickedness*, those which follow it being various forms of its development. We learn how utterly alien this *wickedness* is to the spirit of Christ when we notice the employment of the word to describe the sin of Simon: "Thou hast neither part nor lot in this matter, for thy heart is not right before God" (Acts viii. 22). Such a man had no comprehension of the source of the apostolic powers; the sacred things of God were unknown to one who could treat such gifts as merchandise. And it is full of interest in the present connexion to observe that what our English version there renders "matter" is really, as the margin (R.V.) shows, "word." It was the word of God which was mighty in the first preachers, which was growing and prevailing as they testified unto Christ, and in this "word" a heart like Simon's could have no share. He was no fit member of the fellowship of Christ.

Guile was the sin of Jacob, a sin which brake the bond of brotherhood between him and Esau, and wrought so much misery in the whole of Jacob's family history. Guile was not found in Nathanael. The searching eye of Jesus saw that the sin of the "supplanter" was not in him. Hence he is pointed out as an example of the true Israel, that which the race of Jacob was intended to become.

That *hypocrisy* is a foe to brotherhood our Lord makes evident as he reproaches the Pharisees for this sin. "I thank Thee that I am not as other men are, nor even as this publican," are words which could never rise to the lips of him whose heart was purified by the Spirit of God; and envy brings hatred in its train. It was by envy that Saul was incited to seek the death of David; it was from envy that Joseph's brethren sold him into Egypt; through envy a greater than Joseph was sold to be crucified (Matt. xxvii. 18), and this sin led to war in heaven itself.

From *evil-speaking* these Asian converts themselves had to suffer, and would know by experience its mischievous effects. They were spoken against as evil-doers, as the Apostle notes twice over (1 Peter ii. 12, iii. 15). This evil adds cowardice to its other baneful qualities, for it takes advantage of the absence of him against whom it is directed, and is that vice which in 2 Cor. xii. 20 is described as *backbiting*, a rendering which the Revised Version leaves undisturbed, while those who indulge in it are called *backbiters* (Rom. i. 30). St. James has much to say in its dispraise: "Speak not one against another, brethren. He that speaketh against a brother or judgeth his brother speaketh against the law, and judgeth the law" (James iv. 11). Such a one is intruding into the prerogative of God Himself, and passing sentence where he can have no sure knowledge of the acts which he judges. "Evil-speaking," says one of the Apostolic Fathers,[6] "is a restless demon, never at peace. So speak no evil of any, nor take pleasure in listening thereto." By good works St. Peter instructs his converts to live down such cowardly slanders, that those who revile their good manner of life in Christ may be put to shame thereby. Purity will overcome iniquity, innocence gain the day against deceit.

But the transformation to which the Apostle exhorts them must be verily to become a new creation, and so he goes on to speak of their condition as one akin to that of new-born babes. These by natural instincts turn away from all that will hurt them, and seek only what can nourish and support. To such right inclinations, to such simplicity of desire, must the Christian be brought. He has been born again of the word of God. From this he is to seek his constant nurture, as instinctively as the babe turns to its mother's breast. This is able to save the soul (James i. 21), but it cannot be received unless the vices which war against it be put away, and a spirit of meekness take their place. They seek other and less pure food for their support.

Christians are to *long for the spiritual milk which is without guile*. This food for babes in Christ is the word, which is taken by the Spirit and offered a nurture for the soul. But there must be a longing for, a readiness to accept, what is offered. For the spiritual appeals to the reason of man, and though offered, is not forced on him. The Spirit takes of the things of Christ and shows them unto us. And the purification, the clearing off and putting away corrupt dispositions, about which the Apostle speaks so earnestly, applies an eye-salve to the inward vision which helps us to see things in their true light, and so to long for what is really profitable food without guile, which does not disappoint the hope of those that seek it. *That ye may grow thereby unto salvation.* It is called the word of salvation. "To you," says St. Paul to the men of Antioch (Acts xiii. 26), is the word of this salvation sent forth; and through it is proclaimed the remission of sins. The healthy condition of the life of the soul is evidenced by these two signs: longing for proper food and growth by partaking thereof. For there is no standing still in spiritual life, any more than in the natural life. Where there is no growth, decay has already set in; if there be no waxing of the powers, they have already begun to wane. To the natural human growth there must needs come this waning; the body will decay: but the spiritual increase can continue, must continue, until the stature of the fulness of Christ be attained, till we come to be made like unto Him when we see Him as He is. Watch, then, strive and pray for growth, *if ye have tasted that the Lord is gracious*. The true food once found and appreciated, the joy of this support will be such that no other will ever be desired. Hence St. Peter adopts, or rather adapts, the words of the Psalmist (xxxiv. 9) who tells of the blessedness of trusting in the Lord. The angel of the Lord encampeth round about them that fear Him, and setteth them free. This is the initial stage: the deliverance from the power of evil. Then come the desire and longing for the true strength. "O taste and see that the Lord is gracious; blessed is the man that findeth refuge in Him." The joy of such a refuge can come even to those who are suffering after the fashion of the Asian converts. But the Psalmist's words are full of teaching. God's training is empirical. Spiritual experience comes before spiritual knowledge. Well does St. Bernard say of this lesson, though his words pass the power of translation, "Unless you have tasted you will not see. The food is the hidden manna; it is the new name which no one knows but he who receives it. It is not external training, but the unction of the Spirit, which teaches; it is not knowledge (*scientia*) which grasps the truth, but the conscience (*conscientia*) which attests it."

VI
THE PRIESTHOOD OF BELIEVERS

"Unto whom coming, a living stone, rejected indeed of men, but with God elect, precious, ye also, as living stones, are built up a spiritual house, to be a holy priesthood, to offer up spiritual sacrifices, acceptable to God through Jesus Christ. Because it is contained in Scripture, Behold, I lay in Zion a chief corner-stone, elect, precious: and he that believeth on Him shall not be put to shame. For you therefore which believe is the preciousness: but for such as disbelieve, the stone which the builders rejected, the same was made the head of the corner, and a stone of stumbling and a rock of offence; for they stumble at the word, being disobedient: whereunto also they were appointed. But ye are an elect race, a royal priesthood, a holy nation, a people for *God's* own possession, that ye may show forth the excellencies of Him who called you out of darkness into His marvellous light: which in time past were no people, but now are the people of God: which had not obtained mercy, but now have obtained mercy." —1 Peter ii. 4-10.

Leaving the exhortation to individual duties, the Apostle turns now to describe the Christian society in relation to its Divine Founder, and tells both of the privileges possessed by believers, and of the services which they ought to render. He employs for illustration a figure very common in Holy Scripture, and compares the faithful to stones in the structure of some noble edifice, built upon a sure foundation. Such language on his lips must have had a deep significance. He was the rock-man; his name Peter was bestowed by Christ in recognition of his grand confession: and Jesus had consecrated the simile which the Apostle uses by His own words, "Upon this rock I will build My Church" (Matt. xvi. 18), words which were daily finding a blessed fulfilment in the growth of these Asian Churches.

A rock is no unusual figure in the Old Testament to represent God's faithfulness, and its use is specially frequent in Isaiah and the Psalms. "In the Lord Jehovah is an everlasting rock" (Isa. xxvi. 4), says the prophet; again he calls God "the rock of Israel" (xxx. 29); while the prayers of the Psalmist are full of the same thought concerning the Divine might and protection: "Be Thou my strong rock and my fortress" (Psalm xxxi. 2); "Lead me to the rock that is higher than I" (lxi. 2); "O God, my rock and my Redeemer" (xix. 14).

But the language of the New Testament goes farther than that of the Old. Strength, protection, permanence—these were attributes of the rock of which Isaiah spake and David sang. The life-possessing and life-imparting virtue of the Spirit of Christ is a part of the glad tidings of the Gospel. Through Him were light and immortality brought to light. The rock which lives is found in Jesus Christ. In Him is life without measure, ready to be imparted to all who seek to be built up in Him.

Unto whom coming, a living stone, rejected indeed of men, but with God elect, precious. By purification of thought, and act, and word, that childlike frame has been sought after which fits them to draw near; and they come with full assurance. Jesus they know as the Crucified, as the Lord who came to His own, and they received Him not. Generations of preparation had not made Jewry ready for her King's coming, had failed to impress the people with the signs of His advent; and so they disowned Him, and cried, "We have no king but Cæsar." But the converts know Jesus also as Him who was raised from the dead and exalted to glory. This honour He hath "with God." No other than He could bring salvation. Therefore has He received a name that is above every name. And "with God" here signifies that heavenly exaltation and glory. The sense is[7] as when Jesus testifies, "I speak what I have seen *with My Father*" (John viii. 38)—that is, in heaven—or when He prays, "Glorify me, O Father, *with Thine own self*" (xvii. 5). From this excellent glory He sends down His Spirit, and gives to His people a share of that life which has been made manifest in Him. Their part is but to come, to seek; and every one that seeketh is sure to find.

Ye also, as living stones, are built up a spiritual house. Not because they are living men does the Apostle speak of them as living stones. They may be full of the vigour of natural life, yet have no part in Christ. The life which joins men to Him comes by the new birth. And the union of believers with Christ makes itself patent by a daily progress. He is a living stone; they are to be made more and more like Him by a constant drawing near, a constant drinking in from His fulness of the life which is the light of men. In this light new graces grow within them; old sins are cast aside. By this preparation, this shaping of the living stones, the Spirit fits Christians for their place in the spiritual building, unites them with one another and with Christ, fashions out of them a true communion of saints—saints, who, that they may advance in saintliness, have duties to perform both directly to God and for His sake to the world around. By diligence therein the upbuilding goes daily forward.

First, they are *to be a holy priesthood, to offer up spiritual sacrifices, acceptable to God through Jesus Christ*. From the day when God revealed His will on Sinai, such has been the ideal set before His chosen servants. "Ye shall be unto Me a kingdom of priests and a holy nation" (Exod. xix. 6) stands in the preface of the Divinely given law. And God changes not. Hence the praise of the Lamb's finished work when He has purchased unto God men of every tribe, and tongue, and people, and nation is sung before the throne in the self-same strain: "Thou madest them to be unto God a kingdom and priests" (Rev. v. 10). Under the early dispensation God was leading men up from material sacrifices to pay unto Him true spiritual worship. The Psalmist has learnt the lesson when he pleads, "Offer the sacrifices of righteousness, and put your trust in the Lord" (Psalm iv. 6); and Hosea's sense of what was well-pleasing to God is made clear in his exhortation, "Take with you words and return unto the Lord; say unto Him, Take away all iniquity, and accept that which is good, so will we render as bullocks the offering of our lips" (xiv. 3). The Apostle to the Romans is hardly more explicit than this when he urges, "Present your bodies a living sacrifice" (xii. 1), or to the Hebrews, "Let us offer up a sacrifice of praise to God continually, that is, the fruit of lips which make confession to His name" (xiii. 15).

But the Apostles could add to the exhortations of the prophets and psalmists a ground of blessed assurance, could promise how these living sacrifices, these offerings of praise, had gained a certainty of acceptance through Jesus Christ: "Through Him we have boldness and access in confidence through our faith in Him" (Eph. iii. 12); and in another place, "Having Him as a great Priest over the house of God," that spiritual house into which believers are builded, "let us draw near with a true heart, in fulness of faith, having our hearts sprinkled from an evil conscience and our bodies washed with pure water" (Heb. x. 22). Thus do believers become priests unto God, in every place lifting up holy hands in prayer, prayer which is made acceptable through their great High-priest.

It was only from oral teaching that these Asian Christians knew of those lessons which we now can quote as the earliest messages to the Church of Christ. The Scripture was to them as yet the Scripture of the Old Testament, and to this St. Peter points them for the confirmation which it supplies. And his quotation is worthy of notice both for its manner and its matter: *Because it is contained in Scripture, Behold, I lay in Zion a chief corner-stone, elect, precious: and he that believeth on him shall not be put to shame*. The passage is from Isaiah (xxviii. 16); but a comparison with that verse shows us that the Apostle has not quoted all the words of the prophet, and that what he has given corresponds much more closely with the Greek of the Septuagint than with the Hebrew. The latter concludes, "He that believeth shall not make haste," and contains some words not represented in the version of the Seventy. The variations which St. Peter accepts are such as to assure us that for him (and the same is true for the rest of the Apostles) the purport, the spiritual lessons, of the word were all which he counted essential. Neither Christ Himself nor His Apostles adhere in quotation to precise verbal exactness.[8] They felt that there lay behind the older record so many deep meanings for which the fathers of old were not prepared, but which Gospel light made clear. To somewhat of this fuller sense the translators of the Septuagint seem to have been guided.[9] They lived nearer to the rising of the day-star. Through their labours God was in part preparing the world for the message of Christ. The words which Isaiah was guided to use express the confidence of a believer who was looking onward to God's promise as in the future: "He shall not make haste." He knows that the purpose of God will be brought to pass; that, as the prophet elsewhere says, "the Lord will hasten it in its time" (lx. 22). Man is not to step in, Jacob-like, to anticipate the Divine working.

But "shall not be ashamed" was a form of the promise more suited to the days of St. Peter and these infant Churches. For the name of Christ was in many ways made a reproach; and only men of faith, like Moses and the heroes celebrated with him in Heb. xi., could count that reproach greater riches than the treasures of Egypt. Other and weaker hearts needed encouragement, needed to be pointed to the privileges and glories which are the inheritance of the followers of Jesus. And in this spirit he applies the prophetic words, *For you therefore which believe is the preciousness.* Faith makes real all the offers of the Gospel. It opens heaven, as to the vision of St. Stephen, so that while they are still here believers behold the glory of God to which Christ has been exalted, are assured of the victory which has been won for them, and that in His strength they may conquer also. Thus they receive continually the earnest of those precious and exceeding great promises (2 Peter i. 4) whereby they become partakers of the Divine nature.

But all men have not faith. The Bible tells us this on every page. God knows what is in man, and in His revelation He has set forth not only invitations and blessings, but warnings and penalties. Life and good, death and evil—these have been continually proclaimed as linked together by God's law, but ever with the exhortation, "Choose life." Of such warning messages St. Peter gives examples from prophecy and psalm: *But for such as disbelieve, the stone which the builders rejected, the same was made the head of the corner* (Psalm cxviii. 22), *and a stone of stumbling and a rock of offence* (Isa. viii. 14); *for they stumble at the word, being disobedient.* Here the Apostle touches the root of the evil. The test of faith is obedience. It was so in Eden; it must be ever so. But now, as then, the tempter comes with his insidious questionings, "Hath God said?" and sowing doubts, he goes his way, leaving them to work; and work they do. Now it is the truth, now the wisdom, of the command, that men stumble at. But in each case they disobey. Those leave it unobserved; these despise and set it at nought. And the penalty is sure. For mark the twofold aspect of God's dealing which is set forth in the passages chosen by St. Peter to enforce his lesson. Spite of man's disobedience, God's purpose is not thwarted. The stone which He laid in Zion has been made the head of the corner. Though rejected by some builders, it has lost none of its preciousness, none of its strength. Those who draw near unto it find life thereby; are made fit for their places in the Divine building, in the kingdom of the Lord's house which He will most surely establish as the latter days draw on. But they who disobey are overthrown. The despised stone, which is the sure word of God, rises up in men's self-chosen path, and makes them fall, and at the last, if they persist in despising it, will appear for their condemnation.

Whereunto also they were appointed. The Apostle has in mind the words of Isaiah, how the prophet, in that place from which he has just quoted, declares that many shall stumble and fall, and be broken, and be snared, and be taken. This is the lot of the disobedient. These penalties dog that sin. It is the unvarying law of God. The Bible teaches this from first to last, by precepts as well as by examples. The disobedient must stumble. But the Bible does not teach that any were appointed unto disobedience. Such fatalist lessons are alien to God's infinite love. The two ways are set before all men. God tries us thus because He has gifted us above the rest of creation, that we may render Him a willing service. But neither prophet nor Apostle teaches that to stumble is to be finally cast away. Both picture God's mercy in as large terms as those in which St. Paul speaks of the Jews: "Did God cast off His people? God forbid.... They, if they continue not in their unbelief, shall be grafted in, for God is able to graft them in again" (Rom. xi.).

A hardening in part hath befallen Israel, and to the Church of Christ there is offered the blessedness which aforetime was to be the portion of the chosen people. But the offer is made on like terms of obedient service, and involves large duties. St. Peter marks the likeness of the two offers by choosing the words of the Old Testament to describe the Christian calling, with its privileges and its duties. Believers in Christ are a peculiar treasure unto God from among all people, a kingdom of priests, and a holy nation, even as was said to Israel (Exod. xix. 5, 6) when they came out of Egypt and received the Law from Sinai. But among the dispersion, for whom he writes, there were those who had been heathens, as well as the converts from Judaism. That he may show them also to be embraced in the new covenant, and their calling contemplated under the old, the Apostle points to another of God's promises, where Hosea (i. 10; ii. 23) tells of the grace that was ready to be shed forth on them which in time past were no people, but now are the people of God, which had not obtained mercy, but now have obtained mercy. Thus all, Jew and Gentile, are to be made one holy fellowship, one people for God's own possession.

And this kingdom of God's priests has its duty to the world as well as unto God. Israel in time past was chosen to be God's witness to the rest of mankind, so that when men saw that no nation had God so nigh unto them as Jehovah was whenever Israel called upon Him, that no nation had statutes and judgements so righteous as all the Law which had been given from Sinai, they might be constrained to say, "Surely this great nation is a wise and understanding people," and might themselves be won to the service of a God so present and so holy. And now each member of the Christian body, while offering himself a living sacrifice to God, while delighting to do His will, while treasuring His law, is to exercise himself in wider duties, that God's glory may be displayed unto all men. One of the psalmists, whose words have been in part referred to Christ Himself, testifies how this priesthood for mankind should be fulfilled: "I have published righteousness in the great congregation; lo, I will not refrain my lips, O Lord, Thou knowest. I have not hid Thy righteousness within my heart; I have declared Thy faithfulness and Thy salvation; I have not concealed Thy loving-kindness and Thy truth from the great congregation" (Psalm xl. 9, 10). These were the excellencies which the Psalmist had found in God's service, and his heart ran over with desire to impart the knowledge unto others. With juster reason shall Christ's servants be prompted to a like evangel. They cannot hold their peace, specially while they consider how great blessings those lose who as yet own no allegiance to their Master.

That ye may show forth the excellencies of Him who called you out of darkness into His marvellous light. This theme fills the rest of the letter. The Apostle teaches that in every condition this duty has its place and its opportunities. Subjects may fulfil it, as they yield obedience to their rulers, servants in the midst of service to their masters, wives and husbands in their family life, each individual in the society where his lot is cast, and specially those who preside over the Christian congregations. Wherever the goodness of God's mercy has been tasted, there should be hearts full of thanksgiving, voices tuned to the praise of Him who has done great things for them. Lives led with this aim will make men to be truly what God designs: a holy nation; a kingdom of priests. And ever as men walk thus will the kingdom for which we daily pray be brought nearer.

The opportunities for winning men to Christ differ in modern times from those which were open to the earliest Christian converts; but there is still no lack of adversaries, no lack of those by whom the hope of the believer is deemed unreasonable: and now, as then, the good works which the opponents behold in Christian lives will have their efficacy. These cannot for ever be spoken against. A good manner of life in Christ shall, through His grace, finally put the gainsayers to shame. They shall learn, and gain blessing with the lesson, that the stone which they have so long been rejecting has been set up by God to be the foundation of His Church, the head stone of the corner, and the gates of hell shall not prevail against it.

VII
CHRISTIANS AS PILGRIMS IN THE WORLD

"Beloved, I beseech you, as sojourners and pilgrims, to abstain from fleshly lusts, which war against the soul; having your behaviour seemly among the Gentiles; that, wherein they speak against you as evil-doers, they may by your good works, which they behold, glorify God in the day of visitation. Be subject to every ordinance of man for the Lord's sake: whether it be to the king, as supreme; or unto governors, as sent by him for vengeance on evil-doers and for praise to them that do well. For so is the will of God, that by well-doing ye should put to silence the ignorance of foolish men: as free, and not using your freedom for a cloak of wickedness, but as bondservants of God. Honour all men. Love the brotherhood. Fear God. Honour the king."—1 Peter ii. 11-17.

The Apostle opens his exhortations with a word eminently Christian: *Beloved*. It is a word whose history makes us alive to and thankful for the Septuagint Version. Without that translation there would have been no channel through which the religious ideas of Judaism could have been conveyed to the minds of the Western peoples. There are several Greek words which signify "to love," but bound up with every one of them is some sense which renders it ill-fitted to describe true Christian love and still less suited for expressing the love of God to man. The word in the text has been fashioned to tell of that love which St. Paul describes in his "more excellent way" (1 Cor. xiii.). In classic speech it implies more of the outward exhibition of welcome, than of deep affection. But the translators of the Septuagint have taken it specially for themselves, and use it first to express the love of Abraham for Isaac (Gen. xxii. 2); and, thus consecrating and elevating it, they have brought it at length to great dignity, for they employ it to signify the love of the Lord for His people and the highest love of man to God: "The Lord preserveth all them that love Him" (Psalm cxlv. 20); "The Lord loveth the righteous" (cxlvi. 8). So in the New Testament it can be used of the "well-beloved" Son Himself. With such an expression of their union to each other in the Lord does St. Peter preface his admonitions. They are counsels of love.

I beseech you, as sojourners and pilgrims. The Christian looks for a life eternal. In comparison thereof the best things of this time are of little account, while the evil of the world renders it no safe resting-place. It is but as a lodging for a brief night, and at dawn the traveller sets forward for his true home. Hence the argument of the apostolic entreaty. You have no long time to stay, and none to waste; your motto is ever, "Onward!" *I beseech you to abstain from fleshly lusts, which war against the soul.* Of the perils of life's journey the Psalmist gives us a telling sketch in the first verse of Psalm i.; and if we may accept the words as the outcome of David's experience, they teach us the subtlety of these lusts of the flesh, as they war against the soul. They had led David to adultery and murder. The first stage of the course through which they carry you is described as walking by the counsel of the ungodly. It is not being of their number, but only being ready to accept their advice; and though the course has begun, it is still possible for him who walks to turn round and to turn back. The next step shows captivation. The man stands in the way of sinners, not afraid of his company now, though they have a taint of positive guilt instead of the negative character of ungodliness. But the war against the soul goes on; and the captive at the next stage sinks down willingly, is pleased with his chains, sits in the seat of the scorners, as ready now as they to make a mock at sin. With good reason does St. Peter use most solemn words of entreaty. The peril at all times is great. The flesh warreth against the spirit. We cannot do the things that we would. But for these men the danger was extreme. Some of them had lived in surroundings where such sins were counted a part of religious duty; had the support of long prescription; were sanctioned and indulged in by those of the convert's own blood.

Yet the Apostle does not counsel the new-made Christians to run away from this battle. They owe a duty to those who are out of the way, and must not shrink from it, be it ever so painful: *having your behaviour seemly among the Gentiles.* Their lives are to be led in the sight of their fellow-men, to be so led as to have the approval of a clear conscience, and to be void of offence in the eyes of others. This outward seemliness is what Christian love exhibits as a testimony to Christ's grace and an attraction unto the world, making known unto all men the unsearchable riches of Christ: *that, wherein they speak against you as evil-doers, they may by your good works, which they behold, glorify God in the day of visitation.* The seemly conduct of believers must be continuous, or it will fail of its effect. It is not one display of Christian conduct, nor occasional spasmodic manifestations thereof, which will win men to love the way of Christ. And this is the result without which Christ's people are not to rest satisfied. The evil reports of the adversaries are ill-grounded, but they do not think so; and the only means of removing their perverse view is by a continuous revelation of the excellence of Christ's service. They may rail, but we must bless; they may persecute: we must not retaliate, but returning good always for their evil, make them see at length that this way which they are attacking has a character and a power to which they have been strangers. This enlightenment is implied in the word "behold": *They behold your good works.* It denotes initiation into a mystery. And to unbelievers Christ's religion must be a mystery. The clearing of the vision leads them up to faith. The word in every place where it occurs in the New Testament is St. Peter's own, and he employs it once (2 Peter i. 16) to describe the vision, the insight, into the glory of Christ, which he and his fellows gained at the Transfiguration. Such a sight removes all questionings, and constrains the enlightened soul to join in the exclamation, "Lord, it is good for us to be here." The victory for Christ is to be won on the very ground where the opposition was made. In the very matter over which the enemy reviled, there shall they praise God for that which they erewhile maligned. This it is which constitutes their day of visitation. Some have thought the visitation intended was to be one of punishment for obstinate withstanding of the truth, but it surely harmonises better with the glory of God that the dispensation should be one of instruction and light. We seem to have a notable example of what is meant in the history of St. Paul. He in all earnestness persecuted the Way unto the death. The day of visitation came to him, a day which, while darkening the bodily vision, gave a clearness to the soul. The persecutor became the Apostle to the Gentiles, and the world bore him witness that now he preached the faith of which he had once made havoc (Gal. i. 23). This was God's own conquest, but in the same manner will believers be helped to win their victory. They are to aim at nothing less, never to rest content till the accusers of their good deeds are brought to glory in the performance of the same. So was Justin Martyr won to the side of Christianity: "When I heard the Christians accused and saw them fearless of death and of everything else that is counted fearful, I was sure they could not be living in wickedness and in the love of pleasures" (2 Apol. xii.). Well-doing shall not fail of its reward. Men will testify, as of Isaac of old "We saw plainly that the Lord was with thee, and we said, Let there now be an oath betwixt us" (Gen. xxvi. 28).

The Apostle now turns to one illustration of Christian behaviour wherein the converts might be tempted to think themselves absolved from some portion of their duty. They were living under heathen rulers. Did their freedom in Christ release them from obligations to the civil powers? The question was sure to arise. St. Peter supplies both a rule and a reason: *Be subject to every ordinance of man for the Lord's sake.* Christians, just as other men, hold their place in the commonweal. All that the state requires citizens to do in aid of good government, order, the support of institutions and the like, will fall upon them, as upon others. Whether the demands made upon them in this wise be always for ends of which they would approve, they are not to discuss so long as their rulers provide duly for the social order and welfare. This is the apostolic rule. The reason is, Men are to submit thus for the Lord's sake. The powers that be are ordained of God, and He would have obedience yielded to them. The Bible knows nothing about forms of government; these are to be ordered as men at various times and under various conditions deem most helpful. But the Bible doctrine is that God uses all powers of the world for His own purposes and to work out His will. Of Pharaoh, who had deliberately despised God's messages through Moses, the Divine voice declared that he would long ago have been cut off from the earth, but was made to stand that he might show God's power, and that His name might be declared throughout all the earth (Exod. ix. 15, 16); and of the Assyrian at a later day (Isa. x. 10, 12) God tells how he was used as the rod of the Divine anger, but that the fruit of his stout heart and the glory of his high looks would surely be punished. God employs for His ends instruments with which He is not always well-pleased. These can inflict His penalties, yea even may be made to advance His glory. Pilate was assured by Christ Himself that the power which he was about to exercise was only by Divine permission: "Thou wouldest have no power against Me except it were given thee from above" (John xix. 11); and St. Paul enforces obedience to authorities equally with St. Peter: "He that resisteth the power withstandeth the ordinance of God" (Rom. xiii. 2). Be subject, therefore, *whether it be to the king, as supreme; or unto governors, as sent by him for vengeance on evil-doers and for praise to them that do well.* The order under which these converts were living was superintended by some officer appointed by the Roman emperor, and to this the form of the Apostle's words applies. The king is the Cæsar; the governor is the procurator or subordinate official by whom the imperial power was represented in the provinces. When St. Peter wrote, Nero ruled in Rome, and was represented abroad by ministers often of a like character.

How extreme must after this be the case of those who would claim freedom to resist the rulers under whom they live. God has allowed them to stand, He is using them for His own purposes, they may be the ministers of His vengeance, and to Him alone does vengeance belong. He intends them also to recognise the merit of the doers of good. It may be that they do not fulfil God's intent in either wise, yet while He suffers them to keep their power the Christian's duty is obedience to every civil enactment, for anarchy would be a curse both to him and to others, bringing in its train more hurt than help. When Christians shall be found among those who abide by the law of the lands wherein they dwell, even should their faith not be accepted by their rulers, their good citizenship will hardly fail to disarm hatred and abate persecution. And so they are to range themselves ever on the side of order. *For so is the will of God, that by well-doing ye should put to silence the ignorance of foolish men.* For this end believers are to abide in the world, that through them the world may be renewed. The opponents of their faith suffer, says the Apostle, from lack of knowledge. As he says in another place, "they rail in matters whereof they are ignorant" (2 Peter ii. 12). Had men known, they would not have crucified the Lord of glory; and did they know, they would not persecute His followers. But knowledge will not come without a preacher. Such preachers of the excellence of their faith shall the law-abiding Christians in each community be made. They shall publish the lessons of their own experience; they shall win favour by their example. The world will recognise that these men have a secret which others do not possess, will find that they yield obedience to earthly rulers because they are above all things servants of God. It was through convicting them of their ignorance that Jesus put the Sadducees to silence. "Ye do err," was His argument, "not knowing the Scriptures nor the power of God" (Matt. xxii. 34). And when men are made sensible of such ignorance, they are silenced for very shame (1 Cor. xv. 34). This word "silenced" is very expressive both in the Gospel and here. It implies that a bridle or muzzle is put upon the mouth of ignorance, so that it may either be guided into a better way, or, if not so, be checked from doing harm. For some there are who not only will be ignorant, but foolish also, whom no teaching will profit. But even these will in the end be silenced. So, as says the brother Apostle, "be not overcome of evil, but overcome evil with good" (Rom. xii. 21).

The first part of the Apostle's exhortation in our verse had in view, it may be, more especially the Gentile converts. Their past life had been one of evil-doing in the sight of God; those whom they had left, and who were most likely to be their adversaries, were still walking in the same ways, and were to be won over and conquered for Christ. He now turns more directly to those who had been Jews. These were no longer bound to the observance of the ceremonial law, and we know from the New Testament as well as from Church history that with this release there were exhibited in the lives of many such excesses as made them a disgrace to the Christian name. We find much about these in the Second Epistle. St. Peter would not keep the Jewish converts under the burden of the Law, but he warns them against their besetting danger: *as free, and not using your freedom for a cloak of wickedness, but as bondservants of God.* There were bad Jews, even as there have been bad Christians. These would welcome a rule which set them at liberty from the Mosaic observances, to which their adherence aforetime had been in outward seeming rather than in earnest zeal. To these St. Peter preaches that to lay aside Judaism is not to embrace Christianity. The Leader of the new faith had ever taught a different lesson. He came not to destroy the Law, but to fulfil it, and to set forth God's will in a nobler aspect. Those who would follow Him must take up the cross. His service is a yoke which restrains from all evil. Those who come to Christ come as bondservants of God, free only because they are bound to the observance of the noblest law. They must lay aside the flesh, with its affections and lusts, and not vindicate their freedom by using it as an occasion to riot and self-indulgence.

And the Apostle binds together all his teaching in four closing precepts: *Honour all men; Love the brotherhood; Fear God; Honour the king.* All men, without distinction, are to be honoured, because in all there remains the image of God. It may be defaced, blurred exceedingly. The more needful is it to deal considerately with such, that we may help to restore what has been marred. Those who are our brethren in Christ, the brotherhood, we shall own with affection, seeking to be of one heart and one soul with them, because they belong to Christ. For them we shall have, if we be true to our faith, that mighty love which passeth in excellence both faith and hope. But the exhortation of St. Peter speaks in this wise: Ye who hold your brethren in Christ unspeakably dear, do not allow that love to suffice, to swallow up all regard for other men. They also need your thoughts, your help. The heathen, the unbelievers—these have the strongest possible claim, even their great need. And so with the other pair of precepts. Ye who fear God, which is your foremost duty, do not let that fear lessen your willingness to do honour to your earthly rulers. The feelings toward God and the king differ in character and in degree, but both have their place in proper share in the heart of the true servant of Christ.

VIII
CHRISTIAN SERVICE

"Servants, be in subjection to your masters, with all fear; not only to the good and gentle, but also to the froward. For this is acceptable, if for conscience toward God a man endureth griefs, suffering wrongfully. For what glory is it, if, when ye sin, and are buffeted *for it*, ye shall take it patiently? but if, when ye do well and suffer *for it*, ye shall take it patiently, this is acceptable with God. For hereunto were ye called: because Christ also suffered for you, leaving you an example, that ye should follow His steps: who did no sin, neither was guile found in His mouth: who, when He was reviled, reviled not again; when He suffered, threatened not; but committed *Himself* to Him that judgeth righteously; who His own self bare our sins in His body upon the tree, that we, having died unto sins, might live unto righteousness; by whose stripes ye were healed. For ye were going astray like sheep, but are now returned unto the Shepherd and Bishop of your souls." —1 Peter ii. 18-25.

The Gospel history shows very clearly that during our Lord's lifetime His followers were drawn largely from the ranks of the poor. It was fitting that He who had been proclaimed in prophecy as "the Servant of the Lord" should enter the world in humble estate; and, from the lowly position of the virgin-mother and her husband, the life of Jesus for thirty years must have been spent in comparative poverty and amid poor surroundings. The major part of His chosen disciples were fisherfolk and such-like. And though we read of the wife of Herod's steward among the women who ministered unto Him and of the richer Joseph of Arimathæa as a secret disciple, these are marked exceptions. To the poor His Gospel was preached, and among the poor it first made its way. The question of the chief priests, "Hath any of the rulers believed on Him, or the Pharisees?" (John vii. 48), tells its own tale, as does also the significant record, "The common people heard Him gladly" (Mark xii. 37).

It need not therefore much surprise us if St. Peter, now that he begins to classify his counsels, addresses himself first to "household servants": *Servants, be in subjection to your masters, with all fear.* We have, however, to bear in mind, as we consider the Apostle's exhortation, that most of those whom he addresses were slaves. They had no power of withdrawing themselves, though their service should prove burdensome and grievous. St. Paul, in writing to the same class, nearly always employs the word which means "bondservants." Yet his counsel agrees with St. Peter's. Thus he exhorts that their service be "with fear and trembling" (Eph. vi. 5); in Col. iii. 22, "Obey in all things them that are your masters." And to Timothy and Titus it is given as a part of their charge to "exhort servants to be in subjection to their own masters and to be well-pleasing to them in all things" (1 Tim. vi. 1; Titus ii. 9).

When St. Peter and St. Paul wrote, this slave population was everywhere very numerous. Gibbon calculates that in the reign of Claudius the slaves were at least equal in number to the free inhabitants of the Roman world; Robertson places the estimate much higher. These formed, then, a very large share of the public to which the first preachers had to appeal, and we can understand the importance to the Christian cause of the behaviour of these humble, but doubtless most numerous, members of the society. Their lives would be a daily sermon in the houses of their masters. Hence the very earnest exhortations addressed to them that by their conduct they should adorn the doctrine of God our Saviour in all things; that they should count their masters worthy of all honour; that the name of God and of the doctrine be not blasphemed; that they should be in subjection *with all fear.* Everything in the New Testament concerning slaves goes to show that they were a most important factor in the early Christian societies.

Men wonder nowadays that there is so little said by any of the Apostles about freeing slaves from their bondage. The best men in those times and long before appear to have regarded slavery as one of the institutions with which they were bound to rest content. It flourished everywhere; it was countenanced in the Scriptures of the older dispensation. Eleazar was Abraham's slave, and the Law in many passages contemplates the possession by Israelites of persons who were bought with their money. Hence we find no remonstrance against slave-holding in the New Testament writings, only advice to those who were in such bondage to cultivate a spirit which would render it less galling and to strive that by their behaviour the cause of Christ might be advanced. St. Paul represents the ideas of his age when, writing to the Corinthians, he says, "Wast thou called being a bondservant? Care not for it; but if thou canst be made free, use *it* rather" (1 Cor. vii. 21). Freedom was worth having, but any heroic effort to get rid of the yoke is not encouraged in the Epistles. Yet it must have been a lot which called for the exercise of much moral strength to make it bearable. Even from the house of the Christian Philemon the slave Onesimus found cause to run away. But St. Paul in his letter admits no right on the slave's part to take this course. With the Apostle there is no question that the first duty is to go back to his master. All that he urges is that the common profession of Christianity by slave and master ought to, and doubtless would, alleviate the conditions of servitude. There were in Christianity, as time has shown, germs which would fructify, a spirit which some day would strike on the chains of slaves. But the vision of such a time had not dawned either for St. Paul or St. Peter. Christ has overcome the world in many other matters beside slavery. It is only that Christians are so tardy in awaking to the fulness of His lessons.

So in apostolic days the rights and claims of slave-masters were looked upon as indisputable. Be subject, *not only to the good and gentle, but also to the froward*. There is to be no resistance, no lapse in duty. About service rendered to good masters there might be little apprehension, but even here St. Paul finds occasion for warning. "They that have believing masters," he says, "let them not despise them because they are brethren" (1 Tim. vi. 2). Christian freedom was not without its dangers in many forms, especially to minds wherein liberty was a strange idea. But froward masters are to be faithfully served likewise, and care is to be taken withal to remove every occasion for their frowardness. The apostolic lesson is to make suffering endurable, noble, acceptable to God, by seeing that it be always undeserved. How strange a doctrine this in the eyes of the world! The rule of purely human conduct would be just the opposite. If wrong be undeserved, rebel at once. Christianity supplies a motive for the contrary course: *conscience toward God*. The world's spirit is not His spirit, and to have praise with Him should be the Christian's single aim. Men can at times be patient when rebuke is deserved, but the world sees that that deserves no credit. "What thank have ye?" they cry. But they give no praise for the bearing of unmerited rebuke.

The world counts such conduct weakness, and is still far from comprehending the Divineness of the virtue of yielding patiently to wrong. God has long been teaching the lesson, but it has been slowly learnt. He chose the milder, timid Jacob rather than the fiery Esau. Both had faults in multitude. With the world Esau is oft the favourite. At a later day He stamps with approval the noble mercy of David in sparing Saul, while round Daniel and his companions in Babylon there gathers something of a halo of New Testament sanctity by reason of the noble confession which they made under persecution. These are chapters in the Divine lesson-book. Such lives marked stages in the preparation for the Servant of the Lord. Men, if they would have hearkened, were being trained to estimate such a character at God's value. Now Christ's example is before us, and we are bidden to follow it.

For hereunto were ye called. Strange invitation to be dictated by love, a call to suffering! And yet the Master at first promises nothing else to His followers: "If any man would come after Me, let him deny himself, and take up his cross, and follow Me" (Matt. xvi. 24). And what can a Christian wish for but to be like Christ? And the very reason given ought to make us love the cross. We are called unto suffering because Jesus suffered for us, leaving us an example that we should follow His steps. He has trodden the hard road, the winepress of the wrath of God, alone and for men. At this point the Apostle begins to apply to Christ Isaiah's description of the suffering "Servant of the Lord," "who did no sin, neither was guile found in His mouth" (Isa. liii.). But soon the memory of the scenes he had witnessed is present with him; and his words, though holding to the spirit of Isaiah's picture, become a description of what he himself had seen and heard when Jesus was taken and crucified: *Who, when He was reviled, reviled not again; when He suffered, threatened not, but committed Himself to Him that judgeth righteously.* How the brief words sum up and recall the dark history— Caiaphas, Pilate, and Herod; the mockery, the scourging, the railing crowd, the dying Jesus, and the parting prayer, "Father, into Thy hands I commend My spirit."

So far the Apostle speaks of the example of Christ, which, though far above and beyond us, we are exhorted and called on to follow. And there are many who will go with him thus far who value our Lord's work only for its lofty example. Indeed, it is characteristic of those who deny the mediatorial office of Christ to be loudest in magnifying the grandeur of His character. To His good works, His love for men, His spotless life, His noble lessons, they accord untiring praise, as though thereby they would atone for denying Him that office which is more glorious still. But St. Peter stops at no such half-way house. He knows in whom he has believed, knows Him for the Son of the living God, a Teacher with whom were the words of eternal life. So in pregnant words he sets forth the doctrine of the Atonement as the end of Christ's suffering: *Who His own self bare our sins in His own body upon the tree, that we, having died unto sins, might live unto righteousness.* He bare our sins. The words tell of something beyond our powers to comprehend; but some light is shed on them by a kindred passage (Matt. viii. 17), where the Evangelist applies to the work of Jesus those other words from Isa. liii., "Himself took our infirmities and bare our sicknesses." The narrative in the Gospel has just recorded how Jesus wrought many miracles. First a leper was healed, then the centurion's servant, next Simon's wife's mother, and afterwards many sick and demoniacs beside. There is no record here of the effect produced on Jesus Himself by these exhibitions of miraculous power, but from other passages in the Gospels we do find that He was conscious in Himself of a demand on His power when such cures were wrought. Thus we are told, at the cure of the woman with the issue, that Jesus perceived in Himself that the power proceeding from Him had gone forth (Mark v. 30); and again when many were cured, that "power came forth from Him and healed them all" (Luke vi. 19). Of the woman Jesus says expressly, "Thy faith hath made thee whole"; and the manifestation of eagerness to touch Jesus is a sign of the faith of the others whom the Divine power blessed with health.

The Bible recognises everywhere the analogy between sin and sickness. May we not trace some analogy between the Lord's works of healing and that mightier deliverance from sin won by Christ upon the cross, an analogy which may help, if but a little, to give meaning to the bearing by Christ of human sins? A power went forth when the sick were healed; and through that imparted power they were restored to health, faith being the pathway which brought the Divine virtue to their aid. Thus Jesus bore their diseases and took them away. Look through this figure on the work of our redemption. Christ has borne the burden of sin. He has died for sin that men may die from sin, that sin may be slain in us, the fell disease healed by the power of His suffering. We cannot comprehend what was done for the sick when Christ was on earth, nor what is wrought for sinners by His grace in heaven. Those alone who reap the blessing know its certainty; and they can but say, as the blind man whose sight was restored, "One thing I know: that, whereas I was blind, now I see" (John ix. 25).

To this teaching, that Christ's suffering wrought man's rescue, St. Peter adds emphasis by another quotation from that chapter of Isaiah which he has so much in mind: *by whose stripes ye were healed*. Christ was stricken, and God grants to His sufferings a power to heal the souls of those whom He loves because they strive to love Him. Healing through wounds! Soundness through that which speaks only of injury! Mysterious dispensation! But long ago it had been foreshadowed, and shown also how little connexion there was to be, except through faith, between the remedy and the disease. Those who were bitten of the serpents in the wilderness gazed on the brazen serpent, and were healed. In the dead brass was no virtue, but God was pleased to make of it a speaking sacrament; so has it pleased Him to give healing of sins to those who by faith appropriate the sacrifice on Calvary. Christ has claimed the type for Himself: "I, if I be lifted up from the earth, will draw all men unto Myself" (John xii. 32).

And now, as is so often his wont, St. Peter varies the figure. The wounded sinner finding cure becomes the wandering sheep that has been brought back into the fold: *For ye were going astray like sheep, but are now returned unto the Shepherd and Bishop of your souls.* But the message, the teaching, the love, is all the same. He who before was the great Exemplar, whose footsteps we should follow, is now the Shepherd, the Good Shepherd, who goes before His sheep. This Shepherd has been a Sufferer, too. He has given Himself up as a prey to the wolves that His flock might be saved. Now, with a voice of love, He calls His sheep by name; and hearing, they follow Him.

But He is more than this. Brought within the fold, the sheep still need His care; and it is freely given. He is the Bishop, the Overseer, the Watchman for His people's safety, who, having gathered them within the fold, tends them with constant watchfulness. The figure passes over thus into the reality in the Apostle's closing words. The cure which the great Healer desires to accomplish is in the souls of men. For them His care is bestowed, first to bring them safe out of the way of evil, then for ever to keep them under the sheltering care of His abundant love.

IX
CHRISTIAN WIVES AND HUSBANDS

"In like manner, ye wives, *be* in subjection to your own husbands; that, even if any obey not the word, they may without the word be gained by the behaviour of their wives; beholding your chaste behaviour *coupled* with fear. Whose *adorning* let it not be the outward adorning of plaiting the hair, and of wearing jewels of gold, or of putting on apparel; but *let it be* the hidden man of the heart, in the incorruptible *apparel* of a meek and quiet spirit, which is in the sight of God of great price. For after this manner aforetime the holy women also, who hoped in God, adorned themselves, being in subjection to their own husbands: as Sarah obeyed Abraham, calling him lord: whose children ye now are, if ye do well, and are not put in fear by any terror.

"Ye husbands, in like manner, dwell with *your wives* according to knowledge, giving honour unto the woman, as unto the weaker vessel, as being also joint heirs of the grace of life; to the end that your prayers be not hindered."—1 Peter iii. 1-7.

The Apostle gave at first (ii. 13) the rule of Christian submission generally; then proceeded to apply it to the cases of citizens and of servants. In the same way he now gives injunctions concerning the behaviour of wives and husbands. The precept with which he began holds good for them also. *In like manner, ye wives, be in subjection to your own husbands.* The life and teaching of Jesus had wrought a great change in the position of women, a change which can be observed from the earliest days of Christianity. We can gather in what estimation women were generally held among the Jews at that time from the expression used in the account of our Lord's interview with the woman of Samaria. There it is said (John iv. 27) that the disciples marvelled that Jesus was talking with a woman. Such a feeling must afterwards have been entirely dispelled, for all through the earthly life of Christ we find Him attended by women who ministered unto Him; we read of His close friendship with Mary and Martha, and are told, at the time of His death (Matt. xxvii. 55), that many women beheld the Crucifixion afar off, having followed Him from Galilee. Women were the earliest visitors to the tomb on the great Easter morning, and to them, among the first (Luke xxiv. 22), was the Lord's resurrection made known.

We are not surprised, therefore, in the history of the infant Church, to read (Acts i. 14) that women were present among the disciples who waited at Jerusalem for the promise of the Father, nor to learn how the daughters of Philip the evangelist (Acts xxi. 9) took a share in the labours of their father for the cause of Christ, or that Priscilla (Acts xviii. 26), equally with her husband, was active in Christian good offices. Other examples occur in the Acts of the Apostles: Dorcas, Lydia, and the mother of Timothy; and the constant mention of women which we find in the salutations with which St. Paul concludes his letters makes it clear how large a part they played in the early propagation of the faith. "Fellow-workers," "servants of the Church," "labourers in the Lord," are among the terms which the Apostle applies to them; and we know from the Pastoral Epistles what help the primitive Church derived from the labours of its deaconesses and widows.

To be occupied in such duties was sure to give to women an influence which they had never possessed before; and the women converts, in countries such as these Asiatic provinces, were exposed to the same sort of danger which beset the slave population at their acceptance of the Christian faith. They might begin to think meanly of others, even of their own husbands, if they were still content to abide in heathenism. Such women might incline at times to take counsel for their life's guidance with Christian men among the various congregations to which they belonged and to set a value on their advice above any which they could obtain from their own husbands. They might come to entertain doubts also whether they ought to maintain the relations of married life with their heathen partners. With the knowledge that such cases might occur, St. Peter gives his lesson. And as in the case of slaves, so here, he gives no countenance to the idea that to become a Christian breaks off previous relations. Wives, though they have accepted the faith, have wifely duties still. Like Christian citizens living in a heathen commonwealth, they are not by religion released from their previously contracted obligations; they are to abide in their estate, and use it, if it may be done, for the furtherance of the cause of Christ. Be in subjection to *your own* husbands; they have still their claim on your duty.

There is much gentleness in the Apostle's next words. He knows that there may arise cases where believing wives have husbands who are heathen. But he speaks hopefully, as thinking they would not be of frequent occurrence: *even if any obey not the word*. Wives, especially if they be of such a character as the Apostle would have them be, could not have been won to the faith of Christ without much converse with their husbands on so deep a subject; and the word which was working effectually in the one would often have its influence with the other. It might not always be so. But husbands, though not obeying the word as yet, are not to be despaired of.

And here we may turn aside to dwell on the tone of hope in which St. Peter speaks of these husbands who obey not. For the word ἀπειθοῦντες, by which they are described, is the same that is used in ii. 18 of those who stumble at the word, being disobedient. The lesson here given to Christian wives, not to despair of winning their husbands for Christ, gives warrant for what was said on the former passage: that the disobedience which causes men to stumble need not last for ever, nor imply final obduracy and rejection from God's grace. But this by the way.

The Apostle adds the strongest motive to confirm wives in holding to their married state: *That the husbands may without the word be gained by the behaviour of their wives: beholding your chaste behaviour coupled with fear.* "Without the word" here means that there is to be no discussion. They are so to live as to make their lives a sermon without words, to work conviction without debate; then, when the victory is won, there will remain no trace of combat: all will tell of gain, and nothing of loss.

And once again St. Peter uses his special word (ἐποπτεύειν) as he describes how the husbands shall be affected by the behaviour of their wives. They shall gaze on it as a mystery, the key to which they do not possess. The wives in heathen homes must have been obliged to hear and see many things which were grievous and distasteful. The husbands could hardly fail to know that it was so. If, then, they still found wifely regard and respect, wifely submission, with no assertion of a law of their own, no comparison of the lives of Christian men with those of their own husbands, if a silent, consistent walk were all the protest which the Christian wives offered against their heathen environments, such a life could hardly fail of its effect. There must be a powerful motive, a mighty, strengthening power, that enabled women to abide uncomplainingly in their estate. For this the husbands would surely search, and in their search would learn secrets to which they were strangers, would learn how the tongue was restrained where remonstrance might seem more natural, how pure life was maintained in spite of temptations to laxity, and the marriage bond exalted with religious observance even when reverence for the husband was meeting with no equal return. Such lives would be more powerful than oratory, have a charm beyond resistance, would win the husbands first to wonder, then to praise, and in the end to imitation.

And from describing the grace of such a life the Apostle turns to contrast it with other adornments of which the world thinks highly. *Whose adorning,* he says, *let it not be the outward adorning of plaiting the hair, and of wearing jewels of gold, and of putting on apparel.* We can see from the catalogue in Isaiah (iii. 18-23) that the daughters of Zion in old days had gone to great lengths in this outside bravery, and provoked the Lord to smite them. These had forgotten the simplicity of Sarah. But that in the house of Abraham there were found no such ornaments is hardly to be believed. The patriarch, who sent (Gen. xxiv. 53) to Rebekah jewels of silver and jewels of gold, did not leave his own wife unadorned. Nor does the language of St. Peter condemn Rebekah's bracelets, if they be worn with Rebekah's modesty. The New Testament does not teach us to neglect or despise the body. A misrendering in the Authorised Version, "Who shall change our vile body" (Phil. iii. 21), has long seemed to lend countenance to such a notion. It is one of the gains of the Revised Version that we now read in that place, "Who shall fashion anew the body of our humiliation." Sin has robbed the body of its primal dignity, but it is to be restored and made like unto the body of Christ's glory. And He did not despise the body when He deigned to wear it that He might draw nearer unto us. If these things be present to our thoughts, we shall seek to bestow on the body whatever may make it comely. The mischief arises when the adornment of the outer brings neglect of the inner man, when fine apparel has for its companions the haughtiness, the stretched-forth necks, and wanton eyes which Isaiah rebukes. Then it is that it rightly comes under condemnation. When the jewel is (as Rebekah's was) the gift of some dear one—a parent, a husband, a near kinsman—it rouses grateful reminiscences, and may fitly be prized, and holily worn, and ranked near to the rings of betrothal and of marriage.

Let these be the feelings which regulate womanly adornment, and it may be made a part of the culture of the heart, the inner man, which St. Peter urges the Christian wives to be careful to adorn: Let your adorning *be the hidden man of the heart, in the incorruptible apparel of a meek and quiet spirit, which is in the sight of God of great price.* All Scripture regards man as of twofold nature, the outward and the inward, of which the latter is the more precious. He is a Jew who is one inwardly (Rom. ii. 29); the inward man delighteth in the law of God (Rom. vii. 22); while the outward man perishes the inward man may be renewed day by day (2 Cor. iv. 16), being strengthened with power through God's Spirit. This hidden man is the centre from which all the strength of Christian life comes. Let this be rightly adorned, and the outward life will need no strict rules; there will be no fear of excess, least of all when the inner life is cared for because it is precious before God. Its pure array passeth gold and gems, be they ever so beautiful. This is a grace which never fades, but will flourish through eternity.

The Apostle proceeds to commend it by a noble example. The Old Testament Scriptures do not dwell largely on the lives of women, but a study of what is said will oftentimes reveal deeper meaning in the record and put force into a solitary word. The writer of the Epistle to the Hebrews couples Sarah with Abraham in the list of heroes and heroines of faith, and St. Peter from a single word finds a text to extol the submission which she showed to her husband. He probably refers to Gen. xviii. 12, where she gives the title of "lord" to Abraham, as Rachel in another place (Gen. xxxi. 35) does to her father Laban: *For after this manner aforetime the holy women also, who hoped in God, adorned themselves, being in subjection to their own husbands: as Sarah obeyed Abraham, calling him lord.* A Scripture example which has more in common with the experience of the Asian women is the life of Hannah. Her lot, for a time at least, was as full of grief and disappointment as theirs could be; but her trust in God was unshaken. Her patience under provocation was exemplary, while the picture of her home life is one full of touching affection on the part of both husband and wife; and the mother's gratitude, when her prayer was granted, is set forth in her noble hymn of thanksgiving and in the devotion of her child to the service of the God who had bestowed him. Ruth is another of those holy women who must have been in St. Peter's thoughts, who, though not of the house of Israel, manifested virtues in her life which made her fit to be the ancestress of King David. The Apostle, however, seems to have had a purpose in his special mention of Sarah. As the sons of Israel looked back to Abraham and to the covenant sealed with him, yea, not seldom prided themselves on being his children, so the daughters of Israel counted themselves as Sarah's daughters after the flesh. St. Peter now gives them another ground for that claim. God's promises to Abraham have been fulfilled in Christ, and so Christian Jewesses are more truly than ever daughters of Sarah. *Whose children ye now are.* But to the heathen converts the same door was opened. They by their faith were now made partakers of the ancient covenant. They too were become Sarah's daughters. Let them, one and all, continue in the well-doing which has been commended; let it be seen in the daily round (ἀναστροφὴ) of their lives, led in quietness and humility. The excessive love of adornment against which they are warned marks a condition of boldness and unrest. But unrest may enter into the other actions of their life. Their behaviour is to be coupled with fear and reverence, but it should eschew everything which partakes of flighty irregularity. It should be steady and consistent, running into no extremes either of humiliation or the contrary. *Do well, and be not put in fear by any terror.*

The Apostle now addresses Christian husbands. In his counsel to subjects and slaves he has not dwelt on the duties of rulers and masters.

Perhaps he judged it unlikely that his letter would come to the hands of many such, or it may be he thought the lessons which he had to give were more needed by the subject people, if Christ's cause were to be furthered. But with husbands and wives life has of necessity a great deal in common, and the one partner can hardly receive counsel which is not of interest to the other. To the wives the Apostle spake as though examples of unbelieving husbands might be rare. Christian husbands with unbelieving wives he hardly seems to contemplate. We know from St. Paul (1 Cor. vii. 16) that there were such. But doubtless heathen wives hearkened to Christian husbands more readily than heathen husbands to their Christian wives. The husbands are to use their position as heads of their wives with judgement and discretion: *Dwell with your wives according to knowledge.* The knowledge of which St. Peter speaks is not religious, godly, Christian knowledge, but that foresight and thoughtfulness which the responsibility of the husband calls for. He will understand what things for his wife's sake he should do or leave undone. This knowledge, which results in considerate conduct towards her, will manifest itself in Christian chivalry. The woman is physically the feebler of the two. No burden beyond her powers will be laid upon her; and by reason of her weaker nature regard and honour will be felt to be her due. For the woman is the glory of the man (1 Cor. xi. 7). Such observance will not degenerate into undue adulation nor foolish fondness, apt to foster pride and conceit, but will be inspired by the sense that in God's creation neither is the man without the woman, nor the woman without the man.

But beyond and above these daily graces of domestic and social intercourse, the Apostle would have husband and wife knit together by a higher bond. They are *joint heirs of the grace of life.* Both are meant to be partakers of the heavenly inheritance, and such participation makes their chief duty here to be preparation for the life to come. Those who are bound together not by wedlock only, but by the hope of a common salvation, will find a motive in that thought to help each other in life's pilgrimage, each to shun all that might cause the other to stumble: *That your prayers be not hindered.* They are fellow-travellers with the same needs. Together they can bring their requests before God, and where the two join in heart and soul Christ has promised to be present as the Third. And in praying they will know one another's necessities. This is the grandest knowledge the husband can attain to for the honouring of his wife; and using it, he will speed their united supplications to the throne of grace, and the union of hearts will not fail of its blessing.

X
THEY WHO BLESS ARE BLESSED

"Finally, *be* ye all like-minded, compassionate, loving as brethren, tender-hearted, humble-minded: not rendering evil for evil, or reviling for reviling; but contrariwise blessing; for hereunto were ye called, that ye should inherit a blessing. For he that would love life, and see good days, let him refrain his tongue from evil, and his lips that they speak no guile: and let him turn away from evil, and do good; let him seek peace, and pursue it. For the eyes of the Lord are upon the righteous, and His ears unto their supplication: but the face of the Lord is upon them that do evil. And who is he that will harm you, if ye be zealous of that which is good? But and if ye should suffer for righteousness' sake, blessed *are ye*: and fear not their fear, neither be troubled; but sanctify in your hearts Christ as Lord: *being* ready always to give answer to every man that asketh you a reason concerning the hope that is in you, yet with meekness and fear: having a good conscience; that, wherein ye are spoken against, they may be put to shame who revile your good manner of life in Christ."—1 Peter iii. 8-16.

The Apostle now ceases from his special admonitions, and enforces generally such qualities and conduct as must mark all who fear the Lord. *Finally*, he says—and the word may indicate the close of his counsels; but the virtues which he inculcates are of so important a character that he may very well intend them as the apex and crown of all his previous advice— *be ye all like-minded, compassionate, loving as brethren, tender-hearted, humble-minded*. St. Peter has here grouped together a number of epithets of which all but one are only used in the New Testament by himself, and they are of that graphic character which is so conspicuous in all the Apostle's language. *Like-minded*. If the word be not there, the spirit is largely exemplified in the early history of the Church. How often we hear the phrase "with one accord" in the opening chapters of the Acts. Thus the disciples continued in prayer (i. 14); thus they went daily to the Temple (ii. 46); thus they lifted up their voices to God (iv. 24), for all they that believed were of one heart and one soul (iv. 32). Such lives exhibit harmony of thought, the same aim and purpose. The men may not, will not, always use the same means or follow the same methods, but they will all be seeking one result. Such unity is worth more than uniformity. *Compassionate.* This feeling St. Paul describes (Rom. xii. 15) as rejoicing with them that do rejoice and weeping with them that weep. For the παθήματα of this life are not always sorrowful, though the best of them are not worthy to be compared with the glory that shall be revealed (Rom. viii. 18).*Loving as brethren.* The sense of the brotherhood of Christians is strongly marked in all the New Testament Scriptures. It is the name by which our Lord claims fellowship with men, being not ashamed to call them brethren. It is the designation of the Christian body from the first (Matt. xxiii. 8), is constantly found in the Acts and the Epistles (Acts vi. 3, ix. 30, xi. 29), and has been used of the Church in every age, marking how as one family we dwell in Him. Next comes the word which is not St. Peter's alone: *Tender-hearted.* St. Paul has it (Eph. iv. 32), but it is no Greek notion. It was a Jewish idea that deep feeling was closely connected with some of the organs of the body; and in the Old Testament, as in the story of Joseph (Gen. xliii. 30) and elsewhere (1 Kings iii. 26), we come upon such phrases as "His bowels did yearn upon his brother." This Hebrew notion the LXX. has conveyed into Greek by the word which St. Peter here uses, and which those translators had used and consecrated long before. For them so exalted was the thought contained in it that they employ it in the prayer of Manasses (ver. 7) to express the tenderness of God towards the penitent, the yearning love of the Father, who sees the prodigal afar off, and has compassion. *Humble-minded.* This word and those akin to it are almost a New Testament creation. The heathen had no admiration for the temper it expresses, and where they do use the word it is in a bad sense as signifying "cowardly" and "mean-spirited." Before Christ none had taught, "He that is greatest among you shall be your servant" (Matt. xxiii. 11).

It is manifest that if such harmony, kind feeling, attachment, affection, and humility flourished among believers, these virtues would put discord to the rout, and leave no occasion for rending the oneness of the Christian body. They would also be proof against evil from without, both in deed and speech, neither tempted to *render evil for evil* in their actions nor *reviling for reviling* in their words. They have a duty to the world, and cannot thus belie their Christian profession. They are called to adorn the doctrine of their Saviour, and the Master's sermon has among its prominent precepts "Bless them that curse you." This is the spirit of St. Peter's exhortation, *But contrariwise blessing*; that is, Be ye of those who bless. For there is a law of recompense with God in good things as in evil; the blessers shall be blessed:

For hereunto were ye called, that ye should inherit a blessing. It is as though he urged them thus: Ye were aforetime enemies of God; but ye have been made partakers of His heavenly calling (Heb. iii. 1), that ye may come to blessing. This should move you to bless your enemies. And more than this, the servant of God may receive no blessing from the world, may get curses for his blessing; but yet he knows where to flee for consolation. He can pray with the Psalmist, "Let them curse, but bless Thou" (Psalm cix. 28), conscious that the Lord will stand at the right hand of the needy.

The psalmists knew much of such trials, and it is from the words of one of them (Psalm xxxiv. 12-16) that St. Peter enforces his own lesson. It is a psalm full of the knowledge of the trials of God's servants: "Many are the afflictions of the righteous"; but it is rich also in plenitude of comfort: "The Lord delivereth him out of them all." The father of long ago teaches thus to his children the fear of the Lord: *He that would love life, and see good days, let him refrain his tongue from evil, and his lips that they speak no guile: and let him turn away from evil, and do good; let him seek peace, and pursue it. For the eyes of the Lord are upon the righteous, and His ears unto their supplication: but the face of the Lord is upon them that do evil.* A glance at the Psalm will show that the Apostle has not quoted precisely; and though he has much in common with the Greek of the LXX., he does not adhere closely to that. But he gives to the full the spirit both of the Hebrew and the Greek. The life of which the Psalmist speaks is life in this world. The original explains this by making the latter clause of the verse, "and loveth *many* days, that he may see good." And the love is to be a noble feeling, a desire to make his worth living. Such a life must exhibit watchfulness over words and actions. The precepts begin at the beginning, with control of the tongue. Control that, and you are master of the rest. "It is a little member, but boasteth great things." "The world of iniquity among our members is the tongue, which defileth the whole body" (James iii. 5, 6). It needs to be kept as with a bridle, and not only when the ungodly are in sight, but constantly. But the words of the Psalm contemplate a further danger. Men may give good words with the lips while the heart is full of bitterness. Then the lips are lying, and this is an evil as great as the former, and more perilous to him who commits it, because the sin does not come to the light that it may be reproved, but contrives to wear the mask of virtue.

And the actions need watchfulness also. They must not only possess the negative quality of abstinence from evil, but the positive stamp of good deeds done. "By their fruits ye shall know them." And the work will be no light one. Peace is to be sought, and the Apostle uses a word which implies that a chase is needful to obtain it. St. Paul has a passage very much in the spirit of St. Peter's teaching here, and the words of which picture distinctly the difficulties which the Christian will have to labour against: "Giving diligence to keep the unity of the Spirit in the bond of peace" (Eph. iv. 3). This tells us why our Apostle urges the pursuit of peace. It is the clasp which binds the Christian communion together. From all sorts of causes men are prone to fall apart, to break the oneness; and peace is able to hold them fast. Hence the diligence in seeking it, the earnestness of the pursuit that it may not elude us.

But when all is done, when men have not been sitting with folded hands waiting and dreaming that peace would come without pursuit, but have laboured for it, they do not always attain to it. "I am for peace," says the Psalmist, "but when I speak, they are for war" (Psalm cxx. 7). And so the disappointed struggler is directed to the sure source of consolation amid discomfiture. The Lord marks his efforts, knows their earnest purpose in spite of their ill-success. He beholds also those who have withstood them, but with far other regard. St. Peter has not quoted what the Psalmist says of their fate: "God will root out the remembrance of them from the earth." God's righteous pilgrim is not forgotten. His prayer is heard, and will be answered for good. No shadow has come between him and God, though his lot seem very dark. Neither can the wrong-doer raise a shadow to screen himself from the all-seeing eyes. All things are naked and open before the eyes of Him with whom we have to do.

Thus far St. Peter has used the language of the Psalmist, and among the converts the Jews would be sure to supply from the context those other words, "O fear the Lord, all ye His saints; for they that fear Him lack nothing." The Apostle clothes that same thought in his own words: *And who is he that will harm you, if ye be zealous of that which is good?* He has repeatedly dwelt on the power of goodness to win unbelievers to its side (ii. 12, 15; iii. 1), and the same idea shapes his words now. In those days the Zealots were well known, and their unbounded enthusiasm for their evil cause. Josephus lays the destruction of Jerusalem at their door. The Apostle would have Christ's disciples "zealots" for Him. Let there be nothing half-hearted in their service, and its power will be irresistible. It will avail either to silence and confound the adversaries, or to strengthen the faithful so that the smell of the furnace of persecution shall not pass upon them. They shall be enabled to break the chains with which their foes would bind them as easily as Samson his green withes. *But and if ye should suffer for righteousness' sake, blessed are ye.* If ye endure chastening, God is dealing with you as with sons. He has called Himself your Father; Christ has claimed you for brethren. He, the righteous, suffered; shall we not reckon it for a blessing to be worthy to bear the cross? Only let us be of good courage. He that endureth to the end shall find salvation. *And fear not their fear, neither be troubled.* Again St.

Peter applies the promises of the ancient Scriptures. In the days of Isaiah all Judah was in terror, king and people alike, before the gathering armies of Syria and Israel. In their dread comes the prophetic message, and says to the confederates, "Gird yourselves, and ye shall be broken in pieces," and to the tiny power of Judah, "Let the Lord of hosts be your fear, and let Him be your dread, and He shall be for a sanctuary" (Isa. viii. 12, 13). The condition of these Asian converts was one of heaviness through manifold temptations. While the believer lives here he always has his assailants, and in those early days the rulers of the earth were not seldom among the adversaries of the Christians. Hence the Apostle's exhortation is most apposite: Fear not their fear—the things which they would dread, and with which they will threaten you. For what are they? They may take away your property. Be not troubled; you would soon have had to leave it. The loss a few years sooner is no terrible affliction. They may drive you from one land to another. To strangers and sojourners what can that signify? If they cast you into prison, the Lord who shut the lions' mouths for Daniel is your Lord also; and I, Peter, know how angel-hands have removed chains and opened prison doors. And should they scourge and torture you, do you shrink from thus being made like unto your Master? *Sanctify in your hearts Christ as Lord.*

Isaiah's message to disheartened Judah was, "The Lord of hosts, Him shall ye sanctify." On His word shall ye rely, assured that He, the holy God, will fail neither in wisdom nor power. To think otherwise is not to sanctify Him. The Lord knoweth how to deliver out of temptation. St. Peter, who knew Christ as the Son of the living God, applies to the Son the words first spoken of the Father. The Son is one with the Father. Hence he bids the afflicted converts, suffering for righteousness' sake, not to be afraid of the world's terror, but to sanctify Christ in their hearts as Lord. He is the Emmanuel, whom Isaiah was sent to promise. God has dwelt among men, and will be the God and the Deliverer of all His faithful ones. This sense of "God with us" they know, and with the knowledge comes a power not their own, and they fear no more the fear of their adversaries.

It is against foes of another sort that the Christian has now to hold fast his faith, and sanctify Christ as his Lord. There are those who deny Him all that is supernatural, all that speaks of the Divine in His history; who treat the resurrection and ascension of the Lord as groundless legends, due to the ignorance of His followers; and who leave to the Jesus of the Gospels only the qualities of a better fellow-man. These are the enemies of the cross of Christ.

And of such dangerous teaching it would seem as if St. Peter had been thinking in the words that follow: *Being ready always to give answer to every man that asketh you a reason concerning the hope that is in you.* The believer rests on Christ in faith. But though in his belief there must be much which he cannot fathom, yet it is a belief for men. His service is a reasonable service; he can point to abundance of evidence as ground for his faith; he believes because he has experienced the power of the Spirit, and fears not to trust the Christ whom he has sanctified in his heart as Lord; he knows in whom he has believed. But beside this, he can study the Old Testament; and there he learns how the coming incarnation dominates every portion of the volume, how from the first redemption through the seed of the woman was made known; and he follows the revelation step by step till in the evangel of Isaiah he has predictions almost as vivid and plain as the narrative of the Gospels. Those four narratives are another warrant for his faith, their wondrous agreement amid multitudinous divergences, divergences so marked that none could have ventured to put them forth as history except while the knowledge of those who had seen the Lord and been witnesses of His actions was available to vouch for and stamp as true these varicoloured pictures of the life of Jesus. He has further vouchers in the lives and letters of those who knew and followed the Lord, followed Him, most of them, on the road that led through persecution unto death. And beside all this, there stands and grows the Church built upon this history, strong with the power of this faith and in her holy worship sanctifying Christ as her Lord. These are things to which the Christian appeals. They are not the only reasons for belief, but they are those of which he can make other men cognisant, and to which the world cannot continue always blind; and they have a force against which the gates of hell have not yet been, nor ever will be able, to prevail.

These reasons he gives *with meekness and fear*—with meekness, because in that spirit all the victories of the Lord are to be won; with fear, lest by feeble advocacy the cause of Christ may suffer. And he does not bring words alone with him to the struggle, but the power of a godly life; he is prepared for the conflict by the possession of a *good conscience* before God and men; he bears in mind the prophetic exhortation, "Be ye clean, ye that bear the vessels of the Lord" (Isa. lii. 11). That injunction was given to those who were in their day strangers and pilgrims. But with the good conscience, pureness of heart in the service of the Lord, there need be no haste, no flight. The Lord will go before them; the God of Israel will be their rearward. And the good conscience has lost none of its efficacy: *Wherein ye are spoken against, they may be put to shame who revile your good manner of life in Christ.* Of the Christian's faith and hope his revilers know nothing, but his good life and his reasons for it men can see and hear. And these shall gain the victory. But they must go hand in hand. The deeds must bear out the words. When he testifies that his hope is placed where neither persecutions nor revilings avail against it, his life must show him fearless of what the world can do. His position toward it must be that which St. Peter himself took: "Whether it be right in the sight of God to hearken unto you more than unto God, judge ye" (Acts iv. 19). Men may marvel at what they see in him, but they will take knowledge that he has been with Jesus. He is created, new-created, in Christ Jesus unto good works (Eph. ii. 10). His revilers use him despitefully; but, according to Christ's lesson, he prays for them, and their shafts glance pointless off. Well does St. Paul close his catalogue of the Christian armour "with all prayer and supplication praying at all seasons in the Spirit" (Eph. vi. 18). Thus does the believer wield his weapons effectually. His revilers have no reason for their words; he is careful that they shall have none. As with Peter and John the council could say nothing against their good deed and let them go, finding nothing how they might punish them, so shall it be with others of the faithful; and, for very shame at the futility of their accusations and assaults, the revilers shall be put to silence.

XI

THE REWARDS OF SUFFERING FOR WELL-DOING

"For it is better, if the will of God should so will, that ye suffer for well-doing than for evil-doing. Because Christ also suffered for sins once, the righteous for the unrighteous, that He might bring us to God; being put to death in the flesh, but quickened in the spirit; in which also He went and preached unto the spirits in prison, which aforetime were disobedient, when the long-suffering of God waited in the days of Noah, while the ark was a-preparing, wherein few, that is, eight souls, were saved through water: which also after a true likeness doth now save you, *even* baptism, not the putting away of the filth of the flesh, but the interrogation of a good conscience toward God, through the resurrection of Jesus Christ; who is on the right hand of God, having gone unto heaven; angels and authorities and powers being made subject unto Him."—1 Peter iii. 17-22.

The Apostle comes back to his solemn subject. Why are the righteous called to suffering? The question was perplexing these Asian Christians when St. Peter wrote. Previous ages had pondered over it, Job and his friends among the number; and men ponder over it still. St. Peter has suggested several answers: The faith of Christ's servants after trial will be found praiseworthy at the appearance of their Lord; to bear wrong with patience is acceptable with God; it is a happy lot, Christ has said, to suffer in the cause of righteousness. His next response to the question is more solemn than these: Suffering is sent to the righteous by the will of God. It never comes otherwise, and is meant to serve two several purposes: it is intended to benefit the unrighteous, and to be a blessing and glory to the righteous who endure it.

He shows that this is God's will by two examples. Christ, the sinless, suffered at the hands of sinful men, and for their sakes, as well as for all sinners; and though we only can approach the subject with deep reverence and use the language of Scripture rather than our own about the effect of suffering on Christ Himself, we are taught therein that He was made perfect as the Leader of salvation by the things which He suffered: and the Apostle here describes the sequel of those sufferings by the session on the right hand of God in heaven, where angels and authorities and powers are made subject unto Him.

But God's ordinance in respect of the suffering of the godly has been the same from of old. In the ancient world Noah had found grace in God's sight in the midst of a graceless world. He was made a witness and a preacher of righteousness; and the faithful building of the ark at God's command was a constant testimony to the wrong-doers, whose sole response was mockery and a continuance in the corruption of their way. But God had not left them without witness; and when the Deluge came at length, some hearts may have gone forth to God in penitence, though too late to be saved from the destruction. To Noah and those with him safety was assured; and when the door of the ark was opened, and the small band of the rescued came forth, it was to have the welcome of God's blessing and to be pointed to a token of His everlasting covenant. In this wise St. Peter adds once more to the consolations of those who endure grief and suffering wrongfully, and thus does he set forth the general drift of his argument. But the whole passage is so replete with helpful lessons that it merits the fullest consideration.

For it is better, if the will of God should so will, that ye suffer for well-doing than for evil-doing. For evil-doing suffering is certain to come. It cannot be escaped. God has linked the two together by an unalterable law. Such suffering is penal. But when the righteous are afflicted their lot is not of law, but of God's merciful appointment and selection, and is ordained with a purpose of blessing both to themselves and others. The words of St. Peter are very emphatic concerning God's ordinance: *If the will of God so will.* It is not always clear to men. Therefore St. Paul (Eph. i. 9) speaks of the mystery of the Divine will, but in the same place (i. 5) of the good pleasure thereof. It is exercised with love, and not with anger. It was the feeling[10] with which God looked forth upon the new-created world, and, behold, it was very good (Rev. iv. 11). With the same feeling He longs to behold it rescued and restored. Such is the desire, such the aim, with which God permits trial and distress to fall upon the righteous. And that the sufferers may be kept in mind of God's remedial purpose herein, the Apostle adduces the example of Christ Himself: *Because Christ also suffered for sins once, the righteous for the unrighteous, that He might bring us to God.* The suffering Christ should give pause to all questionings about the sufferings of His servants. Their lot may be hard to explain. But be their lives ever so pure, their purposes ever so lofty, "in many things we offend all," and need not murmur if we be chastened.

But as we think of the sinless Jesus and His unequalled sufferings, we learn the applicability of the prophet's lamentation, "See if there be any sorrow like unto my sorrow" (Lam. i. 12). The burden of the unrighteous world was laid upon the righteous Son of God, and this because of God's love for sinners. Herein was the love of God manifested in us. Sinful men were the material chosen for the display of the Divine love, and God sent His only-begotten Son into the world that we might live through Him. It was of God's ordinance and the Son's obedience that redemption was thus purchased. That we might live, the sinless Christ must die, and ere He died must be put to grief by the opposition of those whom He came to save; must lament and be hindered in His works of mercy by the want of faith among His own kindred, by the persistent sins of those cities in which His mightiest works were wrought; must shed tears of anguish over the city of David, which would know nothing of the things which belonged unto her peace. This was the chastisement of the innocent to gain peace for the guilty, that God might thus commend His love to men, and Christ might bring them back to the Father. And this bringing back is not the mere action of a guide. This He is, but He is far more: He helps those who are coming at every step, and as they draw near they find through Him that the Father's house and the Father's welcome are waiting for their return. Shall men complain, nay shall they not be lost in praise, if God will at all consent to use their trials to extend His kingdom and His glory, and thus make them partakers of the sufferings of Christ? Such a lot had been welcome to St. Peter: "They departed from the presence of the council rejoicing that they were counted worthy to suffer dishonour for the name" (Acts v. 41); and here in his epistle he publishes the joy of such shame, publishes it that others through all ages may suffer gladly, trusting their God to use the pains He sends to magnify His glory. The lesson is for all men at all times. Christ suffered for sins once; but once here means once for all, and proclaims to each generation of sinners that Jesus bore His cross for them.

Being put to death in the flesh, but quickened in the spirit. The suffering of Jesus went thus far, that there might be nothing in the cup of human woe which He had not tasted. His spirit was parted from the flesh, as when we die. The body lay in the grave; the spirit passed to the world of the departed. But the triumph of death was short. After the three days' burial came the miracle of miracles. The dead Jesus returned to life, and that resurrection is made the earnest of a future life to all believers. Thus began the recompense of the righteous Sufferer, and the power of the resurrection makes suffering endurable to the godly, makes them rejoice to be conformed unto Christ's death and forgetful of all things save the prize of the high calling, which lies before them to be won. Nor was it with Christ's spirit during those three days as with the souls of other departed ones. He, the sinless One, had no judgement to await; His stay there was that dwelling in paradise which He foreknew and spake of to the penitent thief.

In which also He went and preached unto the spirits in prison, which aforetime were disobedient, when the long-suffering of God waited in the days of Noah. At this point we come upon a twofold line of interpretation, occasioned by the difficulty which constantly arises of deciding whether πνεῦνα—"spirit" is to be understood of the Divine Spirit or of the spiritual part of man's nature as distinguished from the flesh. Those who have taken the words "quickened in the Spirit" of the previous verse in the former of these senses explain this passage of the preaching of Christ to the antediluvian world through His servant Noah. The Divine fiat had gone forth. The Flood was to come and bring destruction to the bodies of all but Noah and his family. But within those doomed bodies souls were shut up, and these the love of Christ would not willingly give over. They should hear, while still in their prison of the flesh, the offer of His grace; and should they repent, the waves which wrought destruction of the body might release them from the bondage of corruption. This was the purpose of God's long-suffering, which waited and appealed while the ark was a-preparing. Thus did the Divine Spirit of Christ go forth as a herald of mercy to the impenitent, proclaiming that for their souls the door of forgiveness was not yet closed.

Those, on the contrary, who refer "quickened in the spirit" to the human soul of Christ, take this text as an additional authority for the doctrine in the Apostles' Creed that our Lord's human soul after the Crucifixion descended into hell. Thus, they hold, His pure spirit went beyond this world to experience all that human spirits can know before the judgement comes. Thither He came but as a Herald. Death and the grave had no power to detain Him. In mercy to those who had passed away before the Incarnation, He brought the message of the mediatorial work which He had completed in His crucifixion. The sinners before the Flood are singled out for mention by St. Peter as sinners above all men, so sunk in wickedness that but eight were found worthy to be saved from the Deluge. Thus the magnitude of Christ's mercy is glorified. He who goes to seek these must long to save all men. And to carry this message of glad tidings is part of the recompense for the agonies of Gethsemane and Calvary, a portion of what made it a blessing to suffer for well-doing.

Up to the sixteenth century the latter exposition and application of the words found most favour, but at the time of the Reformation the chief authorities[11] expounded them of the preaching of Christ's Spirit through the ministry of the patriarch. For the main argument with which St. Peter is dealing these applications, however interesting in themselves, are not deeply important. He wants to set before the converts a warrant for what he has said about the blessedness of suffering for righteousness. If we accept the application to Noah, the example is a powerful one. His sufferings must have been manifold. The long time between the threatened judgement and its accomplishment was filled with the opposition of sinners and their mockery and taunts over his patient labour on the ark, to say nothing of the distress of soul when he found his preaching falling ever on deaf ears. But his trial had its reward at last when the little band were shut in by God Himself, and the ark bore them safely on the rising waters. And if he could feel that any, though perishing in body, had by repentance been saved in soul, this would make light the burden even of greater suffering than had fallen to the patriarch, to know the joy which comes from converting a sinner from the error of his way and therein saving a soul from death.

And if we refer the words "quickened in the spirit" to the soul of Christ, parted from the body and present in the spirit-world, they are a link to connect this passage with words of the Apostle's sermon on the day of Pentecost. There he does speak of the Lord's descent into hell, and teaches how David of old spake thereof and of the Resurrection "that neither was He left in Hades, nor did His flesh see corruption" (Acts ii. 31). In this sense the quickening in the spirit is the beginning of Christ's victory and triumph. It is the earnest of eternal life to all believers. And how welcome a message to those who, like Abraham, had rejoiced in faith to see the day of Christ, to hear from His own lips the tidings of the victory won! Of the Herald of such a Gospel message, of Him who by His suffering delivered those who through fear of death were all their lifetime subject to bondage, we may, with all reverence, speak as "being made perfect by becoming the Author of eternal salvation to all them that obey Him" (Heb. v. 9).

Wherein few, that is, eight souls, were saved. The building of the ark was the test of Noah's faith, the ark itself the means of his preservation. In the patriarch's sufferings St. Peter has found an apt parallel to the life of these Asian Christians: the same godless surroundings; the same opposition and mockery; the same need for steadfast faith. But if rightly pondered, the Old Testament lesson is rich in teaching. Noah becomes a preacher of righteousness, not for his own generation only, but for all time. He suffered in his well-doing. Nothing stings more keenly than scorn and contempt. These he experienced to the full. He came as God's herald to men who had put God out of all their thoughts. His message was full of terror: "Behold, I do bring a flood of waters upon the earth, to destroy all flesh wherein is the breath of life from under heaven; everything that is in the earth shall die" (Gen. vi. 17). Few heeded; fewer still believed. But when the work of the messenger was over; when the ark was prepared, and the fountains of the great deep were broken up, and the windows of heaven were opened; when he and his were shut in by God, then appeared the blessedness. And if haply there had been any in whom he had beheld signs of repentance, how the thought that some souls were saved, though their bodies were drowned with the rest, would magnify the rejoicing of the rescued; and the overthrow of the ungodly would proclaim how little ultimate bliss there could be in evil-doing. All these things would come home to the hearts of the "strangers of the dispersion."

And were they few in number? Fewer still were those who stood with Noah in the world's corruption. But God was with him; he walked with God, and found grace in His eyes; and God blessed him when the Flood was gone, and by the sign of the covenant, the faithful witness in heaven (Psalm lxxxix. 37), has placed a memorial of the happiness of his well-doing before the eyes of mankind for ever. And it would comfort the believers if they kept in mind the object which St. Peter has so often set before them, and on which he would have them set their desire in their distress. There was hope, nay assurance, that the heathen world around them would be won by their steadfast well-doing to the service of the Lord. Christ did not send his followers on a hopeless quest when He said, "Go, baptize all nations." It was no material ark they were set to fashion; they were exalted to be builders of the Church of Christ. And to put one stone upon another in that building was a joy worth earning by a life of sacrifice.

Saved through water. But God appointed the same waves to be the destruction of the disobedient. With no faith-built ark in which to ride safe, the sinners perished in the mighty waters which to Noah were the pathway of deliverance. A solemn thought this for those who have the offer of the antitype which the Apostle turns next to mention! This double use which God makes of His creatures—how to some they bring punishment, to others preservation—is the theme of several noble chapters in the book of Wisdom (xi.-xvi.), expanding the lesson taught by the pillar of a cloud, which was light to Israel, while it was thick darkness to the Egyptians.

Which also after a true likeness doth now save you, even baptism. Under the new covenant also water has been chosen by Christ to be the symbol of His grace. His servants are baptized into the name of the Father, Son, and Holy Ghost. This is the door appointed for entrance into the family. But the waters of the Flood would have overwhelmed Noah, even as the rest, had he not been within the ark, and the ark would not have been made had he been lacking in faith. So in baptism must no more saving office be ascribed to the water. Even the Divine word, "the word of hearing, did not profit some, because they were not united by faith with them that heard aright" (Heb. iv. 2). Neither does the sign in baptism, though Divinely instituted, profit, being alone. The Christian, having been cleansed by the washing of water with the word, is sanctified by Christ because of his faith. The washing of regeneration must be joined with the renewing of the Holy Ghost. That Spirit does not renew, but convicts of sin those who believe not on Christ (John xvi. 8). In his salvation Noah accepted and acted on God's warning about things not seen as yet, and so his baptism became effectual. In faith, too, Israel marched through the Red Sea, and beheld the overthrow of their heathen pursuers. And baptism mixed with faith is saving now. Those Old Testament deliverances were figures only of the true, and were but for temporal rescue. Christ's ordinance is that to which they testified before His coming, and is coupled with the promise of His presence even unto the end of the world.

And that there may be no place for doubting, the Apostle subjoins a twofold explanation. First he tells us what baptism is not, then what it is and what it bestows. It is *not the putting away of the filth of the flesh*. Were this all, it would avail no more than the cardinal ordinances (with meats and drinks and divers washings) which were imposed of old until a time of reformation. Through them the way into the holy place was not made manifest, nor could be. True baptism is *the interrogation of a good conscience toward God, through the resurrection of Jesus Christ*. This is a spiritual purification, wrought through the might of Christ's resurrection. And the Apostle describes it by the effect which it produces in the religious condition and attitude of him who has experienced it. The sinner who loves his sin dare not question his conscience. That witness would pronounce for his condemnation. So he finds it best to lull it to sleep, or perhaps deaden it altogether. But to him who, being risen with Christ in faith, seeks those things that are above, who strives to make himself spiritually purer day by day, there is no such dread. Rather by constant questioning and self-examination he labours that his conscience may be void of offence towards God and man. That man not only dares, but knows it to be a most solemn duty, thus to purge his conscience. So the effect of baptism is daily felt, and the questioned soul thankfully bears witness to the active presence of the Spirit, for the bestowal of which the Sacrament was the primal pledge.

Others have rendered ἐπερώτημα "an appeal," and have joined it very closely with the words *toward God*. These have found in the Apostle's explanation the recognition of that power to draw nigh unto God which the purified conscience both feels, and feels the need of. There are daily stumblings, the constant want of help; and through Christ's resurrection the way is opened, a new and living way, into the holiest, and the power is granted of appealing unto God, while the sense of baptismal grace already bestowed gives confidence and certainty that our petitions will be granted.

Who is on the right hand of God, having gone into heaven; angels and authorities and powers being made subject unto Him. Now the Apostle turns back to his main subject. The righteous who suffers for, and in, his righteousness, may not only be a blessing to others, but may himself find blessing. We dare only use the words which the Spirit has supplied when we speak of Christ being perfected by what He endured. But the Apostle to the Hebrews has a clear teaching. He speaks of Christ as being "the effulgence of God's glory, and the very image of His person" (Heb. i. 3). Yet he tells that, "though He was a Son, He learned obedience by the things which He suffered, and became thus the Author of eternal salvation unto all them that obey Him" (Heb. v. 8). And he goes further, and teaches that this submission of Christ to suffering was in harmony with the Divine character and according to God's own purpose: "It became Him for whom are all things, and through whom are all things, in bringing many sons unto glory, to make the Author of their salvation perfect through sufferings" (Heb. ii. 10). From all eternity Christ was perfect as the Son of God, but He has suffered that He may be a perfect Mediator. Why this was well-pleasing unto the Father it is not ours to know, nor can we by searching find. But, the sufferings ended, He is crowned with glory; He is exalted to the right hand of the Father; He is made Lord of all. This He taught His disciples ere He sent them to baptize: "All authority hath been given unto Me in heaven and on earth" (Matt. xxviii. 18). Having taken hold of the seed of Abraham and consented to be made lower than the angels, He has now been set "far above all principality, and power, and might, and dominion, and every name that is named, not only in this world, but also in that which is to come" (Eph. i. 21). Thus does St. Paul teach even as St. Peter; and we may believe, though we fail to grasp the manner thereof, that through His humiliation our blessed Lord has been exalted, not only because He receives for ever the praises of the redeemed, but because He has wrought through His suffering that which was well-pleasing in the sight of the Father.

The whole clause before us is worthy of notice for another reason. It was doubtless written before our Gospels were in circulation, when the life and work of Jesus were only published by the oral teaching of the Apostles and their fellows; yet in a summary form it covers the whole field of the Gospel story. Those to whom this Epistle was written had been taught that Jesus was the Christ, had heard of His righteous life among men, of His sufferings, death, and resurrection, had been taught that afterwards He was taken up into heaven. They knew also that the baptism by which they had been admitted into the Christian communion was His ordinance and the appointed door into the Church which He lived and died to build up among men. Thus, without the Gospels, we have the Gospel in the Epistles, and a witness to the integrity of that history of Christ's life which has come down to us in the narratives of the Evangelists. And when all the contributions of the Apostolic Epistles are put side by side, we may easily gather from them that the history of Jesus which we have now is that which the Church has possessed from the beginning of the Gospel.

XII
THE LESSONS OF SUFFERING

"Forasmuch then as Christ suffered in the flesh, arm ye yourselves also with the same mind; for he that hath suffered in the flesh hath ceased from sin; that ye no longer should live the rest of your time in the flesh to the lusts of men, but to the will of God. For the time past may suffice to have wrought the desire of the Gentiles, and to have walked in lasciviousness, lusts, winebibbings, revellings, carousings, and abominable idolatries: wherein they think it strange that ye run not with *them* into the same excess of riot, speaking evil of *you*: who shall give account to Him that is ready to judge the quick and the dead. For unto this end was the gospel preached even to the dead, that they might be judged according to men in the flesh, but live according to God in the spirit."—1 Peter iv. 1-6.

It is always hard to swim against the stream; and if the effort be a moral one, the difficulty is not lessened. These early Christians were finding it so. For them there must have existed hardships of which to-day we can have no experience, and form but an imperfect estimate. If they lived among a Jewish population, these were sure to be offended at the new faith. And when we remember the zeal for persecution of a Saul of Tarsus, we can see that in many cases the better the Jew, the more would he feel himself bound, if possible, to exterminate the new doctrines. Among the heathen the lot of the Christians was often worse. Did the people listen a while to the teaching of the missionaries, yet so unstable were they that, as at Lystra, to-day might see them stoning those whom yesterday they were venerating as gods; and they could easily, by reason of their greater numbers, bring the magistrates to inflict penalties even where the multitude refrained from mob violence. The cry, "These men exceedingly trouble our city" or "These who turn the world upside down are come among us," was sure to find a ready audience; while the uproar and violence which raged in a city like Ephesus, when Paul and his companions preached there, shows how many temporal interests could be banded together against the Christian cause. On individual believers, not of the number of the preachers, the more violent attacks might not fall; but to suffer in the flesh was the lot of most of them in St. Peter's day. Hence the strong figure he employs to describe the preparation they will need: *Arm ye yourselves*—make you ready, for you are going forth to battle. St. Paul also, writing to Rome and Corinth, uses the same figure: "Let us put on the armour of light," "the armour of righteousness on the right hand and on the left."

Forasmuch then as Christ suffered in the flesh, arm ye yourselves also with the same mind. Though some strokes of the foe will fall on the flesh, the conflict is really a spiritual one. The suffering in the body is to be sustained and surmounted by an inward power; the armour of light and of righteousness is the equipment of the soul, which panoply the Apostle here calls the mind of Christ. Now what is the mind of Christ which can avail His struggling servants? The word implies intention, purpose, resolution, that on which the heart is set. Now the intention of Christ's life was to oppose and overcome all that was evil, and to consecrate Himself to all good for the love of His people. This latter He tells us in His parting prayer for his disciples: "For their sakes I sanctify Myself, that they themselves also may be sanctified in truth" (John xvii. 19), while every action of His life proclaims His determined enmity against sin. This brought Him obloquy while He lived in the world, and in the end a shameful death; but these things did not abate His hatred of sin, nor lessen His love for sinners. For still into the city where He reigns there shall in no wise enter anything that defileth (Rev. xxi. 27), though to the faithful penitent "the Spirit and the bride say, Come, and he that is athirst, let him come; he that will, let him take the water of life freely" (Rev. xxii. 17).

Christ bare willingly all that was laid upon Him that He might bring men unto God. This is the spirit, this the purpose, the intent, with which His followers are to be actuated: to have the same strenuous abhorrence of sin, the same devotion in themselves to goodness, which shall make them inflexible, however fiercely they may be assailed. Let them only make the resolve, and power shall be bestowed to strengthen them. He who says, "Arm yourselves," supplies the weapons when His servants need them. Jesus Himself found them ready when the tempter came, and drew them in all their keenness and strength from the Divine armoury. Satan comes to others as he came to Christ, and will make them flinch and waver, if he can. At times he offers attractive baits; at times he brings fear to his aid. But, in whatever shape he comes or sends his agents, let them but cling to the mind of Christ, and they shall, like Him, say triumphantly, "Get thee behind me, Satan."

For he that hath suffered in the flesh hath ceased from sin. God intends it to be so, and the earnest Christian strives with all his might that it may be so. To help men God sends them sufferings, and intends them to have a moral effect on the life. They are not penal; they are the discipline of perfect love desiring that men should be held back from straying. Men cannot always see the purposes of God at first, and are prone to bewail their lot. But here and there a saint of old has left his testimony. One of the later psalmists had discovered the blessedness of God-sent trials: "Before I was afflicted I went astray; but now I observe Thy word"; and, in thankful acknowledgment of the love which sent the blows, he adds, "It is good for me that I have been afflicted, that I might learn Thy statutes" (Psalm cxix. 67, 71). Hezekiah had learnt the lesson, though it brought him close to the gates of the grave; but he testifies, "Behold, it was for my peace that I had great bitterness.... Thou hast cast all my sins behind Thy back" (Isa. xxxviii. 17). God had blotted out the evil record, that he who had suffered in the flesh might cease from sin. It is good for us thus to recognise that God's dispensations are for our correction and teaching, and that without them we should have been verily desolate, left to choose our own way, which would surely have been evil; and though we cannot cease from sin while we are in the flesh, God's mercy places the ideal state before us—*He that hath suffered in the flesh hath ceased from sin*—that we may be strengthened, nevermore to submit ourselves to the yoke of wickedness. How shall he that is dead to sin live any longer therein? Live therein he cannot. Of that old man within him he will have no resurrection, for though the motions, the promptings to evil, are there, the love of evil is slain by the greater love of Christ.

That ye no longer should live the rest of your time in the flesh to the lusts of men, but to the will of God. Christians must live out their lives till God calls them, and for the rest of their time in the flesh they will be among their wonted surroundings. Just as Christian slaves must abide with their masters, and Christian wives continue with their husbands, so each several believer must do his duty where God has placed him. But because he is a believer it will be done in a different spirit. He is daily cutting himself away from what the world counts for life; he has begun to live in the Spirit, and the natural man is weakened day by day; he knows that what is born of the flesh is flesh, and bears the taint of sin: so he refuses to follow where it would lead him. Men often plead for evil habits that they are natural, forgetting that "natural" thus used means human, corrupt nature. The birth of the Spirit transforms this nature, and the renewed man goes about his worldly life with a new motive, new purposes. He must follow his lawful calling like other folks, but the sense of his pilgrimage makes him to differ; he is longing to depart, and holds himself in constant readiness. Worldly men live as though they were rooted here and would never be moved. "Their inward thought is that their houses shall continue for ever, and their dwelling-places to all generations; they call their lands after their own names" (Psalm xlix. 11). To the servant of Christ life wears another aspect. He is content to live on, for God so wills it, and has work for him to do. To continue in the flesh may be, as it was to St. Paul, the fruit of his labour. And he welcomes this owning of his work, and will spend his powers in like service. Yet, with the Apostle, he has ever "the desire to depart and be with Christ, for it is very far better" (Phil. i. 23).

And as he strives to fulfil God's intent by crucifying the old man and ceasing from sin, the Christian rejoices in a growing sense of freedom. To follow the lusts of men was to serve many and hard taskmasters. Riches, fame, luxury, sensual indulgences, riotous living, are all keen to win new slaves, and paint their lures in the most attractive colours; and one appetite will make itself the ally of another, lust hard by greed, so that the chains of him who takes service with them are riveted many times over, and difficult, often impossible, to be cast off. But the will of God is one: "One is your Master"; "Love the Lord your God with all your heart"; "And all ye are brethren"; "Love your neighbour as yourself." Then shall you enter into life. And the life of this promise is not that fragment of time which remains to men in the flesh, but that unending after-life where the natural body shall be exchanged for a spiritual body, and death be swallowed up in victory.

For the time past may suffice to have wrought the desire of the Gentiles. The Apostle here seems to be addressing the Jews who, living among the Gentiles, had, like their forefathers in Canaan, learned their works. The nation was not so prone to fall away into heathendom after the Captivity; yet some of them in the dispersion, like Samson when he went down unto the Philistines, may have been captured and blinded and made to serve. The proximity of evil is infectious. To the Gentile converts St. Peter speaks elsewhere as having been slaves to their lusts in ignorance (i. 14). But whether Jew or Gentile, when they had once tasted the joy of this purer service, this law of obedience which made them truly free, they would be strengthened to suffer in flesh rather than fall back upon their former life. The time would seem enough, far more than enough, to have been thus defiled. All was God's; all that remained must be given to Him with strenuous devotion.

St. Peter seems to place in contrast, as he describes the two ways of life, two words, one by which he denotes the service of God, by the other devotion to the world and its attractions. The former ($\theta \acute{\epsilon} \lambda \eta \mu \alpha$) implies a pleasure and joy; it is the will of God, that which He delights in, and which

He makes to be a joy to those who serve Him. The other (βούλημα) has a sense of longing, unsatisfied want, a state which craves for something which it cannot attain. St. Paul describes it as "led away by divers lusts, ever learning" (but in an evil school), "never able to come to the knowledge of the truth, corrupted in mind, reprobate" (2 Tim. iii. 7). Such is the desire of the Gentiles. The Apostle describes it in his next words: *To have walked in lasciviousness, lusts, winebibbings, revellings, carousings, and abominable idolatries.* How gross heathendom can be our missionaries from time to time reveal to us. All the corruptions which they describe were reigning in full power round about these converts. When men change the glory of the incorruptible God for the likeness of corruptible man or even worse, and worship and serve the creature, their own animal passions, rather than the Creator, there is no depth of degradation to which they may not sink. St. Paul has painted for us some dark pictures of what such lives could be (Rom. i. 24-32; Col. iii. 5-8). But though Christianity in our own land have forced sin to veil some of its fouler aspects, vice has not changed its nature. The same passions rule in the hearts of those who live to the lusts of men, and not to the will of God. The flesh warreth against the Spirit, even if the Spirit be not utterly quenched, and brings men into its slavery. For the sake of Christ, then, and for love of the brethren, the faithful have need still to be proclaiming, *Let the time past suffice,* and by their actions to testify that they are willing to suffer in the flesh, if so be they may thereby be sustained in the battle against sin and may strengthen their brethren to walk in a new way.

Wherein they think it strange that ye run not with them into the same excess of riot, speaking evil of you. The godless love to be a large company, that they may keep one another in heart. Hence they who have been of them, and would fain withdraw, have no easy task; and to win new comrades sinners are ever most solicitous. Their invitations at first will take a friendly tone. Solomon understood them well, and described them in warning to his son: "Come with us," they say: "let us lay wait for blood; let us lurk privily for the innocent without cause; let us swallow them up alive as Sheol, and whole as those that go down into the pit. We shall find all precious substance; we shall fill our houses with spoil. Thou shalt cast thy lot among us; we will all have one purse" (Prov. i. 11-14). This is one fashion of their excess of riot, but there are many more. The Apostle's words picture their life as an overflow, a deluge. And the figure is not strange in Holy Writ. "The floods of ungodly men made me afraid," says the Psalmist (Psalm xviii. 14); and St. Jude, writing about the same time as St. Peter and of the same evil days, calls such sinners "wild waves of the sea, foaming out their own shames" (Jude 14). "Shames," he says, because the floods of excess pour on in overwhelming abundance, and those who escape from them do so only with much suffering in the flesh, sent of God, to set them free from sin.

And if there be no hope of winning recruits or alluring back those who have escaped, the godless follow another course. They hate, and persecute, and malign. Ever since the days of Cain this has been the policy of the wicked, though not all push it so far as did the first murderer (1 John iii. 12). For the life of the righteous is a constant reproach to them. They have made their own choice, but it yields them no comfort; and if one means of making others as wretched as themselves fails, they take another. They point the finger of hatred and scorn at the faithful. To the Greeks Christ's faith was foolishness. The Athenians, full of this world's wisdom, asked about Paul, "What will this babbler say?" and mocked as they heard of the resurrection of the dead. With them and such as they this life is all. But the Christian has his consolation: he has committed his cause to another Judge, before whom they also who speak evil of him must appear.

Who shall give account to Him that is ready to judge the quick and the dead. The Christian looks on to the coming judgement. He can therefore disregard the censures of men. Neither the penalties nor the revilings of the world trouble him. They are a part of the judgement in the present life; by them God is chastening him, preparing him by the suffering in the flesh to be more ready for the coming of the Lord. In that day it will be seen how the servant has been made like unto his Master, how he has welcomed the purging which Christ gives to His servants that they may bring forth more fruit. He believes, yea knows, that in the Judge who has been teaching and judging him here day by day he will find a Mediator and a Saviour. With the unbeliever all is otherwise. He has refused correction, has chosen his own path, and drawn away his neck from the yoke of Christ; his judgment is all yet to come. The Judge is ready, but He is full of mercy. St. Peter's phrase implies this. It tells of readiness, but also of holding back, of a desire to spare. He is on His throne, the record is prepared, but yet He waits; He is Himself the long-suffering Vinedresser who pleads, "Let it alone this year also."

Such has been the mercy of God even from the days of Eden. In the first temptation Eve adds one sin upon another. First she listens to the insidious questioning which proclaims the speaker a foe to God: then without remonstrance she hears God's truth declared a lie; hearkens to an aspersion of the Divine goodness; then yields to the tempter, sins, and leads her husband into sin. Not till then does God's judgement fall, which might have fallen at the first offence; and when it is pronounced, it is full of pity, and gives more space for repentance. So, though the Judge be ready, His mercy waits. For He will judge the dead as well as the living, and while men live His compassion goes forth in its fulness to the ignorant and them that are out of the way.

For unto this end was the gospel preached even to the dead, that they might be judged according to men in the flesh, but live according to God in the spirit. "*Unto this end*"—what does it signify? What but that God has ever been true to the name under which He first revealed Himself: "The Lord God, merciful and gracious" (Exod. xxxiv. 6); that He has been preaching the Gospel to sinners by His dispensations from the first day until now? Thus was the Gospel preached unto Abraham (Gal. iii. 8) when he was called from the home of his fathers, and pointed forward through a life of trial to a world-wide blessing. Heeding the lesson, he was gladdened by the knowledge of the day of Christ. In like manner and unto this end was the Gospel sent to God's people in the wilderness (Heb. iv. 2), even as unto us; but the word of hearing did not profit them. With many of them God was not well pleased. Yet He showed them in signs His Gospel sacraments. They were all baptized unto Moses in the cloud and in the sea, did all eat the same spiritual meat, and all drank the same spiritual drink (1 Cor. x. 2-4), for Christ was with them, as their Rock of refreshing, all their journey through the desert, preaching the Gospel by visitations now of mercy, now of affliction. Unto this end He brought them many a time under the yoke of their enemies; unto this end He sent them into captivity. Thus were they being judged, as men count judgements, if haply they might listen in this life to the gospel of trial and pain, and so live at last, as God counts life, in the spirit, when the final judgement-day is over. They are dead, but to every generation of them was the Gospel preached, that God might gather Him a great multitude to stand on His right hand in the day of account.

_ Some have applied the words of this verse to the sinners of the days of Noah, connecting them closely with iii. 19; and truly, though they be but one example out of a world of mercies, they are very notable. They were doomed; they were dead while they lived: "Everything that is in the earth shall die" (Gen. vi. 17). Yet to them the preacher was sent, and unto this end: that though they were to be drowned in the Deluge, and so in men's sight be judged, their souls might be saved, as God would have them saved, in the great day of the Lord. But every visitation is a gospel, a gospel unto this end: that through judgement here a people may be made ready in God's sight to be called unto His rest.

Few passages have more powerful lessons than this for every age. The world is full of suffering in the flesh. Who has not known it in many kinds?

But it is in consequence, to those who will hear, very full of Gospel sermons. They cry aloud, Sin no more; the time past may suffice to have wrought the will of the Gentiles. Suffering does not mean that God is not full of love; rather it is a token that, in His great love, He is training us, opening our eyes to our wrong-doings that we may cast them off, and giving us a true standard to judge between the desire of the Gentiles and the will of God. And though men may look on us as sore afflicted, our Father, when the rest of our time in the flesh shall be ended, will give us the true life with Him in the spirit.

XIII
CHRISTIAN SERVICE FOR GOD'S GLORY

"But the end of all things is at hand: be ye therefore of sound mind, and be sober unto prayer: above all things being fervent in your love among yourselves; for love covereth a multitude of sins: using hospitality one to another without murmuring: according as each hath received a gift, ministering it among yourselves, as good stewards of the manifold grace of God; if any man speaketh, *speaking* as it were oracles of God; if any man ministereth, *ministering* as of the strength which God supplieth: that in all things God may be glorified through Jesus Christ, whose is the glory and the dominion for ever and ever. Amen."—1 Peter iv. 7-11.

But the end of all things is at hand. Well-nigh two thousand years have passed away since the Apostle wrote these words. What are we to think of the teaching they convey? For it is not St. Peter's teaching only. Those who laboured with him were all of the same mind; all gave the same note of warning to their converts. St. Paul exhorts the Philippians, "Let your moderation be known unto all men. The Lord is at hand" (Phil. iv. 5); and in the first letter to the Corinthians the last words before his benediction are to the same purport: "Maran atha" (1 Cor. xvi. 22); that is, The Lord cometh. St. James preaches, "Stablish your hearts, for the coming of the Lord draweth nigh" (James v. 8). To the Hebrews the Apostle writes, "Yet a little while, and He that shall come will come, and will not tarry" (Heb. x. 37). While St. John, who lived longer than any of the rest, conveys the warning even in more solemn tones: "Little children, it is the last hour" (1 John ii. 18). Are we to look on these admonitions as so many mistaken utterances? Are we to think that the disciples had misunderstood the Lord's teaching, or would they say the same words if they were with us to-day?

We may allow that those who had been present at the Ascension, and had heard the words of the angels declaring that "this same Jesus should so come as they had seen Him go into heaven" (Acts i. 11), might expect His return to judge the world to be not far distant. But, in whatever they say in reference thereto, their main concern is that men should be ready. "In such an hour as ye think not the Son of man cometh," is the ground-text of all their exhortations. Now had arrived the fulness of the time (Gal. iv. 4) in which God had sent forth His Son, born of a woman; and if we take the verb of St. Peter's sentence ἤγγικε, "has come near", we feel that he viewed the new era on which the world had entered in this light. And so did the other Apostles. One says, "Now once in the end of the ages hath Christ been manifested" (Heb. ix. 26); another teaches that things of old "were written for our admonition, upon whom the ends of the ages are come" (1 Cor. x. 11). God has spoken aforetime in many portions and in many ways, but in the end of these days He hath spoken in His Son (Heb. i. 2). All things are now summed up in Christ; He is the end of all things. Prophecy, type, sacrifice, all have passed away. There will come no new revelation; no word more will be added to the Divine book. Its lessons will find in each generation new illustrations, new applications, but will admit no change of form or substance. The Christian dispensation, be it long or short, is the last time; it will close with the Second Advent. And continual preparedness is to be the Christian's attitude. And this is the purport of St. Peter's next exhortations, which are as forceful to-day as they were eighteen hundred years ago.

Be ye therefore of sound mind. Exactly the counsel which should follow the previous lesson. It was misinterpreted at first, as it has been since. We know how unwisely the Thessalonians behaved when they had been told by St. Paul, "The day of the Lord so cometh as a thief in the night" (1 Thess. v. 2). The Apostle learnt that they were sorely disturbed, and wrote them a second letter, from which we can gather how far they had wandered from soundness of mind. At first the Apostle speaks gently: "Be not quickly shaken from your mind, nor yet be troubled, either by spirit, or by word, or by epistle as from us, as that the day of the Lord is now present" (2 Thess. ii. 2). But soon he shows us how the excitement had operated. Some among them had begun to walk disorderly, apparently thinking that they might live upon the community, working not at all, but being busybodies. These made, no doubt, the approach of the day of the Lord their pretext. St. Paul bids such men in quietness to work and eat their own bread. To be found at their duty was the best way of preparing for the end.

How soundness of mind may serve the Church of Christ is seen in the settlement of that murmuring which arose (Acts vi. 1) as soon as the Christian disciples began to be multiplied in Jerusalem. It was the Grecian Jews who complained that their widows were neglected. The Apostles wisely withdrew from the distribution about which the complaint was made, and more wisely still gave the oversight into the hands of Greeks (as the forms of all their names bear witness) who would be fully trusted by the murmurers. "And the word of God increased." The pages of Church history supply examples in abundance of the need in religious matters for this soundness of mind. We need not go back to very ancient times. What sore evils led to and arose out of the peasant war in Germany in the days of the Reformation, followed by those excesses which disgraced the name of Christianity in Münster and other parts of Westphalia! And in our own land both at that time and subsequently the unwise enthusiasm of those who acted as though whatever had been must be wrong hindered sorely the temperate efforts of the more conservative and sober minds; while undue prominence given to single doctrines of the Gospel has many times warped men's minds; and does so still, making the cause of Christ to be hardly spoken of. A sense of proportion is a gift which the Church may fitly pray for in her members, and that, while they seek to foster the sevenfold graces of the Holy Spirit, they may ever keep in mind the mercy of Him who bestows only a portion on each of us as we can receive it, and makes no man the steward of them all.

And be sober unto prayer. The Apostle selects one example wherein the sound mind ought to be sought after, and he has chosen it so as to be of general application. The wisdom to which he is exhorting is needed for all men, both those who teach and those who hear, those who serve tables and those who are served thereby. Many members of the Christian body, however, will not be concerned with such special duties. But all will pray, and so to prayer he applies his precept. *Be sober.* A sound mind will preserve us from extravagance in our approach unto God. For even here extravagance may intrude. The Corinthian Church had gone very far wrong in this respect. Over-elated, losing soundness of mind, through the bestowal of certain gifts, they had introduced such irregularities into their religious meetings that St. Paul speaks of occasions when they might have been regarded as madmen (1 Cor. xiv. 23). These were public prayers. St. James applies the same standard to private prayers: "Ye ask, and receive not, because ye ask amiss" (James iv. 3). There is no true prayer in your petitions. You have selected in your own hearts what you would fain have and do, and you come before God with these as your supplications. There is no thought in them of yielding to God's will, but only the sense that if your petitions were granted you would reap a present satisfaction. Ye ask amiss. Many a heart can testify to the proneness to err thus by want of sobriety.

Above all things being fervent in your love among yourselves. Soundness of mind and sobriety should dominate every part of the believer's life; but there are other virtues of pre-eminent excellence, unto which, though they be far above him, he is encouraged to aspire. Of these St. Peter, like St. Paul (1 Cor. xiii. 13), places love at the summit, above all things. The word he uses signifies that perfect love which is the attribute of God Himself. To frail humanity it must ever be an ideal. But the Apostle in his second epistle (2 Peter i. 7) has given a progressive list of graces to be sought after in a holy life, a series of mountain summits each above the other, and each made visible through the one below it. Here, too, love comes as the climax; and the Revised Version marks it as far above mere human affection: "In your love of the brethren supply also love." Here is no anticlimax, if we once appreciate the grandeur of the concluding term.

In the present verse, however, the Apostle exhorts that this Divine quality is to be exercised by the converts among themselves, and exercised with much earnestness and diligence. It is to be the grace which pervades all their lives, and extends itself to every condition thereof. But we understand why St. Peter has used this word for love as soon as we come to the clause which follows: *For love covereth a multitude of sins.* To cover sin is Godlike. It has been often asked, Whose sins are covered by this love, those of him who loves, or of him who is loved? The question can have but one answer. There is nothing in the New Testament to warrant such a doctrine as that love towards one's fellow-men will hide, atone for, or cancel any man's sins. When our Lord says of the woman who was a sinner, "Her sins, which are many, are forgiven; for she loved much" (Luke vii. 47), it is not love to the brethren of which He is speaking, but love to God, which she had manifested by her actions toward Himself; and when He presently adds, "Thy faith hath saved thee," He tells us the secret of her availing love. But when men are animated by that love toward their neighbours which shows likest God's, they are tender to their offences; they look to the future more than to the past, hoping all things, believing all things; they have tasted God's mercy in the pardon of their own sins, and labour to do thus unto others, to cast their sins out of sight, to put them, as God does when He forgives, behind their back, as though in being forgiven they were also forgotten. The phrase is quoted by St. Peter from Prov. x. 12, where Solomon says, "Love covereth *all* sins," and our Lord's words to St. Peter himself (Matt. xviii. 22) about forgiving until seventy times seven times practically set no limit to the extension of pardon to the repentant. Thus taught, the Apostle uses the noble word ἀγάπη of human tenderness to offenders, because he would urge men to a boundless, all-embracing, Godlike pity for sinners.

Using hospitality one to another without murmuring. We need only reflect on the narrative of the Acts of the Apostles to realise how large a part hospitality must have played in the early Church as soon as the preachers extended their labours beyond Jerusalem. The house of Simon the tanner, where Peter was entertained many days (ix. 43); the friends who at Antioch received Paul and Barnabas and kept them for a whole year (xi. 26); the petition of Lydia, "Come into my house, and abide there" (xvi. 15); and Jason's reception of

Paul and Silas at Thessalonica (xvii. 7), are but illustrations of what must have been the general custom. Nor would such welcome be needed for the Apostles alone. The Churches must have been very familiar with cases of brethren driven from their own country by persecution, or severed from their own kinsfolk by the adoption of the new faith. To such the kind offices of the Christian congregations must have been constantly extended, so that hospitality was consecrated into a blessed and righteous duty. To be "given to hospitality" (Rom. xii. 13) is reckoned among the marks whereby it shall be known that believers, being many, are one body in Christ; and from the salutations in the last chapter of the Epistle to the Romans we can frame a picture of the large work of lodging and caring for strangers as it entered into the duties of a Christian life. The brethren at Rome are exhorted to receive and help Phœbe, the bringer of the Epistle, because she had been a succourer of many, and of Paul himself. Of Priscilla and Aquila, who are next named, we know that they were friends and fellow-workers with St. Paul in Corinth, and that in Ephesus they showed their Christian love toward the stranger Apollos; and not only so, but they provided a place where the brethren might assemble for their worship. Later on is mentioned Mary, who bestowed much labour on the brethren, Urbanus, a helper in Christ, and the households of Aristobulus and Narcissus, whole families made friends through the extension of hospitality. Of the mother of Rufus St. Paul speaks tenderly as his own mother also. The coupling together of Philologus and Julia suggests that they were husband and wife and had opened their doors to the brethren, and the notice of Nereus and his sister points to similar good offices. And from whatever place the Epistle was sent to Rome, there Tertius, St. Paul's amanuensis, was under the hospitable roof of Gaius, whom he speaks of as the host of the whole Church. Doubtless at times the burden might fall heavily on some of the poorer brethren. Hence the need for the Apostle's addition *without murmuring*. The word is the same which is used (Acts vi. 1) of the complaints of the Grecians. And in this matter, as in all, a sound mind would be called for, that loads might be placed by the Churches only on such as were able to bear them.

The intimate fellowship that would grow out of such exercise of kind offices must have been a power to encourage greatly the labourers for Christ. As they dwelt together, hours not given to public ministrations would be spent in private converse, and would knit the members together, and forward the common work. As St. Paul writes to Philemon, who appears to have been eminent in good offices, the hearts of the saints were refreshed by this godly intercourse. In friendly communion the love of all would wax warmer, zeal become more earnest, the weak would be strengthened, and the strong grow stronger.

According as each hath received a gift, ministering it among yourselves, as good stewards of the manifold grace of God. The close connexion between *gifts* and *grace* is better marked in the Greek than it can be in the English. The χαρίσματα are bestowed upon us by the χάρις of God. But every word in the sentence is full of force. Each hath received a gift. None can plead his lack of faculty; none can claim exemption from the duty of ministering; none is so poor but he has something that he can lay out for the brethren. All have time; all have kind words: the least can give, what is the best of gifts, a good example. But what we have is not our own; it is received: and humility would teach us to believe that God has bestowed on us the powers which we are best fitted, by place and opportunities, to use in His service. None can say of any gift, "It is all my own; I may do with it as I please." God has set the world about us full of His exchangers. The poor, the feeble, the doubting, the fearful—these are God's bankers, with whom we may put out our gifts to usury. And Himself is the security for all that we deposit thus: "Inasmuch as ye did it unto one of the least of these My brethren, ye did it unto Me." Hence we live under the responsibility of stewardship. And every man's gift is given to profit withal (πρὸς τὸ συμφέρον, 1 Cor. xii. 7). The Greek implies that it must be shared with others. Nor can any of us make it a profit to himself till he have found the way to make it profitable to his brethren.

That he may give more precision to his counsel, the Apostle proceeds to speak of gifts under two heads into which they are naturally divided. First come those which St. Paul (Rom. xii. 6-8) ranges under the head of prophecy, embracing therein teaching and exhortation likewise: *If any man speaketh, speaking as it were oracles of God.* The first Christian preachers must have gained their knowledge of the life and teaching of Jesus by listening to the narratives of the twelve, and must have gone forth to give their teaching orally. The training of those who were appointed to minister in the various places whither the apostolic missions penetrated must have been of the same kind. In those first years there was work to be done which would seem more important than the writing of a Gospel history. When such preachers published to the congregations what they had learnt of the Master's lessons, their sermons would be orally given, and though conveying the same instruction, would be liable to constant modifications of words. It was from such oral teaching that the variations found in the Gospel narratives probably had their origin. The preachers gave the spirit, and as nearly as possible the text, of what they had been taught. Perhaps by memoranda or otherwise, they would refresh their knowledge of the apostolic words, so as to adhere as much as might be to what they had first received. The word λόγια—oracles—which the Apostle here employs, seems intended to remind such preachers and teachers that they now, as the Jews of old, had received "living oracles" (Acts vii. 38), words by which spiritual life was conveyed, to deliver to the Church. Those of them who were Jews would call to mind how God's prophets had constantly prefaced their message with "Thus saith the Lord" or concluded it with the Divine accrediting, "I am the Lord"; and that the Christian prophet must bear in mind that he is only an ambassador, and must abide by his commission, if he would speak with authority, that as a steward he must ever think of the account to be some day given of the "oracles of God" (Rom. iii. 2) with which he was entrusted, and must "handle aright the word of truth" (2 Tim. ii. 15). For all such is St. Peter's admonition, *If any man speaketh, speaking as it were oracles of God.*

And next he turns to those gifts which are to be exercised in deeds, and not in words: *If any man ministereth, ministering as of the strength which God supplieth.* Under "ministry" St. Paul classes (Rom. xii. 7, 8) giving, ruling, showing mercy. These are duties which secure the temporal condition of the Church and her members. The New Testament story suggests many offices which could be discharged by those who had not devoted themselves in a special manner to the ministry of the word. How much service would be called for by those collections for the saints which St. Paul urges so frequently upon the Churches! How many houses would find employment in such labours as were exhibited in the home of Dorcas! How many a traveller, bent on his secular work, would carry apostolic messages or letters to the flocks of the dispersion! To these may be added those offices of mercy which St. James describes as θρησκεία, outward acts of religion, to visit the widows and fatherless in their affliction. The strength which God supplieth embraces every faculty or possession, be it wealth, administrative skill, or special knowledge. The physician and the craftsman alike may spend their powers for Christ. All may be consecrated, ministered, as supplied of God. And it is a gain to the Church when, following the apostolic pattern, these duties of external religion are severed from the prophecy, the spiritual work of the teacher.

That in all things God may be glorified through Jesus Christ, whose is the glory and the dominion for ever and ever. Amen. This is to be the thought which animates all who minister: that each man's service may be so rendered to his brethren that it will work for the glory of God. And Christ has led the way. He testifies in His final prayer, "I glorified Thee on the earth, having accomplished the work which Thou hast given Me to do" (John xvii. 4). Of our work we can use no such words. We are but unprofitable servants. In many things we offend all. But all may labour in the Christlike spirit; and thus through Him, through service rendered in His name and for His sake, will God be glorified. The thought of Jesus humbling Himself, taking the form of a servant, testifying of Himself, "The Son of man came not to be ministered unto, but to minister, and to give His life a ransom for many," can give a dignity to lowliest labour, and at the same time can impart consolation to the true labourers, for whom this mighty ransom has been paid, their inheritance won, their salvation achieved; while the Conqueror of sin and death, their Redeemer, has taken His seat at God's right hand, where worshipping spirits ever praise Him, saying, "Worthy art Thou, our Lord and our God, to receive the glory, and the honour, and the power" (Rev. iv. 11).

XIV
THE BELIEVER'S DOUBLE JOY

"Beloved, think it not strange concerning the fiery trial among you, which cometh upon you to prove you, as though a strange thing happened unto you: but insomuch as ye are partakers of Christ's sufferings, rejoice; that at the revelation of His glory also ye may rejoice with exceeding joy. If ye are reproached for the name of Christ, blessed *are ye*; because the *Spirit* of glory and the Spirit of God resteth upon you."—1 Peter iv. 12-14.

After the benediction in ver. 11, we might have supposed that the exhortations of the Apostle were ended. But he now proceeds to make general application of the lessons which above (ii. 19) he had confined to a particular class: the Christians who were in slavery. And the times appear to have called for consolation. The Churches were in great tribulation. St. Peter speaks here, more than in any other passage of the Epistle, as if persecution were afflicting the whole Christian body: *Beloved*—the word embraces them all—*think it not strange concerning the fiery trial among you, ... as though a strange thing happened unto you.* His strong word implies extreme suffering. St. John uses it (Rev. xviii. 9, 18) of the burning up of the mystical Babylon, and it is found nowhere else in the New Testament. A trial meriting this description was harassing the Asian Christians; but spite of the intensity of suffering, which may be inferred from his language; he bids the converts not to wonder at it or deem it other than their proper lot: "Think it not strange."

He does not enter upon reasons for his admonition, or he might have selected a goodly list of Old Testament saints who for their faith were called to suffer. For the Jewish brethren, Joseph and David, Elijah and Micaiah, David and his companions in exile, Job and Nehemiah, would have been forcible examples of suffering for righteousness. The Apostle, however selects only the loftiest instance. Christ, the Master whom they were pledged to serve, had suffered, and had said, besides, that all who would follow Him must take up the cross. Need they wonder, then, if in their case they found the Lord's teaching coming true?

But, in describing the purpose of their trials, the Apostle introduces some words which place their affliction in a distinct light: *Which cometh upon you to prove you*—literally, for your proving (πρὸς πειρασμὸν ὑμῖν). And the word is that which is constantly used of *temptation*, whether sent of God or coming in some other way. When viewed as a process of proving, the believers would be able to find some contentment under their persecutions. God was putting them to the test. He would know if they are in earnest in His service, and so they are cast into the furnace, God's wonted discipline. The prophet Zechariah tells both of the process, and the God-intended result: "I will refine them as silver is refined, and will try them as gold is tried; they shall call on My name, and I will hear them: I will say, It is My people; and they shall say, The Lord is my God" (Zech. xii. 9). And the Psalmist bears like testimony: "The Lord trieth the righteous" (Psalm xi. 5), and says that for those who are found faithful the end is blessedness: "We went through fire and through water, but Thou broughtest us out into a wealthy place" (Psalm lxvi. 12).

Such thoughts would yield comfort to those for whom St. Peter immediately wrote. They were suffering for Christ's sake; their faith in Him was being tested. But the Apostle's words are left for the edification of all generations of believers. Throughout all time and everywhere there has been abundance of grief and pain. How may sufferers to-day participate in the apostolic consolation? How may they learn to think it not strange that they are afflicted?

The Apostle's words supply the answer to such questions. And they are no light or infrequent questionings both for ourselves and others. Men are prone to lament over temporal losses or bodily sufferings, their own or others', in tones which convey the idea that such trials will in the end be compensated and made efficacious for the future blessing of the sufferer. The New Testament has no such doctrine. "The trial which cometh upon you to prove you," is St. Peter's expression. There is much suffering in the world which is in no sense a participation of the sufferings of Christ, in no sense a God-sent trial for proving the faith of the sufferer.

Here, if honestly questioned, the individual conscience will give the true answer; and if that inward witness condemn the life for no excesses, of which suffering is the appointed fruit, if the bodily pains be not the outcome of a life lived to the flesh, nor the sorrow and poverty the result of follies and extravagance aforetime, then, with the anguish and distress which God hath sent (for we may then count them as of His sending), the Spirit will have bestowed light that we may discern their purpose, light which will show us God's hand weaning us from the world and making us ready for going home, or, it may be, giving to others through us His teaching in message and example. Then the enlightened and pacified soul will be able to rejoice amid pain, conscious of purification; and will out of the midst of sorrow see God's designs justified. Satan will look on such times as his opportunity, and suggest to the Christian that he is unduly afflicted and forgotten of God; but the joy which comes from being able to look trouble in the face, as sent by a Father, drives away despondency and puts the enemy to rout. He is triumphant who can rest on a faithful God, with an assurance that with the temptation He will also make the way of escape, that he may be able to endure it (1 Cor. x. 13).

But dare we then pray, as Christ has taught us, "Lead us not into temptation"? Yes, if we ponder rightly on the purport of our petition. Christ does not bid us pray to God not to try us; He Himself made no such prayer for His disciples; He was Himself submitted to such trial: "It pleased the Lord to bruise Him; He hath put Him to grief" (Isa. liii. 10). Nay, one Evangelist (Mark i. 12) tells us how He was not led, but *driven* forth, of the Spirit into the wilderness to be tempted of the devil. Yet He taught the prayer to His disciples, and He did so because He knew both what was in man, and what was in the world. In the latter since sin entered, the tempter has found manifold enticements to lead men astray. All that belongs to the lust of the flesh, the lust of the eyes, or the pride of life, riches, influence, beauty, popularity, prosperity of every kind, may be used as tests of faith, may be made to glorify God; but they can also be perverted in the using. And there dwell within man strong desires, which he is prompted to gratify at times, without heeding whether their gratification be right or wrong; and when desire and opportunity meet, there is peril to the tempted.

"How oft the sight of means to do ill deeds
Makes deeds ill done!"

And when desire has once gained the mastery, the next yielding is sooner made; the forbidden path becomes the constant walk; the moral principle—the Godlike in the conscience—is neglected; men grow weaker, are led away of their own lusts and enticed.

On the other hand, if the unlawful desire be resisted from the first, each succeeding conflict will offer less hardship, each new victory be more easily gained, and the virtuous act will become a holy habit; the man will walk with God. For this end God uses the evil, of which Satan is the father, to be a discipline, and turns the snares of the enemy into a means of strength for those whom he would captivate. Knowing all this, Christ has left us His prayer. In it He would teach us to ask that God should protect us in such wise that the desire to sin which dwells within us may not be roused to activity by opportunities of indulgence, or if we are thrown where such opportunities exist, the desire may be killed in our hearts. Thus our peril will be lessened, and we shall be helped to walk in the right way, through His grace. Our strong passions will grow weaker, and our weak virtues stronger, day by day.

And such a petition should check all overweening confidence in our own power to withstand temptation, all overreadiness to put ourselves in the way of danger that we may show our strength, and that we can stand though others may fall. The sin and folly of such presumption would be constantly present to St. Peter's mind. He could not forget how his own faith failed when he would make a show of it by walking to meet Jesus over the sea of Galilee. Still less could he forget that utterance of self-confidence, which thought scorn of trials to come, "Though I should die with Thee, yet will I not deny Thee." It needed but the timid suggestion of a servant-maid to call forth that manifestation of feebleness for which only tears of deepest penitence could atone, and which remained the darkest memory in the Apostle's life. He above all men knew to the full the need we have to pray, "Lead us not into temptation."

And in respect of courting trial, even when the suffering to be encountered would be allowed by all men to be suffering for righteousness' sake, the New Testament gives us many lessons that we should not offer ourselves to unnecessary danger. Our Lord Himself (John viii. 59), when the Jews took up stones to cast at Him, hid Himself and conveyed Himself out of harm's way. At another time we are told, "He would not walk in Judæa because the Jews sought to kill Him" (John vii. 1). St. Paul, too (2 Cor. xi. 33), to avoid uncalled-for suffering, was let down by the wall of Damascus, and afterwards made use of the dissensions of the Pharisees and Sadducees (Acts xxiii. 6) to divert the storm which their combined animosity would have raised against him. In this spirit St. Peter gives his counsel. "Make sure," he would say, "that the trials you bear are sent to prove you. Let constant self-questioning testify that they *are* proving you; then wonder not that they are sent, but *rejoice inasmuch as ye are partakers of the sufferings of Christ.*" He who thus learns the blessing of trial thanks the Lord for his troublous days. He has a double joy, rejoicing in this life, sorrowful yet alway rejoicing; and is assured that at the revelation of Christ's glory his joy shall be still more abundant.

If ye are reproached for the name of Christ, blessed are ye. It was a joy to the Apostles (Acts v. 41) at the beginning of their ministry that they were counted worthy to suffer dishonour for the name. Their offence is described as speaking in the name of Jesus, and filling Jerusalem with their teaching. The feeling of their persecutors was so strong that they were minded to slay them, but upon wiser counsel they only beat them and let them go. St. Paul's commission to Damascus (Acts ix. 14) was to bind all that called upon the name of Christ, and his work after his conversion was to be "to bear Christ's name before the Gentiles and kings and the children of Israel." What such preaching would be, we gather from St. Peter's words (Acts ii. 22). They taught men that Jesus of Nazareth, a Man approved of God by powers, and wonders, and signs, had been crucified and slain by the Jews, but that God had raised Him from the dead; that He was now exalted by the right hand of God and was ordained of God (Acts x. 42) to be the Judge of quick and dead; that to Him all the prophets bare witness that through His name every one that believeth on Him should receive remission of sins. St. Paul and the rest preached the same doctrine. All that had happened in Christ's life was "according to the Scriptures" (1 Cor. xv. 3, 4) of the Old Testament; Christ and Him crucified (1 Cor. ii. 2), Jesus and the resurrection (Acts xvii. 18), are the topics constant in his letters and on his lips. And for their doctrine and their faith preachers and hearers suffered persecution and reproach.

In our land suffering such as theirs is no more laid upon us, but for all that the reproach of Christ has not ceased. Our days are specially marked by a desire for demonstration on every subject, and it comes to pass thereby that those who are willing in spiritual things to walk by faith rank in the estimation of many as the less enlightened portion of the world, and are pictured as such in much of our modern literature. All that tells of miracle in the life of Jesus is by many cast altogether aside, as alien to the reign of law under which the world exists; and the Gospel narratives of the virgin-birth, the wonderful works, the Resurrection, and the Ascension are treated as the invention of the fervid imaginations of the first followers of Jesus; while to cling to them as verities, and to their importance and significance in the work of the world's salvation, stamps men as laggards in the march of modern speculation. To accept the New Testament story as the fulfilment of predictions in the Old is reckoned by many for ungrounded superstition; and among the unbelieving there are keen eyes still which gladly mark the slips and stumblings of professing Christians, and throw the obloquy of individuals broadcast upon the whole body.

To hold fast faith at such a time, to accept the Gospels as true and their teaching as the words of eternal life, to see in Christ the Redeemer appointed from eternity by the foreknowledge of God, and to believe that in Him His people find remission of sins, to see and acknowledge above the reign of law the power of the almighty Lawgiver—these things are still beset with trials for those who will live in earnest according to such faith; and if we receive less of the blessing which St. Peter here speaks of as accompanying the reproach of Christ, may we not fear that we exhibit less of the zeal and fervour of the Christians to whom he wrote?

Because the Spirit of glory and the Spirit of God resteth upon you. In the former clause the Apostle, speaking of the joy of believers, exhorted the converts to a present rejoicing, even in the midst of sufferings, because these were borne for Christ's sake, that so, when He shall appear in whose name they have suffered, their rejoicing may be still more abundant. In like manner he seems here to regard their blessedness in a double aspect. The Spirit of glory rests upon them. A power is imparted to them whereby they accept their pains gladly, and therein glorify God, and the same Spirit fills them with a sense of future glory. Like Stephen before his persecutors, they become filled with the Holy Ghost, their spirits are lifted heavenwards, and even now they behold the glory of God, and Jesus sitting on the right hand of God. Thus suffering is robbed of its sting, and Christ's reproach becomes a present blessing.

St. Paul combines the same thoughts in his appeal to the Roman Christians. "Let us rejoice," he urges, "in the hope of the glory of God" (Rom. v. 2). This is the glory to be revealed in the presence of Jesus Christ, that eternal weight of glory which affliction worketh for us more and more exceedingly. But he continues, "Let us rejoice also in our tribulations," knowing that by them we may glorify God in our bodies, and that they are the pledge of glory to come. "For tribulation worketh patience, and patience probation, and probation hope, and hope putteth not to shame" — it will not be disappointed; fruition will surely come — "because the love of God hath been shed abroad in our hearts through the Holy Ghost which was given unto us." This is the Spirit of God of which St. Peter here speaks. It rests like the cloud of glory above the cherubim, and bestows all spiritual power and blessing; it rests on the suffering believer, and gives him rest.

The Authorised Version has here retained a clause which appears to have been at first but an explanatory note, written in the margin of some copy, and then to have been incorporated with the text: "On their part He is evil-spoken of, but on your part He is glorified." We cannot regret the preservation of such a note. It dates back to very early times. The student who made it could write in the language of the New Testament and in its spirit also. It gives us the sense which was then felt to have most prominence and to be the most important. The way of Christ was evil-spoken of, and it could be no strange thing in those days for His followers to be put to fiery trial. Yet the writer feels that the blessedness of the believer is most secured who, regardless of blasphemers around him, strives with all his powers that in his body, whether by life or by death, Christ shall be magnified.

XV
THE RIGHTEOUS HAVE JUDGEMENT HERE

"For let none of you suffer as a murderer, or a thief, or an evil-doer, or as a meddler in other men's matters: but if *a man suffer* as a Christian, let him not be ashamed; but let him glorify God in this name. For the time *is come* for judgement to begin at the house of God: and if *it begin* first at us, what *shall be* the end of them that obey not the gospel of God? And if the righteous is scarcely saved, where shall the ungodly and sinner appear? Wherefore let them also that suffer according to the will of God commit their souls in well-doing unto a faithful Creator."—1 Peter iv. 15-19.

The Apostle now goes one step farther in his exhortations. The brethren are suffering for Christ's cause, and may draw comfort from Christ's example, and be encouraged to patience under their persecutions. But these very sufferings, he would have them see, are God's judgement on His servants in this world, that they may be counted worthy of the kingdom of God, for which they are called to suffer. They must be watchful not to deserve punishment for offences that bring disgrace on themselves and on the cause of Christ.

For let none of you suffer as a murderer, or a thief, or an evil-doer, or as a meddler in other men's matters. He appears to divide these offences into two classes, made distinct by the recurrence of ὡς, "as." The first three concern crimes of which the laws of any land would naturally take cognisance. "Evil-doer" was the word employed by the Jews when they brought our Lord to Pilate: "If he were not an evil-doer, we should not have delivered him up unto thee" (John xviii. 30). The last-named offence, meddling in other men's matters, would bring upon the Christians social odium and render them generally unpopular; and it was precisely the kind of conduct likely to prevail in such a time. We have already found the Apostle exhorting Christian subjects not to think lightly of the duty of obedience to heathen rulers, and the like counsel was given to Christian slaves with heathen masters and to Christian wives with heathen husbands. Such persons would often be tempted to step beyond their province with advice, and perhaps remonstrance, and to display a sense of superiority in so doing which would be galling to those who were of another mind. St. Peter's word to describe this fault is his own, but the idea that such fault needed checking is not wanting in the teaching of St. Paul, and may be taken as evidence that such an interfering spirit prevailed. He speaks of those "who work not at all, but are busybodies" (2 Thess. iii. 11), and to Timothy of those who are "tattlers and busybodies" (1 Tim. v. 13).

St. Peter has ranged these offences in a descending order, placing the least culpable last; and their compass embraces all that rightly might come under the ban of the law or incur the just odium of society. To suffer for such things would disgrace the Christian name; but there is no shame in suffering as a Christian, but rather a reason for giving glory to God. That the name was bestowed as a reproach seems probable from Acts xi. 26, and still more from the mocking tone in which it is used by Agrippa (Acts xxvi. 28); and in the earliest apologists we find this confirmed. "The accusation against us," says Justin Martyr, "is that we are Christians"; and in another place, "We ask that the actions of all those who are accused before you should be examined, so that he who is convicted may be punished as a malefactor, but not as a Christian."

But if a man suffer as a Christian, let him not be ashamed, but let him glorify God in this name. That is, let him be thankful and show his thankfulness that he has been called to bear the name of Christ and to suffer for it. The Authorised Version, adopting a different reading, has "on this behalf." But the sense is nothing different. He is to rejoice that this lot has befallen him, for it is of God's great mercy that we are purified here by trial; he who has not been tried has not entered on the way of salvation. "Let me fall into the hand of the Lord," was the petition of David; and they are more blessed who feel that hand in their correction than those who are cut away from it. It is a terrible lot to think of, if we be abandoned by Him to worldly prosperity. St. Paul congratulates the Philippians "because to them it had been granted, in the behalf of Christ, not only to believe on Him, but also to suffer on His behalf" (Phil. i. 29); and to another Church (Eph. iii. 13) he declares that his own tribulations, endured for their sakes, ought to be to them a glory, because they made known how precious those believers were in the sight of their heavenly Father for whose sake He allowed another to be afflicted that they might be drawn more effectually unto Him. And if this be so, how much cause have they to bless and glorify God who may be permitted to think that He is using their afflictions for a like purpose.

For the time is come for judgement to begin at the house of God. The time is come. Why does the Apostle speak thus? Because the final era of Divine revelation has begun. God has spoken unto men by His Son, and He by His incarnation and death has brought life and immortality to light. The new and living way is opened. We live in the fulness of time, when the faithful, having the testimony of those who companied with Christ, can love Him, though they see Him not, can rejoice in Him, and can receive, with full assurance, the end of their faith, even the salvation of their souls. Such souls have their judgement here. With them God's judgement is neither postponed, nor is it penal. It is disciplinary and corrective both for themselves and others. They are the house of God, the pillar and ground of the truth, and can be set forth as the salt of the earth, the light of the world. Of such judgement and its purpose St. Paul also speaks to the Corinthians: "When we" (the servants of Christ) "are judged" (by suffering in this life), "we are chastened of the Lord, that we may not be condemned with the world" (1 Cor. xi. 32). All chastening while it lasts is grievous, yet afterward it yieldeth peaceable fruit unto them that have been exercised thereby. And by such chastisement God prepares Him witnesses to the truth and preciousness of Christianity; and so long as this time, which is now come, shall continue, so long will God try, and make judgement of, His servants in every generation.

In St. Peter's words we have an echo of prophecy. When the hand of the Lord carried Ezekiel in vision back from Babylon to Jerusalem, he heard the voice of God commanding the destroyers, "Begin at My sanctuary" (Ezek. ix. 6). Yet in that evil age some were found who had been sighing and crying for all the abominations that were done in the midst of the city. These holy ones, living in a naughty world, were God's witnesses, feeling His judgements, but receiving His mark on their foreheads, that they should not be destroyed with the sinners. Years passed away, and at length the Lord of the Temple has Himself come. He began His judgement at the house of God, casting out all that defiled it. But it then had become a mere "house of merchandise"; nay, at a later day He named it "a den of thieves." At last He left it for ever. Then it ceased to be God's house, and though it was spared some forty years, its fate was fixed when He went forth from it (Matt. xxiv. 1, 2) and said that not one stone of it should be left upon another. Henceforth He will have other temples in the hearts of those who worship Him in spirit and in truth. These are now the house of God. With them He exercises judgement constantly for their instruction and amendment. But it shall turn unto them for a testimony in the end. Not a hair of their head shall perish; in their patience they shall win their souls.

And if it begin first at us, what shall be the end of them that obey not the gospel of God? The Apostle joins himself with those of the house of God who will feel the pressure of temporal judgement. He is not forgetful of the Lord's saying, "Simon, behold Satan asked to have you that he might sift you as wheat, but I made supplication for thee that thy faith fail not" (Luke xxii.

31). He knows that he will be tried, but the end to him and all the faithful is that they may be brought into the Father's home. To those who obey not the Gospel the doom pronounced against the Temple answers the Apostle's question. They have had their days of probation, and are like to Jerusalem at the time of the Lord's lamentation, "If thou hadst known in this day the things which belong unto peace! but now they are hid from thine eyes" (Luke xx. 42). They cannot be said to disobey a law of which they have not heard; the glad tidings have been preached unto them, but have found no welcome. As of the doomed city, so of them, it may be said, "Ye would not." After their hardness and their impenitent heart, they have treasured up for themselves wrath in the day of the revelation of the righteous judgement of God.

And if the righteous scarcely is saved, where shall the ungodly and sinner appear? The righteous is he who follows after righteousness, but who feels that, in the midst of his efforts of faith, he needs to cry, "Lord, I believe; help Thou mine unbelief." It is of God's mercy that He accepts the aim and purpose of our lives, and counts not by their results. All men are beset with temptation; in many things we all offend. Works of righteousness bear the taint; they come many a time from wrong motives. The best of us need both the Father's chastisement, and, like Peter, the Saviour's prayers, and the Holy Spirit's guidance. This is what the Apostle means by "scarcely saved." By Divine help Christ's servants are brought nearer and nearer to the ideal, "Be ye holy." But though they live not in sin, sin lives in them; and the warfare with evil is not ended till the burden of the flesh is laid aside. And as there are degrees in the progress of the righteous up the hill of faith, so are there in the falling away of the wicked; and St. Peter in his language appears to have had this in mind, for of the ungodly and sinner he uses a verb in the singular (φανεῖται). Where shall *he* appear? The man begins as the ungodly, a negative character: he thinks not of God; has no reverence for His law; puts Him away from all his thoughts. But in this state he will not long remain. There is no standing still in things spiritual. He who does not advance goes backward, and the ungodly soon becomes the wilful sinner. So sure is this development that the Apostle combines the two aspects of the wicked man's life, and asks, not, Where shall they, but Where shall he, appear?

For the judgement which for the righteous begins at God's house, and is wrought out in the trials of this life, awaits the disobedient when life is ended. The Apostle leaves his solemn question unanswered; but at that day there remaineth no more sacrifice for sins, only a fearful expectation of judgement. It is a fearful thing to fall into the hands of the living God then. Hence the greater blessedness of those who are taken into God's hand of judgement now. And thus the Apostle comforts the sufferers.

Wherefore let them also that suffer according to the will of God commit their souls in well-doing unto a faithful Creator. Again St. Peter goes back in thought to the words of Christ, "Father, into Thy hands I commend My spirit" (Luke xxiii. 46); and on these he builds his final exhortation, which contains within it consolation in abundance. The test of the faithful is his perfect trust. "Though He slay me, yet will I trust in Him" (Job xiii. 15), was the confession which marked Job as more righteous than his advisers. The Revised Version has varied the rendering of the final words in that passage in such wise as to explain how the trust is to be exhibited: "I will wait for Him" — wait, sure that the event will be for my comfort and His glory. This is the spirit which waxes strong in trial. "They that wait upon the Lord shall renew their strength" (Isa. xl. 31), says the prophet. "None that wait on the Lord shall be ashamed," is an oft-repeated testimony of the psalmists (Psalms xxv. 3; xxxvii. 34; lxix. 6); and one whose name is a synonym for suffering tells us, "The Lord is good unto them that wait for Him" (Lam. iii. 25). To such trust St. Peter here exhorts, bidding specially them that suffer to rest on the Lord. Though they be punished in the sight of men, yet is their hope full of immortality, for the souls of the righteous are in the hand of God, a trust which they repose in Him while they live here, a treasure guarded by Him in the world to come. St. Paul knows of the efficacy of this perfect trust, for he writes to Timothy, "We labour and strive," counting bodily suffering as nothing, "because we have our hope set on the living God, who is the Saviour of all men, specially of them that believe" (1 Tim. iv. 10).

The Apostle links a holy life most closely with this trust in God. In well-doing commit your souls unto Him. No otherwise can His guardianship and aid be hoped for. But the Lord knoweth the way of the righteous, and with Him to know is to watch over and help. Nor should men sorrow when they suffer according to God's will. Rather it is cause for gladness. For conscience must tell them that they need to be purged from much earthly dross which clings about them. So the fire of trial may be counted among blessings.

And with two words of exceeding comfort St. Peter strengthens the believers in their trust. God is faithful; His compassions fail not: they are new every morning. In moments of despair the sorrowing Christian may feel tempted to cry out, with the Psalmist, "Hath God forgotten to be gracious? hath He in anger shut up His tender mercies?" (Psalm lxxvii. 10), but as he looks back on the path where God has led him he is convinced of the unwisdom of his questioning, and cries out, "This is my infirmity; I will remember the years of the right hand of the Most High."

And this faithful God is our Creator. In the council of the Godhead it was said in the beginning, "Let us make man in our image." And God breathed into his nostrils the breath of life, which made of him a living soul. From

God's hand he came forth very good, but sin entered, and the Divine image has been blurred and defaced. Yet in mercy the same heavenly conclave planned the scheme for man's restoration to his first estate. The love which spake to Zion of old speaks through Christ to all mankind. "Can a woman forget her sucking child? Yea, she may forget; yet will I not forget thee" (Isa. xlix. 15). In the fulness of time God has sent His Son to take hold upon the sons of men, to wear their likeness, to live on earth and die for the souls which He has made. Trust, says the Apostle, in this almighty, unchanging love; trust God, your Father, your Creator. He will succour you against all assaults of evil; He will comfort and support you when it is His desire to prove you; He will crown you, with your Lord, when trials are no more.

XVI
HOW TO TEND THE FLOCK

"The elders therefore among you I exhort, who am a fellow-elder, and a witness of the sufferings of Christ, who am also a partaker of the glory that shall be revealed: Tend the flock of God which is among you, exercising the oversight, not of constraint, but willingly, according unto God; nor yet for filthy lucre, but of a ready mind; neither as lording it over the charge allotted to you, but making yourselves ensamples to the flock. And when the chief Shepherd shall be manifested, ye shall receive the crown of glory that fadeth not away." — 1 Peter v. 1-4.

St. Peter's last lesson was full of consolation. He showed that it was from God's hand that judgements were sent upon His people to purify them and prepare them for His appearing. With this thought in their minds, he would have the converts rejoice in their discipline, confident in the faithfulness of Him who was trying them. He follows this general message to the Churches with a solemn charge to their teachers. They are specially responsible for the welfare of the brethren. On them it rests by the holiness of their lives and the spirit in which they labour to win men to the faith. *The elders therefore among you I exhort, who am a fellow-elder, and a witness of the sufferings of Christ, who am also a partaker of the glory that shall be revealed: Tend the flock of God which is among you.* Therefore — because I know that the blessed purpose of trial is not always manifest, and because the hope of the believer needs to be constantly pointed to the faithfulness of God — I exhort you to tend zealously those over whom you are put in charge. "Elders" was the name given at first to the whole body of Christian teachers. No doubt they were chosen at the beginning from the older members of the community, when the Apostles established Churches in their missionary journeys. "They appointed for them elders in every Church" (Acts xiv. 23); and it was the elders of the Church of Ephesus that Paul sent for to Miletus (Acts xx. 17). And St. Peter here contrasts them very pointedly with those of younger years, whom he addresses afterwards. But after it became an official title the sense of seniority would drop away from the word.

It is clear from this passage that in St. Peter's time they were identical with those who were afterwards named bishops. For the word which follows presently in the text and is rendered "exercising the oversight" is literally "doing the work of bishop, or overseer." And in the passage already alluded to (Acts xx. 15-28) those who at first are called elders are subsequently named bishops: "The Holy Ghost hath made you bishops to feed the Church of God" (R.V.). As the Church grew certain places would become prominent as centres of Christian life, and to the elders therein the oversight of other Churches would be given; and thus the overseer or bishop would grow to be distinct from the other presbyters, and his title be assigned to the more important office. This had not come about when St. Peter wrote.

The humility, which he is soon about to commend to the whole body, the Apostle manifests by placing himself on the level of those to whom he speaks: "I, who am a fellow-elder, exhort you." He has strong claims to be heard, claims which can never be theirs. He has been a witness of the sufferings of Christ. He might have made mention of his apostleship; he might have told of the thrice-repeated commission which soon supplies the matter of his exhortation. He will rather be counted an equal, a fellow-labourer with themselves. Some have thought that even when he calls himself a witness of Christ's sufferings he is not so much referring to what he saw of the life and death of Jesus, as to the testimony which he has borne to his Master since the pentecostal outpouring and the share which he has had of sufferings for Christ's sake. If this be so, he would here too be reckoning himself even as they, as he clearly intends to do in the words which follow, where he calls himself a sharer, as they all are, in the glory to which they look forward. Thus in all things they are his brethren: in the ministry, in their affliction, and in their hope of glory to be revealed.

He opens his solemn charge with words which are the echo of Christ's own: "Feed My sheep"; "Feed My lambs." Every word pictures the responsibility of those to whom the trust is committed. These brethren are God's flock. Psalmists and prophets had been guided of old to use the figure; they speak of God's people as "the sheep of His pasture." But our Lord consecrated it still more when He called Himself "the good Shepherd, that giveth His life for the sheep." The word tells much of the character of those to whom it is applied. How prone they are to wander and stray, how helpless, how ill furnished with means of defence against perils. It tells, too, that they are easy to be led. But that is not all a blessing, for though docile, they are often heedless, ready to follow any leader without thought of consequences.

But they are God's flock. This adds to the dignity of the elder's office, but adds also to the gravity of the trust, a trust to be entered on with fear and trembling. For the flock is precious to Christ, and should be precious to His shepherds. To let them perish for want of tending is treachery to the Master who has sent men to His work. And how much that tending means. To feed them is not all, though that is much. To provide such nurture as will help their growth in grace. There is a food store in God's word, but not every lesson there suits every several need. There must be thoughtful choice of lessons. The elders of old were, and God's shepherds now are, called to give much care how they minister, lest by their oversight or neglect—

"The hungry sheep look up, but are not fed."

But tending speaks of watchfulness. The shepherd must yield his account when the chief Shepherd shall appear. Those who are watchmen over God's flock must have an eye to quarters whence dangers may come, must mark the signs of them and be ready with safeguards. And the sheep themselves must be strengthened to endure and conquer when they are assailed; they cannot be kept out of harm's way always. Christ did not pray for His own little flock of disciples that they should be taken out of the world, only kept from the evil. Then all that betokens good must be cherished among them. For even tiny germs of goodness the Spirit will sanctify, and help the watchful elder, by his tending, to rear till they flourish and abound.

To his general precept St. Peter adds three defining clauses, which tell us how the elder's duty may be rightly discharged, and against what perils and temptations he will need to strive: *exercising the oversight, not of constraint, but willingly, according unto God.* How would the oversight of an elder come to be exercised of constraint in the time of St. Peter? Those to whom he writes had been appointed to their office by apostolic authority, it may have been by St. Paul himself; and while an Apostle was present to inspire them enthusiasm for the new teaching would be at its height: many would be drawn to the service of Christ who would appear to the missionaries well fitted to be entrusted with such solemn charge and ministry. But even an Apostle cannot read men's hearts, and it was when the Apostles departed that the Churches would enter on their trial. Then the fitness of the elders would be put to the test. Could they maintain in the Churches the earnestness which had been awakened? Could they in their daily walk sustain the apostolic character, and help forward the cause both by word and life? Christianity would be unlike every other movement whose officers are human if there were not many failures and much weakness here and there; and if the ministrations of elders grew less accepted and less fruitful, they would be offered with ever-diminishing earnestness, and the services, full of life at the outset, would prove irksome from disappointment, and in the end be discharged only as a work of necessity.

And every subsequent age of the Church has endorsed the wisdom of St. Paul's caution, "Lay hands hastily on no man." Fervid zeal may grow cool, and inaptitude for the work become apparent. Nor are those in whom it is found always solely responsible for a mistaken vocation. As St. Paul's words should make those vigilant whose office it is to send forth men to sacred ministries, so St. Peter's warning should check any undue urging of men to offer themselves. It is a sight to move men to sorrow, and God to displeasure, when the shepherd's work is perfunctory, not done willingly, according to God.

In some texts the last three words are not represented, nor are they found in our Authorised Version. But they have abundant authority, and so fully declare the spirit in which all pastoral work should be done that they might well be repeated emphatically with each of these three clauses. To labour *according to God*, "as ever in the great Taskmaster's eye," is so needful that the words may be commended to the elders as a constant motto. And not only as in His sight should the work be done, but with an endeavour after the standard which is set before us in Christ. We are to stoop as He stooped that we may raise those who cannot raise themselves; to be compassionate to the penitent, breaking no bruised reed, quenching no spark in the smoking flax. The pastor's words should be St. Paul's, "We are your servants for Jesus's sake," his action that of the shepherd in the parable: "When he findeth it, he layeth it on his shoulders rejoicing." Such joy comes only to willing workers.

Nor yet for filthy lucre, but of a ready mind. We do not usually think of the Church in the apostolic age as offering any temptation to the covetous. The disciples were poor men, and there is little trace of riches in the opening chapters of the Acts. St. Paul, too, constantly declined to be a burden to the flock, as though he felt it right to spare the brethren. The lessons of the New Testament on this subject are very plain. When our Lord sent forth His seventy disciples, He sent them as "labourers worthy of their hire" (Luke x. 7); and St. Paul declares it to be the Lord's ordinance that they which proclaim the Gospel should live of the Gospel (1 Cor. ix. 14). To serve with a ready mind is to seek nothing beyond this. But it is clear both from St. Paul's language (1 Tim. iii. 3; Titus i. 7) and from this verse that there existed temptations to greed, and that some were overcome thereby. It is worthy of note, however, that those who are given up to this covetousness are constantly branded with false teaching. They are thus described by both the Apostles. They teach things which they ought not (Titus i. 11), and with feigned words make merchandise of the flock (2 Peter ii. 3). The spurt of self-seeking and base gain (which is the literal sense of St. Peter's word) is so alien to the spirit of the Gospel that we cannot conceive a faithful and true shepherd using other language than that of St. Paul: "We seek not yours, but you."

Neither as lording it over the charge allotted to you, but making yourselves ensamples to the flock. This, too, is a special peril at all times for those who are called to preside in spiritual offices. The interests committed to their trust are so surpassingly momentous that they must often speak with authority, and the Church's history furnishes examples of men who would make themselves lords where Christ alone should be Lord. Against this temptation He has supplied the safeguard for all who will use it. "My sheep," He says, "hear My voice." And the faithful tenders of His flock must ever ask themselves in their service, Is this the voice of Christ? The question will be in their hearts as they give counsel to those who need and seek it, What would Christ have said to this man or to that? The same sort of question will bring to the test their public ministrations, and will make that most prominent in them which He intended to be so. Thus will be introduced into all they do a due proportion and subordination, and many a subject of disquiet in the Churches will thereby sink almost into insignificance. At the same time the constant reference to their own Lord will keep them in mind that they are His servants for the flock of God.

While he warns the elders against the assumption of lordship over their charges, the Apostle adds a precept which, if it be followed, will abate all tendency to seek such lordship. For it brings to the mind of those set over the flock that they too are but sheep, like the rest, and are appointed not to dominate, but to help their brethren. *Making yourselves ensamples to the flock.* Christ's rule for the good shepherd is, "He goeth before them, and the sheep follow him" (John x. 4). The weak take in teaching rather from what they see than from what they hear. The teacher must be a living witness to the word, a proof of its truth and power. If he be not this, all his teaching is of little value. The simplest teacher who lives out his lessons in his life becomes a mighty power; he gains the true, the lawful lordship, and—

"Truth from his lips prevails with double sway."

The Apostles knew well the weight and influence of holy examples. Hence St. Paul appeals continually to the lives of himself and his fellow-workers. We labour, he says, "to make ourselves an ensample unto you that ye should imitate us" (2 Thess. iii. 9); Timothy he exhorts, "Be thou an ensample to them that believe" (1 Tim. iv. 12), and Titus, "In all things showing thyself an ensample of good works" (Titus ii. 7). Nothing can withstand the eloquence of him who can dare to appeal to his brethren, as the Apostle does, "Be ye imitators together of me, and mark them which walk so as ye have us for an ensample" (Phil. iii. 7), and "Be ye imitators of me, even as I also am of Christ" (1 Cor. xi. 1). Such pattern shepherds have been the admiration of every age. Chaucer, among his pilgrims, describes the good parson thus:—

"The lore of Christ and His Apostles twelve
He taught, and first he followed it himself."

Such are the lives of shepherds who remember that they are even as their flocks: frail and full of evil tendencies, and needing to come continually, in humble supplication, to the source of strength and light, and to be ever watchful over their own lives. These men seek no lordship; there comes to them a nobler power, and the allegiance they win is self-tendered.

And when the chief Shepherd shall be manifested, ye shall receive the crown of glory that fadeth not away. For their consolation the Apostle sets before the elders their Judge in His self-chosen character. He is the chief Shepherd. Judge He must also be when He is manifested; but while He must pass sentence on their work, He will understand and weigh the many hindrances, both within and without, against which they have had to fight. Of human weakness, error, sin, such as besets us, He had no share; but He knows whereof we are made, and will not ask from any of us a service beyond our powers. Nay, His Spirit chooses for us, would we but mark it, the work in which we can serve Him most fitly. And He has borne the contradiction of sinners against Himself. In judging His servants, then, He will take account of the wilfulness of ears that would not hear and of eyes that would not see, of the waywardness that chose darkness rather than light, ignorance rather than Divine knowledge, death rather than life.

Therefore His feeble but faithful servants may with humble minds welcome His appearing. He comes as Judge. *Ye shall receive.* It is a word descriptive of the Divine award at the last. Here it marks the bestowal of a reward, but elsewhere (2 Peter ii. 13) the Apostle uses it for the payment to sinners of the hire of wrong-doing. But the Judge is full of mercy. Of one sinner's feeble efforts He said, "She hath done what she could. Her sins are forgiven." And another who had laboured to be faithful He welcomed to His presence: "Enter into the joy of thy Lord." To share that joy, to partake of His glory, to be made like Him by beholding His presence—this will be the faithful servant's prize, a crown of amaranth, unwithering, eternal.

XVII
BE CLOTHED WITH HUMILITY

"Likewise, ye younger, be subject unto the elder. Yea, all of you gird yourselves with humility, to serve one another: for God resisteth the proud, but giveth grace to the humble. Humble yourselves therefore under the mighty hand of God, that He may exalt you in due time; casting all your anxiety upon Him, because He careth for you."—1 Peter v. 5-7.

Having admonished the shepherds, the Apostle now turns to the flock, and his words recall the exhortations which he has given several times before. In ii. 13 he taught Christian subjects the duty of submission, even should it be their lot to live under heathen rulers. A few verses further on in the same chapter he repeated this teaching to Christian slaves with heathen masters, and the third chapter opens with advice of the same character to the wives who were married to heathen husbands. And now once more, with his favourite verb "be subject," he opens his counsel to the Churches on their duty to those set over them. The relation between the elders and their flock will not be as strained, or not strained after the same manner, as between Christians and heathens in the other cases, but the same principle is to govern the behaviour of those who hold the subject position. The duly appointed teachers are to be accepted as powers ordained of God, and their rule and guidance followed with submission.

Likewise, ye younger, be subject unto the elder. He teaches that as there is a duty of the elders to the younger, so there is a reciprocal duty which, in like manner and with the same thoroughness, must be discharged by the younger to the elders. In those early days the congregation could fitly be spoken of as "the younger." Naturally the teachers would be chosen from those who had been the first converts. The rest of the body would consist not only of those younger in years, but younger in the acceptance of the faith, younger in the knowledge of the doctrines of Christ, younger in Christian experience. And if the Churches were to be a power among their heathen surroundings, it must be by their unity in spirit and faith; and this could only be secured by a loyal and ready following of those who were chosen to instruct them.

But lest there may be any undue straining of the claim to submission, there follows immediately a precept to make it general: *Yea, all of you gird yourselves with humility, to serve one another.* Thus will be realised the true idea of the Christian body, where each member should help all, and be helped of all, the rest, eye and hand, head and feet, each having their office, and each ministering therein as parts of the one body. This idea of general humility was altogether unknown to the world before Christ's coming. The word, therefore, is one coined for Christian use: lowliness of mind, a frame wherein each deems others better than himself. And with it the Apostle has coupled another word for "gird yourselves," which is well fitted to be so placed. It is found nowhere else, and is full of that graphic character of which he is so fond. The noun from which it is derived signifies "an outer garment," mainly used by household servants and slaves, to cover their other clothing and keep it from being spoiled. It appears to have been bound round the waist by a girdle. The word is a complete picture. St. Peter sees in humility a robe which shall encompass the whole life of the believer, keeping off all that might sully or defile it; and into the sense of the word comes the lowly estate of those by whom the garment in question was worn. It was connected entirely with the humblest duties. Hence its appropriateness when joined with "serve one another."

And one cannot in studying this striking word of the Apostle but be carried in thought to that scene described by St. John where Jesus "took a towel and girded Himself" (John xiii. 4) to wash the feet of His disciples. St. Peter gained much instruction from that washing, and he has not forgotten the lesson when he desires to confirm the brethren in Christian humility. "I have given you an example, that ye also should do as I have done to you," was the Lord's injunction; and this the Apostle delivers to the Churches. And verily Christ spake of Himself more truly than of any other when He described the master's treatment of his watchful servants: "He shall gird himself, and make them sit down to meat, and shall come and serve them" (Luke xii. 37). Such has been the Lord's humiliation, who took upon Him our flesh, and now bids us to His banquet, where, through His Spirit, He is ever waiting to bless those who draw near.

How this exhortation to humility in dealing with one another is connected with the verse (Prov. iii. 34) by which the Apostle supports it does not perhaps immediately appear. *For God resisteth the proud, but giveth grace to the humble.* But a little reflection on the characteristics of pride towards men soon makes us conscious that it is very closely united with pride towards God. The Pharisee who despises the publican, and thanks God in words that he is not such a one, feels in his heart no thankfulness nor care for God at all. His own acts have made him the pattern of goodness which he conceives himself to be. And we discover the like in every other exhibition of this spirit. The term (ὑπερήφανοι) by which these haughty ones are described indicates a desire to be conspicuous, to stand apart from and above their fellows. They are self-centred, and look down upon the rest of the world, and forget their dependence upon God.

St. Peter in his quotation has followed the Septuagint. In the Hebrew the first half of the verse is, "He scorneth the scorners." And this is the manner of God's dealing. He pays men with their own coin. Jacob's deceit was punished in kind by the frequent deceptions of his children, so that at last he could hardly credit their report that Joseph is still alive. David was scourged for his offences exactly according to his own sin. But the word which the Apostle has drawn from the Septuagint is also of solemn import. It declares a state of war between God and man. God *resisteth* the proud; literally, He setteth Himself in array against them. And their overthrow is sure. They that strive with the Lord shall be broken to pieces. The Psalmist rejoices over the contrary lot: "The Lord is on my side; I will not fear. What can man do unto me?" (Psalm cxviii. 6). He had realised the feebleness of human strength, even for man to rely on, much more if it stand in opposition to God. "It is better to trust in the Lord than to put any confidence in man," be it in ourselves or in others. So out of his distress he called upon the Lord. It is the sense of need which makes men humble; and to humbled souls God's blessing comes: "He answered me, and set me in a large place."

And as though He would mark humility as the chief grace to prepare men for His kingdom, the Lord's first words in His sermon on the mount are a blessing on the lowly-minded: "Blessed are the poor in spirit, for theirs is the kingdom of heaven"—not shall be, but *is* theirs even now. God's favour to the humble is a present gift. How the sense of this swells the thanksgivings of Hannah and the Virgin Mary! And to teach the lesson to His disciples, when they were far from humility and were anxious only to know which of them should be above the rest in what they still dreamt of as an earthly kingdom, He took a little child and set him before them, as the pattern to which His true followers must conform. This childlike virtue gives admission to the kingdom of heaven; its possessors have the kingdom of God within them.

And St. Peter feeds the flock as he himself was fed. *Humble yourselves therefore under the mighty hand of God, that He may exalt you in due time.* The Apostle may be referring in these words to the trials which were upon the converts when he wrote to them. These he would have them look upon as God's discipline, as a cause for joy rather than sorrow. Christian humility will not rebel against fatherly, merciful correction. How the good man bows before the hand of God we see in Moses when God refused to let him go over into Canaan: "I besought the Lord, saying, O Lord God, Thou hast begun to show Thy servant Thy greatness and Thy strong hand.... Let me go over, I pray Thee, and see the good land that is beyond Jordan. But the Lord was wroth with me for your sakes, and hearkened not unto me" (Deut. iii. 23). And so the meek prophet, who knew that his withdrawal was for the people's sake, having sung, "Happy art thou, O Israel; who is like unto thee, a people saved by the Lord?" (Deut. xxxiii. 29), went up unto Mount Nebo and died there, when his eye was not dim, nor his natural force abated. Hence his praise: "There hath not arisen a prophet since in Israel like unto Moses." Humility was his dying lesson.

But as the Apostle has just been speaking of the duty owed to the elders as teachers, it is perhaps better to apply the words of the exhortation in that sense. Those who were set over the Churches were so set in the Lord. For the time they represented His hand, the hand of care and guidance to those who were submissive. In honouring them, the younger were honouring God. Thus the lesson would be, Bend your hearts to the instruction which He imparts through their words; yield your will to His will, and order your life to be in harmony with His providence; live thus that He may exalt you. For the hand which may seem heavy now will be mighty to raise you in due time. And that time He knows. It is His time, not yours. If it tarry, wait for it. It will surely come; it will not tarry, when the Divine discipline has done its work.

Casting all your anxiety upon Him, because He careth for you. When men do this the due time has come. Till this stage is reached there can be no true humility. But how slow men are in reaching it! We are willing to bring to God a little here and there of our sorrow and our feebleness, but would fain still carry a part of the load ourselves. Human pride it is which cannot stoop to owe everything to God; want of faith, too, both in the Divine power and the Divine love, though our tongues may not confess it. What a powerful homily on this verse is the conduct of the youthful David when he went forth against the Philistine! "The Lord," he says to Saul, "that delivered me out of the paw of the lion and out of the paw of the bear, He will deliver me out of the hand of this Philistine." And when the king offered his own coat of mail, though tempted thereby, he put the armour away, saying, "I cannot go with these, for I have not proved them." He knew that God had given him skill with the humbler weapons, and it was God's battle in which he was to engage. So with his stones and his sling he went forth, telling the defiant challenger, "I come to thee in the name of the Lord of hosts." The action is a comment on the Psalmist's words, "Commit thy way unto the Lord, trust also in Him, and He shall bring it to pass" (Psalm xxxviii. 5).

But neither the young hero by his example, nor the Apostle in his exhortation, teaches a spirit of careless indifference and neglect of means. David chose him five smooth stones out of the brook. These he could use. With these God had delivered him aforetime. And in every condition men are bound to use the best means they know to ensure success, and the Christian will pour out his prayers for guidance and foresight in temporal concerns. That done, the counsel of Christ, on which St. Peter's exhortation is grounded, is, "Be not overanxious; your heavenly Father knoweth your needs." And he who has grown humble under the mighty hand of God in trials has learnt that the same hand is mighty to save: "He careth for you." When this perfect trust is placed in God, the load is lifted. It is, as the Psalmist says literally, *rolled* upon the Lord (Psalm xxxviii. 5).

How salutary this teaching for both the elders and the congregations among these Christians of the dispersion, and how full the promise of help and blessing. The teachers had been placed in the midst of difficulties and charged with a mighty responsibility; but robed in the garment of humility, casting aside all self-trust, coming only in the name of the Lord, the burden would be raised by the almighty arms and made convenient to their powers. And to the younger the same lowly spirit, loving thoughts toward those who cared for their souls, would be fruitful in blessing. For the same God who resisteth the proud showers His grace upon the humble. It falls on them as the dew of Hermon, which cometh down upon the mountains of Zion. Unto them Christ has proclaimed His foremost blessing; has promised, and is giving, the kingdom of heaven to humble souls, and will give them life for evermore.

XVIII
THROUGH PERILS TO VICTORY

"Be sober, be watchful: your adversary the devil, as a roaring lion, walketh about, seeking whom he may devour: whom withstand steadfast in your faith, knowing that the same sufferings are accomplished in your brethren who are in the world. And the God of all grace, who called you unto His eternal glory in Christ, after that ye have suffered a little while, shall Himself perfect, stablish, strengthen you. To Him *be* the dominion for ever and ever. Amen.

"By Silvanus, our faithful brother, as I account *him*, I have written unto you briefly, exhorting, and testifying that this is the true grace of God: stand ye fast therein. She that is in Babylon, elect together with *you*, saluteth you; and *so doth* Mark my son. Salute one another with a kiss of love.

"Peace be unto you all that are in Christ." —1 Peter v. 8-14.

Not only had these Asian Christians to suffer from the opposition and calumnies of the heathen and from the estrangement of former friends: there were perils within the Churches themselves. There were weak brethren, who fell away when trials came, and infected others with their despondency; there were false brethren, with whom faith was a mere consent of the understanding, and not the spring of a holy, spiritual life. These spake of the liberty of Christ as though it were an emancipation from all moral restraints. Such dangers asked for firmness both in the elders and their hearers. To withstand them there must be a constant growth in Christian experience, whereby the faithful might wax steadfast, and attain to the strength and stature of the fulness of Christ. These dangers became more manifest before St. Peter wrote his second letter, where we find them described in dark colours.

Here to the converts, exposed to the assaults of these temptations, he enjoins the same well-ordered frame of mind which before (i. 13) he commended to them as they looked forward to the hope in store for them, and also (iv. 7) in their prayers, that their petitions might be such as suited with the approaching end of all things. *Be sober*, he says again, and combines therewith an exhortation which without sobriety is impossible: *Be watchful.* If the mind be unbalanced, there can be no keeping of a true guard against such dangers as were around these struggling believers. And it is impossible not to connect such an exhortation from his lips with those words of Christ, which one Evangelist says were expressly addressed to St. Peter, "Watch and pray, that ye enter not into temptation" (Mark xiv. 37, 38). He who had received this admonition was conscious that, as in his own case, so with these his converts, the spirit might be willing, but the flesh was weak, and the enemy mighty.

Your adversary the devil, as a roaring lion, walketh about, seeking whom he may devour. In the days of Job, when God asked of Satan, "Whence comest thou?" his answer was, "From going to and fro in the earth and from walking up and down in it" (Job i. 7). Of this Old Testament language the Apostle here makes partial use in his description of the enemy of mankind. He walketh about in the earth, which is his province, for he is called the prince of this world (John xii. 31) and the god of this world (2 Cor. iv. 4). And the Greek word ἀντίδικος, "adversary," which St. Peter uses as a translation of the Hebrew "Satan," is well chosen, for it describes not an ordinary enemy, but one who acts as an opponent would in a court of law. Such was Satan from the first, an accuser. In Job's case he accused the Patriarch to his God: "Doth Job serve God for nought?" "Put forth Thine hand now, and touch all that he hath, or touch his bone and his flesh, and he will curse Thee to Thy face." In earlier days he appears as the accuser of God Himself: "Ye shall not surely die, for God doth know that in the day ye eat thereof then your eyes shall be opened, and ye shall be as God, knowing good and evil" (Gen. iii. 4, 5). And with such-like suggestions he assails the faithful continually, speaking either to their unguarded hearts, or by the words of his servants, of whom he has no lack. St. Paul dreaded his power for the Thessalonian converts: "I sent that I might know your faith, lest by any means the tempter had tempted you, and our labour should be in vain" (1 Thess. iii. 5). And St. Peter's words are dictated by the same fear; he has the same wish to keep the flock steadfast in their faith. To them Satan's whisperings would be after this sort: "You are forgotten of God"; "Love could never leave you so long in trial." Or his agents would say in scorn, "How can you talk of freedom, when your life is one long torment? What is the profit of faith, when it gives you no liberty?" And such questions are perilous to feeble minds. The Apostle marks the great danger by a comparison which Ezekiel (xxii. 25) had used before him, speaking of the tempter as a roaring lion, ever hungry for his prey. There is but one weapon which can vanquish him. "This is the victory that hath overcome the world, even our faith" (1 John v. 4). St. Peter's lesson is the same as St. John's.

Whom withstand steadfast in your faith, knowing that the same sufferings are accomplished in your brethren who are in the world. The steadfast faith must be the firm foundation of God; and the same thoughts, which St. Paul commends as a correction of those who have erred concerning the truth, are those most fit to be urged upon St. Peter's converts to render them steadfast. "The Lord knoweth them that are His" (2 Tim. ii. 19), and with the Lord to know is to care for and to save. And "let every one that nameth the name of the Lord depart from unrighteousness." This is the perfect law, the law of true liberty, and he who continueth therein, being not a hearer that forgetteth, but a doer that worketh, shall be blessed in his doing. Thus resting on God and thus ruling himself, he shall be kept from the snares of the enemy, and having withstood in the evil day, shall still be made able to stand.

And to such steadfastness the brethren are to be moved by the knowledge that others are in the same affliction. How shall such knowledge minister support? The mere knowledge that others bear a like burden does not strengthen our own shoulders; to hear of others' pains will not relieve our own. Not so. But just as it is a power in warfare when men see their leader before them, facing the same perils, hear his voice cheering them by his courage, inspiring them with his hope; just as it is a support to brave men to find brave brethren at their side in the conflict, animated by the same spirit, marching forward to the same victory, so is it in the Christian struggle. All Christians are to be steadfast, the elders like the leaders of an army, the younger like the soldiers who follow, that, moving with one spirit against the foe, feeling that each is like-minded with all the rest, while all are equally conscious of the importance of victory, they may grasp hands as they go forward, and be heartened thereby, being sure that in the danger they will have helpers at their side.

And that he may give the more emphasis to this idea of unity, in which, though the suffering is common to all, yet the hope is also common, and the victory is promised to all, the Apostle does not speak of the converts as a multitude of brethren, but uses a noun in the singular number, naming them (as the margin of the Revised Version indicates) "a brotherhood" (ἀδελφότης). And when they regarded themselves as "a brotherhood in the world," the thought would have its comforting as well as its painful aspect. The world, as Scripture speaks of it, is void of faith. Hence the believer, while he lives in it, is amid jarring surroundings, and is sure to suffer. "In the world ye shall have tribulation." But it is not to last for ever, nor for long. "The world passeth away, but he that doeth the will of God abideth for ever." And though the brotherhood in the world must suffer, yet there is that other brotherhood beyond; and there the suffering will not be remembered for the glory that shall be revealed in us.

And the God of all grace, who called you unto His eternal glory in Christ, after that ye have suffered a little while, shall Himself perfect, stablish, strengthen you. Being now about to sum up the great work of Christian advancement, in which from first to last the power is bestowed by God, St. Peter finds no title more fitting to express the Divine love than "the God of *all* grace." The invitation to become partakers of the glory which Christ has won by His sufferings, won that He may bestow it upon men, was God's free call. Our sufferings, the discipline which the Father employs to purge and purify us, are to last but a little while. Then those whom He has called He will also justify, and those whom He justifies He will in the end glorify. Thus St. Paul (Rom. viii. 30) describes the operations of Divine grace. St. Peter, with the same lesson, uses words more after his own graphic manner. He gives us a picture of God's work in its several stages. First God will complete in all its parts the work which He has begun. He will make it so that He can pronounce it very good, as He did when the worlds *were perfected* in the first creation (Heb. xi. 3), making His people to be so *perfected* that they may be as their Master (Luke vi. 40). Then He will sustain and support that which He has brought to its best estate. There shall not be, as in the first creation, any falling away. New gifts shall be bestowed by the Holy Spirit, through the ministration of the word. It was for such a purpose that St. Paul longed to visit the Roman Church, that he might impart unto them some spiritual gift, to the end that they might be *established*. And what has been perfected and established shall also by the same grace be made strong, that it may endure and withstand all assaults.

In many ancient texts a fourth verb is given, which the Authorised Version renders "settle." It signifies "to set on a firm foundation," and it is of the figurative character which marks St. Peter's language, and, beside this, is not uncommon in the New Testament (Matt. vii. 25; Luke vi. 48; Heb. i. 10, etc.). But the verbs immediately preceding have no direct reference to a building, and the addition arises probably from a marginal note, made to illustrate the text and by some later scribe incorporated with it. The whole passage brings to mind Christ's injunction to the Apostle, "When thou art converted, strengthen thy brethren."

To Him be the dominion for ever and ever. Amen. A fitting doxology to follow the Apostle's enumeration of the riches of Divine grace. He who feels that every gift he has is from above will with ready thankfulness welcome God's rule, and seek to submit himself thereto, making it the law of his life here, as he hopes it will be hereafter.

By Silvanus, our faithful brother, as I account him, I have written unto you briefly. Silvanus was that Silas who accompanied St. Paul in his second missionary journey through the districts of Phrygia and Galatia (Acts xvi. 6), to which St. Peter addresses his letter. To send it by the hand of one known and esteemed among these Churches for his former labours and for his friendship with the great Apostle of the Gentiles would secure acceptance for it, while the bearer would testify to the unity of the doctrine preached by the two Apostles. He who had been a faithful brother to St. Paul was so also to St. Peter, and was by him commended to the Churches. For the expression, *I account him*, implies no doubt or question in the Apostle's own mind. It is the utterance of a matured opinion. The verb (λογίζομαι) is that which St. Paul uses: "I *reckon* that the sufferings of this present time are not worthy to be compared with the glory which shall be revealed in us" (Rom. viii. 18). To St. Paul something of the future glory had been shown, and he had felt abundance of present suffering. He had taken account of both sides, and could speak with certainty. The brevity of St. Peter's letter could be supplemented by the words of his messenger. For Silas himself was a prophet (Acts xv. 32), and fitted to exhort and confirm the brethren.

Exhorting, and testifying that this is the true grace of God: stand ye fast therein. The grace in its several stages has just been summarised: the calling, the perfecting, stablishing, strengthening; and the whole letter is occupied in showing that at every advance God puts His servants to the test. But the Apostle knows that agents of the adversary are busily scattering the tares of doubt and disbelief where God had sown His good seed. The wrestling is not against flesh and blood alone, but against the world-rulers of this darkness, against the spiritual host of wickedness. Hence the form of his exhortation: *Stand fast.*

She that is in Babylon, elect together with you, saluteth you; and so doth Mark my son. Salute one another with a kiss of love. It is most natural to refer these words to a Church, and not to any individual. Some have interpreted them as an allusion to St. Peter's wife, whom, as we know from St. Paul (1 Cor. ix. 5), he sometimes had as a companion in his travels. But there is a degree of inappropriateness in speaking of a single person as elect along with these various Churches of Asia, whereas the Church in Babylon might fitly have such a distinction. It is unnecessary, too, to explain Babylon (as some have done) as intended for Rome. There was no conceivable reason in St. Peter's day why, when he was writing to lands under Roman dominion, if he meant to speak of the city in Italy, he should not call it by its real name. The Mark here named was most probably the John whose surname was Mark (Acts xii. 12), whose mother was a friend of St. Peter's from the earliest days of his apostolic labours. He, too, had been a companion of St. Paul for a time, and made another link between the two great Apostles. St. Peter calls him "son" because it is likely that both the mother and her son were won to the new teaching by him, and he employs the term of affection just as St. Paul does of Timothy, his convert (1 Tim. i. 2, 18; 2 Tim. i. 2). The salutation by a kiss is frequently mentioned. It is called "a holy kiss" (Rom. xvi. 16; 1 Cor. xvi. 20; 2 Cor. xiii. 12; 1 Thess. v. 26) in St. Paul's language. We find from Justin Martyr[12] that it had come to be used in his day as part of the ceremonial preceding the Holy Communion. It was to be a token of perfect love, according to the name which St. Peter here gives it. An evil construction was soon put upon it by the enemies of the faith; and after a long history it fell into disuse, even in the East, where such manner of salutation is more common than in the West. In his final words the Apostle has embodied the benediction of which the kiss was meant to be the symbol.

Peace be unto you all that are in Christ. This is the bond which unites believers into one fellowship. To be in Christ is to be of the brotherhood which has been so significantly marked just before for its unity. And in these last clauses we have examples of the force of the tie. Individuals are brought by it into close communion, as Peter himself with Silas and with Mark, whom he speaks of in terms of family love. To the Churches Silas is commended as a brother in the faith, which faith establishes a bond of strength between the distant Churches which have been called into it together. Well might the heathen, wonderstruck, exclaim, "See how these Christians love one another!" And the Apostle's own words mark the all-embracing character of the love: *all that are in Christ.* They are all brethren, children of the common Father, inheritors of the same promises, pilgrims on the same journey, sustained by the same hope, servants of the same Lord, and strengthened, guided, and enlightened by the one Spirit, who is promised to abide with Christ's Church for ever.

THE SECOND EPISTLE OF ST. PETER

XIX
THE SAVING KNOWLEDGE OF GOD

"Simon Peter, a servant and apostle of Jesus Christ, to them that have obtained a like precious faith with us in the righteousness of our God and Saviour Jesus Christ: Grace to you and peace be multiplied in the knowledge of God and of Jesus our Lord; seeing that His Divine power hath granted unto us all things that pertain unto life and godliness, through the knowledge of Him that called us by His own glory and virtue; whereby He hath granted unto us His precious and exceeding great promises; that through these ye may become partakers of the Divine nature, having escaped from the corruption that is in the world by lust." — 2 Peter i. 1-4.

In the salutation of this second letter the Apostle describes himself in fuller form than in the first: *Simon Peter, a servant and apostle of Jesus Christ.* Some have seen in this description a testamentary character, as though the Epistle contained his parting counsels. The words form an epitome of his whole life. As Simon, son of Jonas, he lived his life in Judaism until Christ's call summoned him to be a fisher of men. "Peter" is the Christ-given name, which marked an advance in spiritual illumination, an advance that fitted him to be one of the chief heralds of God manifest in the flesh. As a servant (or rather, bondservant) of Jesus Christ, he stands on the same level with those to whom he writes, though the service to which he has been called may be in character different from theirs. Jesus had said to the twelve, and through them to the whole body of believers, "One is your Master, even the Christ. But he that is greatest among you shall be your servant" (Matt. xxiii. 10). And here comes forward that other aspect of Christian service. The servants of Christ are, for His sake, servants to all the brotherhood (2 Cor. iv. 5). As an apostle he speaks with authority, an authority greater than can be possessed by any future age. The solemn character of the office is stamped by Christ's words, "As My Father sent Me, even so send I you"; and the Churches are reminded, as they think of the apostolic office, that the Lord who commissioned the twelve to be His servants said, "He that heareth you heareth Me, and He that despiseth you despiseth Me."

St. Peter does not, as in his former letter, name the Churches to which he is writing; but afterwards (iii. 1) he states that this is his second letter to them. We may therefore conclude that the same persons are addressed as before. Here he speaks of them as *them that have obtained a like precious faith with us in the righteousness of our God and Saviour Jesus Christ*. Some have thought that here the Apostle's words are specially addressed to those among the converts who had been won from heathendom, and now were made partakers of the same faith with himself and others who, like him, had been born Jews, and so heirs in part to God's precious promises. But, as he has just made mention of his apostolic office, it seems easier to refer "us" to the Apostles. If this be the sense, then—though in the allusion to his office and authority they must have recognised the points wherein his communing with Christ had made him to differ from them—these words set forward that aspect of the Christian life wherein all the faithful are equal. The graces, gifts, and opportunities which God bestows are according to men's power to improve them; but faith, in its saving efficacy and preciousness, is the same for every believer. And when he speaks of this faith as being in the righteousness of our God and Saviour Jesus Christ, we see that he is thinking of righteousness in that sense in which he uses the word afterwards in this Epistle (iii. 13): as that perfect righteousness which belongs to the new heavens and the new earth, and hence to God Himself.

To this righteousness each "stranger and sojourner" in the world is striving to attain by faith, and by each exercise thereof he is raised nearer to his lofty aim. His faith, like the patriarch's of old, is counted unto him for righteousness. The fruit of each man's faith will be ἰσότιμος—"alike precious"—when the journey is ended. For it will be salvation in the presence of the perfect righteousness. As in the Saviour's parable the welcome was the same to him who had rightly used his two talents as to him who had done the like with five, so each faithful servant of Christ, working righteousness according to his power here, shall be called up into the joy of his Lord. For the joys of heaven all will not have the same capacity; but for each, according to his power to receive it, there will be fulness of joy. Nor should the word "obtained" pass unnoticed. It is the word used of Judas (Acts i. 17), who *obtained* part of the apostolic ministry on the call of Jesus. So here, too, the call into the faith is of God; and it is when men obey it that they progress in Divine graces and go forward unto righteousness.

Grace to you and peace be multiplied in the knowledge of God and of Jesus our Lord. The first words are the same with the Apostle's prayer in the opening of the First Epistle. And to no stage of the Christian life can such a wish be inappropriate. To grow in grace, and so in peace, is the Christian's daily bread; and the thought of this seems to be uppermost in St. Peter's mind in this letter, that thus the falling away, to which he sees the converts are likely to be exposed, may be counteracted. The danger was arising from the boastful parade of a knowledge (γνῶσις) falsely so called (1 Tim. vi. 20). Before this letter was written teachers had risen within the Church who professed to have a deeper and more mysterious interpretation of the doctrines of the Gospel. This esoteric enlightenment they specially named "knowledge," and led men astray by profitless inquiries concerning the absolute nature of God and the manner of His communication with the world. To this teaching St. Paul is referring when he speaks of "foolish questions" and "endless genealogies," and it is this which St. Peter rebukes so vehemently in the next chapter of this letter. As an antidote for the poison, he urges the converts to seek after a true and full knowledge (ἐπίγνωσις) of the Father and the Son. No single word can adequately represent this term, which became the watchword of all the Christian teachers. It is that knowledge of the truth which St. Paul so often commends to Timothy (1 Tim. ii. 4; 2 Tim. iii. 7) and speaks of as that acknowledging of the truth, allowing it to be effective on the life, which follows repentance (2 Tim. ii. 25); it is specially the knowledge of God and of things Divine; it is that knowledge which must temper religious zeal (Rom. x. 2) that it may be effective; it is the knowledge against which if a man sin (Heb. x. 26) he is verily reprobate. And this true knowledge can only come of faithful service. He shall know the Lord who loves to do His will. Do the works, and ye shall know of the doctrine.

Seeing that His Divine power hath granted unto us all things that pertain unto life and godliness. The work, though great, becomes not impossible; the dangers and difficulties, though abundant, are not insurmountable. For it is not on us that the victory depends. God hath begotten us again unto a lively hope through Christ's resurrection; and Christ has promised to be with His servants all the days, even unto the end of the world. There is a free gift of Divine power for all our needs, everything to foster the spiritual life and to guide into the way of holiness. Wisdom will be given that we may understand God's will and choose aright, strength to persevere in the midst of trial, boldness to make confession of the Lord before men, and watchfulness lest we, as did the teachers of error, wax overconfident. All things are granted; all things may be ours.

Through the knowledge of Him that called us by His own glory and virtue. Here the same full knowledge (ἐπίγνωσις) of which the Apostle has just been speaking is to become the channel of all our blessings: to know God, who has made Himself to be known through Christ Jesus. God's glory and virtue—that is, His Divine power—have been manifested in Him. The disciples beheld them in Christ's miracles. "This beginning of His signs did Jesus, ... and manifested His glory; and His disciples believed on Him" (John ii. 11), and of His whole life St. John says, "We beheld His glory, glory as of the only-begotten from the Father. He dwelt among us full of grace and truth" (John i. 14). This is what St. Peter means by "virtue." And still in the hearts of men through the Spirit the same manifestation is given. He illumines them, to give the light of the knowledge of the glory of God in the face of Jesus Christ.

Whereby He hath granted unto us His precious and exceeding great promises. In Christ God has offered men all the blessings of the new covenant: repentance; faith; justification; eternal life. He, with the Son and the Spirit, comes unto the faithful and makes His abode with them. Thus they are made members of Christ's mystical body. He dwells in their hearts by faith; He gives them power to become sons of God: they are adopted of God, who sent His only-begotten Son into the world that they might live through Him. These are the precious promises granted, but not forced upon men, set forth in all their greatness in the life and love of Jesus; and men are invited to choose them. And the choice is made by patiently doing the will of God so far as it is revealed to each man; after that we shall receive the promises (Heb. x. 36).

That through these ye may become partakers of the Divine nature. This is the Divine scheme for man's restoration; this is the change of which St. Paul speaks to the Corinthians (2 Cor. ii. 18), and which he illustrates by the glorified face of Moses. The prophet was called up into Mount Horeb, and drew near to the presence of Jehovah; the Lord spake with him face to face out of the midst of the fire, and his countenance was illumined by the eternal glory. But the radiance was bestowed on Moses alone; the people might not draw near: and the glory shed on him was transient, so that he veiled his face lest the people should mark its passing away. But since the manifestation of God in Christ all men may draw near, and be made partakers of unfading glory. It is not with Zion as with Sinai. The way is open to all, nor will the glory pass away from those who have been blessed with it. For now we all, with unveiled face, reflect as a mirror the glory of the Lord, and, with progress in holiness, are transformed into the same image, as from the Lord the Spirit. Thus men *become*—for it is a gradual process—partakers of the Divine nature, and being drawn more near to God while they live here, are fitted through His mercy, when the last call comes, to go up higher and sit down at the marriage-supper of the Lamb, their life having been a constant putting on of the wedding garment.

Having escaped from the corruption that is in the world by lust. This is the victory that overcometh the world, but it is a conquest which men cannot win unaided, nay, where the truest bravery, the surest hope, is in speedy flight. Like Lot from Sodom must the Christian hasten away from the lusts of the world, casting no look behind him, nor tarrying to dally with them for a moment. For the flesh is weak, and the prince of this world is mighty in his evil domain, and, that he may lead men astray, will ofttimes transform himself into an angel of light; and within the soul of man he has his confederate powers, the cravings of this human nature, which thinks the baits of the enemy are pleasant to the eyes, and it may be they look fit to make one wise. And so in the eyes of the tempted ones, as in the eyes of the senseless bird of the Proverbs, the net seems spread in vain; in their own fancy they seem able to go on without being entangled, and Satan encourages the delusion. After that the stages are easy, but they are all downhill. Men first walk after their own lusts; then they are led by them, then obey them, and at last become their slaves. This is the corruption, the ruin, from which the Christian is aided to flee through seeking the glory of God as it is set before him in the Saviour's works and words. Drawn by these, he turns away his gaze from the world and its lusts; his eyes no longer behold vanity to love it. He has begun to learn of Jesus, and every new lesson makes him stronger in the faith; and by degrees he is enabled to bring forth into light, and bear witness to, the knowledge which he has gained of the glory of God as it shines in the face of Jesus Christ. So not he alone, but those who behold his escape and mark his growth in grace, may give God the praise, saying, "This hath God wrought," for they shall perceive that it is His work.

XX
WHO SHALL ASCEND INTO THE HILL OF THE LORD?

"Yea, and for this very cause adding on your part all diligence, in your faith supply virtue; and in *your* virtue knowledge; and in *your* knowledge temperance; and in *your* temperance patience; and in *your* patience godliness; and in *your* godliness love of the brethren; and in *your* love of the brethren love. For if these things are yours and abound, they make you to be not idle nor unfruitful unto the knowledge of our Lord Jesus Christ. For he that lacketh these things is blind, seeing only what is near, having forgotten the cleansing from his old sins. Wherefore, brethren, give the more diligence to make your calling and election sure: for if ye do these things, ye shall never stumble: for thus shall be richly supplied unto you the entrance into the eternal kingdom of our Lord and Saviour Jesus Christ."—2 Peter i. 5-11.

The Apostle has just set forth in all their fulness the riches of Divine grace: the precious faith, followed by the bestowal of all helps toward life and godliness, and with the large promises of God to rely on for the future, promises whereby those who seek to renounce the things which are not of the Father, but of the world, may become partakers of the Divine nature. These blessings are assured, are in store, but only for those who manifest a desire to receive them. How this desire shall be shown, how it shall constantly grow stronger and be ever fulfilling, until it attain perfect fruition in Christ's eternal kingdom, is the next instruction. *Yea, and for this very cause adding on your part all diligence, in your faith supply virtue.* The plenteousness of the Divine bounty is proclaimed that it may evoke an earnest response from all who receive it. What shall I render unto the Lord for all the benefits which He hath done, and is doing, unto me? is to be the heart's cry of the feeblest of God's saints. For the boundless ocean of grace asks that there should be mingled with it some drops of human duty. God will heal the bite of the serpents in the wilderness, but to gain the blessing the wounded ones, even in their suffering, must turn their eyes to the appointed symbol of healing. Christ's power will cure ten lepers, but He first sends them away to do their little in the path of obedience: "Go, show yourselves to the priest." Thus the Apostle's exhortation here, *Adding on your part all diligence.* The diligence of which he speaks is that sort of endeavour which springs from a sense of duty: an earnest zeal and will to accomplish whatever it finds to do; that does not linger till some great work offers, but hastens to labour in the immediate present. This is the spirit in which Christian advance will be made. And the lines on which such progress will go he now describes as though each new step were evolved from, and were a natural development of, that which preceded it. The faith which the Christian holds fast is the gift of God, and it contains the germs of every grace that can follow. These the believer is to foster with diligence.

St. Peter begins his scale of graces thus: *In your faith supply virtue.* Here virtue means the best development of such power as a man possesses. It may be little or great, but in its kind it is to be made excellent. And here it is that the Christian workers in every sphere must surpass others. They work from a higher motive. What they do is a constant attestation of their faith, is done as in God's sight, and in the confidence that in every act it is possible to give Him glory. There can be no carelessness in such lives, for they are filled with a sense of responsibility, which is the first-fruit of a living faith. And in St. Peter's figurative word the believer is said to supply each grace in turn because he contributes by his careful walk to wake it into life, to make it active, and let it shine as a light before men. *And in your virtue knowledge,* he continues. For, with duty rightly done, there comes illumination over the path of life: men understand more of God's dealings, and hence bring their lives into closer harmony with His will. And we have Christ's own assurance, "If any man willeth to do His will, he shall know of the teaching" (John vii. 17). And the same is true not only of the Lord's own lessons, but of all the promptings of the Spirit in men's hearts. If they hearken to the voice which whispers, "This is the way," it will become at every stage plainer, and there will be shown to them not only the how, but the wherefore.

And in your knowledge temperance. There is a knowledge which puffeth up, giving not humility, which is the fruit of true knowledge, but self-conceit. Of the evil effects thereof the Apostle knew much. Out of it grew extravagance in thought, and word, and action; and its mischief was threatening the infant Churches. Against it the temperance which he commends is to be the safeguard, and it is a virtue which can be manifested in all things. He who possesses it has conquered himself, and has won his way thus to stability of mind and consistency of conduct. "His heart is fixed, trusting in the Lord," and so he can go forward to the Apostle's next stage of the heavenward journey: *And in your temperance patience.* This is the true sequence of spiritual self-control. Life is sure to supply for the godly man trials in abundance. But he is daily striving to die unto the world. The effort fixes his mind firmly on the Divine purposes, and lifts him above the circumstances of time. He is a pilgrim and sojourner amidst them, but is in no bondage to them, nor will he be moved, even by great afflictions, to waver in his trust. He can look on, as seeing Him that is invisible, and can persevere without being unduly cast down.

And in your patience godliness. The mystery of godliness—that is, Godlikeness—was made known by the Incarnation. The Son of God became man, that men might through Him be made sons of God. And godliness in the present world is Christ made manifest in the lives of His servants. Toward this imitation of Christ the believer will aspire through his patience. He takes up the cross and bears it after his Master, and thus begins his discipleship, of which the communion with Christ waxes more intimate day by day. Such was the godliness of St. Paul. It was because he had followed the Lord in all that He would have him to do that the Apostle was bold to exhort the Corinthians, "Be ye imitators of me;" but he adds at once, "as I am of Christ" (1 Cor. xi. 1). And when he sends Timothy to recall his teaching to their minds he says, "He shall put you in remembrance of my ways which are in Christ." By such a walk with Christ His servants are helped forward towards the fulfilment of the two tables of the moral law, to which St. Peter alludes in his next words: *And in your godliness love of the brethren; and in your love of the brethren love.* The last-named love (ἀγάπη) is that highest love, the love of God to men, which is set up as the grand ideal towards which His servants are constantly to press forward; but from this the love of the brethren cannot be severed, nay it must be made the stepping-stone unto it. For, as another Apostle says, "he that loveth not his brother, whom he hath seen, cannot love God, whom he hath not seen" (1 John iv. 20). But love of the brethren is not to be narrowed in the verse before us or elsewhere to love of those who are already known to the Churches as brethren in the Lord. The Gospel of Christ knows no such limits. The commission of the Master was, "Go ye forth into all the world." All mankind are to be won for Him; all are embraced in the name of brethren. For if they be not so now, it is our bounden duty to endeavour that they shall be so. And in thus interpreting we have the mind of Christ with us, who came to seek and to save them that were lost, to die for the sins of the whole world, and who found His brethren among every class who would hear His words and obey them. We have with us, too, the acts of God Himself, who would have all men come to the knowledge of the truth, and who, with impartial love, maketh His sun to rise on the evil and on the good, and sendeth His rain upon the just and the unjust, that thus even the evil and unjust may be won to own His

Fatherhood. Such Divine love is the end of the commandment (1 Tim. i. 5), and terminates the list of those graces the steps whereto St. Paul has more briefly indicated when he says the love which is most like God's springs from a pure heart, a good conscience, and faith unfeigned. In this way shall men be borne upward into the hill of the Lord.

The knowledge of Christ is a lesson in which we cannot be perfected till we behold Him as He is, but yet through it from the first we receive the earnest and pledge of all that is meant by life and godliness, and the culture of the Divine gifts will yield a rich increase of the same knowledge. *For if these things are yours and abound, they make you to be not idle nor unfruitful unto the knowledge of our Lord Jesus Christ.* Men in this life can draw nearer unto this full knowledge, and the bliss of each new gain prompts to more zealous exertion. There can be no relaxation of effort, no remissness, in such a quest. For hope is fostered by the constant experience of a deepening knowledge, and receives continual pledges that the glory to be revealed is far above what is already known. The enlightened vision grows wider and ampler; and the path, which began in faith, shineth more and more unto the perfect day. The world offers other lights to its votaries, but they lead only into darkness. *For he that lacketh these things is blind, seeing only what is near, having forgotten the cleansing from his old sins.* He who has taken no heed to foster within him the light which is kindled by faith, and which can only be kept alive by the grace of the Divine Spirit, is blind, yea blind indeed, for he is self-blinded. He has quenched the inward light which was of God's free gift, and made the light within him to be darkness, a darkness, like Egypt's, which may be felt. Such a man has no insight into the glories of the celestial vision, no joy of the widening prospect which captivates the gaze of the spiritual man. He can see only things close at hand, and is as one bowed downward to the earth, groping a dreary way, with neither hope nor exaltation at the end. For he has forgotten—nay, St. Peter's words are stronger and very striking— λήθην λαβών—he has taken hold upon forgetfulness, made a deliberate choice of that course which obliterates all remembrance of God's initial gift of grace to cleanse him from his old sins. Unmindful of this purification, he has admitted into the dwelling where the Spirit of God would have made a home other spirits more wicked than those first cast out. They have entered in, and dwell there. There is a marked contrast between this expression and the word used for God's gift of faith (ver. 1). That a man receives (λαχών) as the bounty of his Lord's love; and if treasured and used, it proves itself the light of life for this world and the next. The wrong path he chooses for himself (λαβών), and its close is the blackness of the dark.

Wherefore, brethren, give the more diligence to make your calling and election sure. "Wherefore, brethren"—because such terrible blindness as this has fallen upon some, who left their first grace unimproved and allowed even the memory of it to fade away—do you give the more diligence in your religious life. The true way to banish evil is to multiply good, leaving neither room nor time for bad things to spread themselves. When the peril of such things is round about you, it is no time for relaxed effort. Your enemy never relaxes his. He is always active, seeking whom he may devour, and employs not the day only, but the night, when men sleep, to sow his tares. Let him find you ever watchful, ever diligent to hold fast and make abundant the gifts which God has already bestowed upon you. In the foreknowledge of the Father, you are elect from the foundation of the world; and your call is attested by the injunction laid upon you, "Ye shall be holy, for I am holy." Your inheritance is in store where nothing can assail it. God only asks that you should manifest a wish, a longing, for His blessings; and He will pour them richly upon you. He has made you of a loftier mould than the inanimate and irrational creation. The flower turns to the sun by a law which it cannot resist. From the Sun of righteousness men can turn away. But the Father's will is that your eyes should be set on the hope which He offers. Then of a certainty it will be realised. Lift up your eyes to the eternal hills, for from thence your help will come. The promise is sure. Strive to keep your hope equally steadfast. For now you belong to the household of Christ; now you are through Him children of the heavenly Father: to this sonship you are elect and have been called, and to it you shall attain if you hold fast your boldness and the glorying of your hope unto the end.

For if ye do these things, ye shall never stumble. The way will be hard, and may be long, the obstacles in your path many and rugged, heaped up by the prince of this world to bar you from advancing and make you faint-hearted; but down into the midst of the danger there shall shine from the Father of lights a ray which shall illumine the darkness and make clear for you the steps in which you ought to tread, and the rod and staff of God's might will support and comfort you.

For thus shall be richly supplied unto you the entrance into the eternal kingdom of our Lord and Saviour Jesus Christ. In his first words in this passage the Apostle exhorted the believers to supply something, as it were, of their own towards their spiritual advancement; but when the demand was fully understood, behold God had made ready the means for doing everything which was asked for! Within the precious faith which He bestowed was enfolded the potentiality of every other grace. There they lay, as seeds in a seed-plot. All that men were bidden to do was to give them culture. Then God's Spirit would operate as the generous sunshine, and cause each hidden power to unfold itself in its time and bloom into beauty and strength. In this verse the Divine assistance is more clearly promised. What men bestow shall be returned unto them manifold. Do your diligence, says the Apostle, and there shall be supplied unto you from the rich stores of God all that can help you forward in your heavenward journey. The kingdom of God shall begin for you while you are passing through this present life. For it can be set up within you. It has been prepared from all eternity in heaven, and will be enjoyed in full fruition when this life is ended. But it is a state, and not a place. The entrance thereto is opened here. The believer is beckoned into it; and with enraptured soul he enjoys through faith a foretaste of the things which eye hath not seen, nor ear heard, nor heart of man conceived, the things which God has prepared for them that love Him. Over those joys Christ is King, but He is also the door; and those who enter through Him shall go in and out, and shall surely find pasture, even life for evermore.

XXI
THE VOICE HEARD IN THE HOLY MOUNT

"Wherefore I shall be ready always to put you in remembrance of these things, though ye know them, and are established in the truth which is with *you*. And I think it right, as long as I am in this tabernacle, to stir you up by putting you in remembrance; knowing that the putting off of my tabernacle cometh swiftly, even as our Lord Jesus Christ signified unto me. Yea, I will give diligence that at every time ye may be able after my decease to call these things to remembrance. For we did not follow cunningly devised fables, when we made known unto you the power and coming of our Lord Jesus Christ, but we were eye-witnesses of His majesty. For He received from God the Father honour and glory, when there came such a voice to Him from the excellent glory, This is My beloved Son, in whom I am well pleased: and this voice we *ourselves* heard come out of heaven, when we were with Him in the holy mount." — 2 Peter i. 12-18.

Up to this point the Apostle has spoken of God's abundant grace and the consequent duties of believers. And he has set forth these duties in the most encouraging language. He has pictured first the gift of Divine power, and the precious promises of God, whereby men may be helped to walk onward and upward; and when the labour is ended he has pointed to the door of Christ's eternal kingdom, open to admit the saint to His everlasting rest. Now he turns to describe the duty which he feels to be laid upon himself, and faithful is he in the discharge thereof. "Strengthen thy brethren," is constantly ringing in his ears. *Wherefore*, he says, *I shall be ready always to put you in remembrance of these things*. He dreads that taking hold of forgetfulness—that λήθην λαβών—of which he has spoken before, and against which constant diligence is needed. So far as in him lies, the perilous condition shall come upon none of them. The verb in the best texts expresses far more than that which is rendered in the Authorised Version, "I will not be negligent." It implies a sense of duty and the intention of fulfilling it; it bears within it, too, the thought (which is strengthened by the word *always*) that there may be need for such reminding, if not from internal weakness, yet by reason of external dangers. And to bring to the mind of the Churches the gracious bounty of God in Christ, and to set down the steps whereby the graces bestowed should be fostered and increased, is a subject worthy of an Apostle, a theme which no amount of exhortation can exhaust, and one which ought to prompt the hearers to gratitude and obedience.

Though ye know them, and are established in the truth which is with you. Knowledge of things that pertain unto godliness is barren unless it be wrought out in the life. Yet knowledge and practice do not always go hand in hand. This was one of the lessons taught by Jesus as He washed the disciples' feet: "If ye know these things, blessed are ye if ye do them" (John xiii. 17). St. Peter longs that the converts should make this blessedness their own. His life's work is to watch for them, that they be not remiss in doing. To none can such a duty more peculiarly belong than to him who holds Christ's special commission to feed the flock. By "the truth which is with you" the Apostle appears to be alluding to the varying degrees of advancement which there must be among the members of the Churches. All have travelled some way along the road which he has shown them; all have some of the truth within their grasp. They have set their feet on the path, though they be planted with different degrees of firmness. What is needed for each and all is to press forward, not to rest in the present, but to hasten to what lies beyond. For the truth of God is inexhaustible.

Perhaps, too, he thought, as he spake of the truth present with them, that he was of necessity absent and would soon be removed altogether, and the only way by which he could serve them was by his epistle. He could never forget that among those to whom he was writing were the Galatians, over whose falling back from the truth St. Paul had so greatly lamented: who had run well, but had fainted ere the course was over; who had received some truth to be present with them, even the faith of the crucified Jesus, but had been beguiled into letting it slip. Thought of these things shapes his words as he writes, "I shall be ready *always* to put you in remembrance." He rejoices that they are "established," but yet sends them an admonition. Let him that thinketh he standeth take heed lest he fall.

And I think it right. The word marks the solemn estimate which the Apostle takes of his duty. It is a just and righteous work. Danger is abroad, and he has been made one of Christ's shepherds. Many motives prompt him to write his words of counsel and warning. First, his love for them as his brethren, some of them, perhaps, his children in Christ. Like St. Paul, he has them in his heart. Then, he will fulfil to the utmost the charge which the Lord gave him. He is conscious, too, that opportunities for the fulfilment of his trust will soon come to an end. *As long as I am in this tabernacle,* he says. It is but a frail home, the body; and with St. Peter age was drawing on. He saw that the time of his departure could not be far off, and this left no excuse for remitting his admonitions. He must be urgent so long as he can. *To stir you up by putting you in remembrance.* The work of the Apostle will be thoroughly done (διεγείρειν), and be of that nature for which the Holy Ghost was promised to himself and his fellows. "He shall bring to your remembrance all that I said unto you" (John xiv. 26). Thus would St. Peter, like St. Paul, impart unto the converts some spiritual gift, that he, with them, may be comforted, strengthened, each by the other's faith. So he proceeds to dwell on that Divine manifestation by which his own belief had been confirmed. And there would be memories of St. Paul's lessons also to call to their minds, and many of these would be awakened by an appeal like this. The falling away of the Galatians had been from a different cause, but the memory of the past would warn, and might strengthen, them all in the future against their new dangers.

Knowing that the putting off of my tabernacle cometh swiftly, even as our Lord Jesus Christ signified unto me. Such a motive makes the appeal most touching. He will soon be removed. To this he looks forward without alarm. His concern is for them, not for himself. He regards his death as the stripping off of a dress: when its use is past it is parted with without regret. To him, as to his brother Apostle, to die would be gain. But he must have had constantly in mind the Master's prophecy, "When thou art old, thou shalt stretch forth thine hands, and another shall gird thee and carry thee whither thou wouldest not" (John xxi. 18). And in the word "swiftly" he no doubt alludes, not only to the old age in which the end would naturally come, but also to some sharp stroke by which his departure would be brought to pass. The stretching out of his hands would be a preliminary to the prison and the cross. In the Gospel it is said that Christ's words give the sign (σημαίνων), the indication, by what death he should die. The Apostle employs a stronger word (ἐδήλωσε) here: "made it evident." The English version renders both verbs by "signify," but St. Peter's own expression marks how growing age had made clearer to him the manner in which his death should be accomplished. And the mention of Jesus brings vividly before him the thought of the scene he is about to describe, so vividly that some of the language of the Transfiguration scene is reproduced by him.

Yea, I will give diligence that at every time ye may be able after my decease to call these things to remembrance. Jesus is related (Luke ix. 31) to have conversed with Moses and Elias of His decease (ἔξοδος) which He should accomplish at Jerusalem. The word is rare in this sense, being commonly used, as in Heb. xi. 22, of the *departing* of the children of Israel from Egypt. But it is deeply printed in St. Peter's mind; and he, who looks forward to drinking of his Master's cup and dying somewhere as He died, employs the same word concerning his own end. And the word is another indication of the calm with which he can look forward to his death. As with Christ, there is no reluctance, no shrinking. The change will be but a departure, a passing from one stage to another, the putting off the worn garment of mortality to be clothed upon by the robe which is from heaven.

His letters are the only means whereby he can speak after he has been taken from them. Hence his earnestness in writing. "I will give diligence." I have urged diligence on you; I will apply the lesson to myself, and make it possible that afterwards on every occasion you may have it before you. When dead, he will yet speak to them; so that in each new trial, in each time of need, they may strengthen their faith or be warned of their danger. "At every time," he says; and thus his strengthening words of admonition are a legacy through the ages to the Church for evermore.

For we did not follow cunningly devised fables. Here the Apostle speaks in the plural number, and it may well be that he means to include St. Paul with himself and James and John. For the evidence which converted that Apostle, though not the same as that vouchsafed to St. Peter, was of the same kind. The Lord had appeared unto him in the way, had made His glory seen and felt, and fixed for ever in the Apostle's heart the reality of His power and presence. His cry, "Lord, what wilt Thou have me to do?" came from a heart conquered and convinced. He too followed no cunningly devised fable.

By the word (σεσοφισμένοι) which is rendered "cunningly devised" we are reminded of the (σοφία) wisdom which St. Paul so earnestly disclaims in his first letter to the Corinthians. "I came not with excellency of speech or of *wisdom*," he says; "my preaching was not in persuasive words of *wisdom*, that your faith should not stand in the *wisdom* of men, but in the power of God." The *wisdmom* which he speaks is not of this world, but God's *wisdom* in a mystery (1 Cor. ii. 1-7). St. Paul also warns against giving "heed to fables, which minister questionings rather than a dispensation of God which is in faith" (1 Tim. i. 4; cf. also iv. 7 and 2 Tim. iv. 4). In another place (Titus i. 14) he calls them "Jewish fables," a name which is of the same import as the "Jewish vanities" of Ignatius,[13] a name by which he intimates that they darken and confuse the mind. The legends of the Talmud, the subtleties of the rabbinical teaching, and the allegorising interpretations of Philo are the delusions to which both the Apostles refer. The evidence on which they ask credence for their teaching is of another kind. "That which was from the beginning," is the testimony of another Apostle, "that which we heard, that which we have seen with our eyes, that which we beheld, and our hands handled, concerning the word of life, ... that declare we unto you also, that ye also may have fellowship with us" (1 John i. 1-3). St. Peter had seen, and so had St. Paul; and they constantly appealed to, and rested their teaching on, facts and the historic reality of Christ's life and work.

When we made known unto you the power and coming of our Lord Jesus Christ. This is the contrast to that mythic and allegorical teaching to which he has just alluded. From it men could derive neither help in the present, nor hope for the future. It generated superstition, and its followers believed a lie. Often it denied the continuity of revelation, and cast aside all the records thereof. Like theosophic dreams in every age, it was always unprofitable, nearly always pernicious. On the other hand, the teaching of Christ's Apostles proclaimed a power which could save men from their sins, and imparted a hope that stretched out beyond the present, looking for the time when the Lord would reappear. All power is given unto Christ. He is made Redeemer and Lord, and is to be at last the Judge of men. The assurance of His coming had been proclaimed by St. Peter in his former letter as a consolation under affliction. Faith, tried by suffering, will be found unto praise, and glory, and honour at the revelation of Jesus Christ (1 Peter i. 7). This is the climax of the glad tidings of the Gospel. But Christ comes to His people through all the days; and they are conscious of His coming, and inspired thereby and enabled for their work.

But we were eye-witnesses of His majesty. He has already (1 Peter iii. 22) spoken of the fact of Christ's ascension; he is now about to describe what was seen on the holy mount. These things are facts and verities, and not fables. But yet there was more revealed in them than either eye could grasp, or tongue could tell. They were God's truth in a mystery, which supplied new thought for a whole life-time. So for "eye-witnesses" the Apostle uses a word akin to that which twice over he employs in the former Epistle (ii. 12; iii. 2) to describe the effect which Christian lives, when fully scanned, shall have upon the unbeliever. They shall have power to stop the mouths of opponents and to win them to the faith which before they maligned. Such deep insight into the power, and work, and glory of Jesus was imparted to the Apostles at the Transfiguration. They were initiated into the wisdom of God, and henceforth became prophets of the Incarnation; they were convinced that the Jesus with whom they companied was very God manifest in the flesh. The voice from heaven proclaimed it; it was attested by the glorified presence of Moses and Elijah, and by the majesty which for a moment broke through the veil of Christ's flesh. Later on they saw Him risen from the dead, beheld His ascension into glory, and heard from the angels the promise of His return. Not without much meaning does the Apostle use a special pronoun (ἐκείνου) as he dwells on this scene of His majesty. For he would impress on his converts the identity of that Jesus whom he had known in the flesh with the very Son of God sent down from heaven.

For He received from God the Father honour and glory. For the bright cloud which overshadowed them on the mountain-top was the visible token of the presence of God, as of old the cloud of glory had been, where God dwelt above the cherubim; while the honour and glory of Jesus were manifested when He was proclaimed to be the very Son of God. *When there came such a voice to Him from the excellent glory, This is My beloved Son, in whom I am well pleased.* To express the magnificence of the glory which he beheld, the Apostle uses a word not found elsewhere in the New Testament. The Septuagint has it to describe the splendour of Jeshurun's God, who rideth in His *excellency* on the skies (Deut. xxxiii. 26). And it is this outward brightness of the shroud of the Godhead which tells all that human powers can receive of the majesty which it hides, just as His palace, the heavens, declares constantly the glory of God.

The words spoken by the heavenly voice vary here from the records of each of the three Gospels. In one case the variation is slight, but there is no precise agreement. Had the Epistle been the work of some forger of a later age than St. Peter's, we may rest assured that there would have been complete accord with one Evangelist or the other. There is a like diversity in the records of the words of the inscription above Christ's cross. Substantial truth, not verbal preciseness, is what the Evangelists sought to leave to the Church; and their fidelity is proved by nothing more powerfully than by the diverse features of the Gospel narratives.

And this voice we ourselves heard come out of heaven, when we were with Him in the holy mount. We learn here why the Apostles were taken with Jesus to witness His transfiguration. Just before that event we find (Matt. xvi. 21; Mark viii. 31; Luke ix. 22) it recorded by each of the Synoptists that Jesus had begun to show unto His disciples how He must suffer and die at Jerusalem. To Peter, who, as at other times, was the mouthpiece of the rest, such a declaration was unacceptable; but at his expression of displeasure he met the rebuke, "Get thee behind Me, Satan." He, and the rest with him, felt no doubt that such a death as Jesus had spoken of would be, humanly speaking, the ruin of their hopes. What these hopes were they did not formulate, but we can learn their character from some of their questionings. Now, on the top of Tabor, these three representatives of the apostolic band behold Moses and Elias appearing in glory, and Christ glorified more than they; and the subject of which they spake was the very death of which they had so disliked to hear: the decease which He was about to accomplish ($\pi\lambda\eta\varrho o\tilde{\upsilon}v$) in Jerusalem (Luke ix. 31). The verb which the Evangelist uses tells of the fulfilment of a prescribed course, and thus St. Peter was taught, and the rest with him, to speak of that death afterwards as he does in his former letter. "Christ was verily foreordained" to this redeeming work "before the foundation of the world." They heard that He who was to die was the very Son of God. The voice came from the glory of heaven; and from henceforth their hearts were still, even Peter's voice being less heard than before. Down from the mountain they brought much illumination, much solemn pondering. We can feel why it was that "they held their peace, and told no man in those days any of the things which they had seen"; we can feel, too, that from henceforth the scene of this vision would be the holy mount. God's voice had been heard there attesting the Divinity of their Lord and Master; the place whereon they had thus stood was for evermore holy ground.

XXII
THE LAMP SHINING IN A DARK PLACE

"And we have the word of prophecy *made* more sure; whereunto ye do well that ye take heed, as unto a lamp shining in a dark place, until the day dawn, and the day-star arise in your hearts: knowing this first, that no prophecy of Scripture is of private interpretation. For no prophecy ever came by the will of man: but men spake from God, being moved by the Holy Ghost." —2 Peter i. 19-21.

The rendering of the first words in this passage must be reckoned among the distinct improvements of the Revised Version. As the translation stands in the Authorised Version, "We have also a more sure word of prophecy," it conveys a sense which many must have found perplexing. The Apostle had just dwelt on the confirmation of faith, both for himself and those to whom he preached, which was ministered by the vision of the glory of Jesus and by the proclamation of His Divinity by God's voice from heaven. Could any prophetic message vie in his estimate with the assurance of such a revelation? Now what St. Peter meant is made clear. *And we have the word of prophecy made more sure* — more sure because we have received the confirmation of all that the prophets spake dimly and in figure. The Apostle and the rest of the Jewish people had been trained in the ancient Scriptures, and gathered from them, some more and some less, light concerning God's scheme of salvation. There were, however, but few who had attained a true insight into what was revealed. They had dwelt, as a rule, too exclusively on all that spake of the glory of the promised Redeemer and of His coming to reign and to conquer. That there should be suffering in His life, they had put out of sight, though the prophets had foretold it; and so when Christ spake of His crucifixion, soon to come to pass in Jerusalem, St. Peter exclaimed — and he had the feelings of his nation with him — "That be far from Thee." The voice on the holy mount and the words of Moses and Elias had opened their eyes to the full drift of prophetic revelation; and by the illumination of that scene of glory, where yet the lot of suffering was contemplated as near at hand, there had been given to them a grasp of the whole scope of prophecy, and their partial and distorted conception of the work of Christ was banished for ever.

Whereunto ye do well that ye take heed. The idea of a volume of New Testament Scriptures had not entered St. Peter's mind. He knows that St. Paul's letters (iii. 15, 16) are read by some, who do not all profit by the privilege; and his own letters he intends to be an abiding admonition to the Churches. The need, too, of a record of Christ's life and works, a gospel, must have begun to be felt. But yet he points the converts to the ancient records of Israel as a guide to direct their lives. They had heard the Gospel story from the lips of himself and others. Thus they had the key to unlock what hitherto had seemed hard to understand, and could study their prophetic volume with a new and perfect light. This he means by "ye do well." Ye go to the true source of guidance, drink of the fountain of true wisdom, and gain strength and refreshment when it is much needed. Duly to take heed of these records is to search out their lessons and labour after that deeper sense which is enshrined beneath the word. Given as they were at various times and in various fashions, and given to point on to God's purposes in the future, these Scriptures must needs have been dark to those who first received them, nor could the men whom God chose to deliver them have been fully conscious of all they were meant to declare as the ages rolled on and brought their fulfilment nearer. Nor are they all luminous even yet, but they grow ever more so to those who take heed.

As unto a lamp shining in a dark place. Spite of all the light we can compass, the world will always be in one sense a dark place. It is a world of beauty, full of the tokens of God's handiwork, the indications of His love. But evil has also made an entrance; and the trail of the serpent is evident in the sorrow, the disease, the wickedness, that abound on every side. And problems continually present themselves which even to the saints are hard to be solved. Many a psalm records the conflict which has to be passed through ere God's ways can be reconciled to men. We must go into His house, draw near to Him, feel to the full His Fatherhood, ere our hearts can be contented. Nay, the disquiet breaks out again and again. So God, in His mercy, has provided His lamp for those who will use it; and to those who take heed it furnishes ever new light. The history, the prophecy, the devotion, the allegory, of the holy volume are all full of illustrations of the firm purpose of redemption, of the eternal, unchanging love of Jehovah, thwarted only by the perverseness of those whom He is longing to save from their sins. And to call God's revelation in His word a lamp is a striking and instructive figure. It is something which you can take with you, and carry into the dark places whither your lot may send you, and use its light just where and when you need it. But its light must be fed by the constant oil of diligent study, or its usefulness will not be found to the full.

And the truth is the same if we apply the lesson to nations and Churches as it is for individuals. The records were given to a nation chosen to keep the knowledge of God alive in the world. The word spoken did not profit, as it was meant to do, because it was not mixed with faith in them that heard it. And there is the same faith needed still. The light of a lamp in a dark place shines but a little way; but by the rays of the Divine lamp men are to walk, in faith that the steps beyond will become clear in their turn. And thus alone will the problems of life be really solved, the religious contentions, the social difficulties, the trials of family life, the individual doubts and fears: all are elements of darkness; all need to be illumined by the lamp which God has provided. Oh that men would burnish it by diligent heed, and keep its radiance at the full by constant seeking thereunto!

Until the day dawn, and the day-star arise in your hearts. The day has begun to dawn for those who will lift up their heads to its breaking. The day-star from on high hath visited the earth in the person of Christ, but the full day will not be till He returns again. Yet His coming into the world was meant to lighten every man, and to win all men to walk in His light. "I, if I be lifted up, will draw all men unto Me," is His own promise. And in that decease of which He spake with Moses and Elijah He has been lifted up. But He has left it to them that love Him to lift Him up constantly before the eyes of men, to exalt Him by their lives; and our lax performances make the progress of His *drawing all men*, to halt. We fail to make due use of the lamp which He has put ready to our hand, and which only needs to be grasped. The perfect day will not come to us in this life, but He gives to His faithful ones glimpses of the dawn. They learn the presence of the Sun of righteousness, though as yet they see Him only through the mists and darkness of life; and they are cheered with the certainty of the coming day. And the daystar of the Spirit is kindled in the hearts of those who ask Him to dwell there; and they are led forward into greater and greater truth, into richer and fuller light. And for the same end the Spirit is promised to the Church of Christ: that she may be enabled having used the lamp first given with all faithfulness, to open to men the ways of God more fully, and, amid the changes of times and varying vicissitudes and needs of men and nations, to prove that the only satisfaction to the soul is the increasing knowledge of the oneness of God's purpose and eternity of His love. To such a power she will be helped by giving heed to the lamp in every dark place and seeking in its light the elucidation of all hard questions.

Knowing this first, that no prophecy of Scripture is of private interpretation. The Greek words need to be taken account of before we can gather the true meaning of this clause. That which is translated "is" is much more frequently rendered "comes to pass," and bears the sense of "arises," "has its origin."

"Interpretation" is the translation of a word which occurs here only in the New Testament, and implies the "loosing" of what is complicated, the "clearing" of what is obscure. The lesson which the Apostle would give relates to the right appreciation of the Old Testament Scriptures, which contain the prophecy which he has called above "the lamp in a dark place." He intends to say something which may incline men to follow its guidance. The prophetic writings furnish us with illustrations how the problems which arose in the lives of the men of old time, both about events around them and also about the dispensations of Divine providence, found their solution. Thus they furnish rules and principles for time to come; and that men may be induced to confide in their guidance is the object of St. Peter's words. He bids the converts know that these unravellings and clearings of the ways of God are not men's private interpretation of what they beheld. This was not the manner in which they came to be known. They are not evolved out of human consciousness, pondering on the facts of life and the ways of God, nor are they the individual exposition of those whom God employed as His prophets. They are messages and lessons which came from one and the same impelling power, from one and the same illuminating influence, even from God Himself, and so are uniform in spirit and teaching from first to last; and He from whom and through whom they are given can say by the mouth of the last of the prophetic body, "I am Jehovah; I change not" (Mal. iii. 6).

Although the Apostle uses in this Epistle the word "Scriptures" (iii. 16) for the writings of New Testament teachers, it is not likely that he in mind included them among the prophetic Scriptures of which he here speaks. We, knowing the flood of light which the Gospels and Epistles pour upon the Old Testament, can now apply his words to them, fully perceiving that they are a true continuation of the Divine enlightenment, another spring from the same heavenly fountain.

Those who would explain "interpretation" as the judgement which men now exercise in the study and application of the words of Scripture forget the force of the verb (γίνεται) "comes to pass," and that the Apostle is exalting the source and origin of the words of prophecy, that he may the more enforce his lesson, "Ye do well to take heed to them."

For no prophecy ever came by the will of man. Prophecy makes known what never could have entered into the mind or understanding of men, nor were the prophetic words that have come down to us written because men wished to publish views and imaginations of their own. Man is not the source of prophecy. That lay above and beyond the human penmen. Nay, men could not, had they so willed, have spoken of the things there written for the enlightenment of the ages. These are deep things, belonging to the foreknowledge of God alone, by whom His Son was foreknown as the Lamb without spot before the foundation of the world. Of this the book of prophecy tells from first to last: of the seed of the woman to bruise the serpent's head; of the family from which a seed should come in whom all the earth should be blessed; of the rod to spring from the stem of Jesse; of the king who was to rule in righteousness; of the time when the kingdom of the Lord's house should be established on the top of the mountains, and all nations should flow into it; of the day when all men should know the Lord from the least to the greatest, when the earth should be full of the knowledge of the Lord as the waters cover the sea. Such tidings came not into the thoughts of men except as they were put there from the Lord; and they tell of things yet to come that are beyond the grasp of men unless they be spiritually-minded and enlightened. For not only are the prophetic Scriptures God's special gift: the insight into their full meaning comes also from Him. Beyond the physical sense it is true, "The hearing ear and the seeing eye, the Lord is the Maker of them both" (Prov. xx. 12).

But men spake from God, being moved by the Holy Ghost. The Authorised Version translates a text which had, "*Holy* men of God spake as they were moved by the *Holy* Ghost." And this repetition of an adjective is after St. Peter's manner, though the oldest manuscripts do not support it here. Compare the thrice-repeated "righteous" in the notice of Lot in the next chapter (ii. 7, 8). And the Authorised Version describes most truly the agents whom God chooses. He will have none but holy men to be the heralds of His truth. A Caiaphas may be constrained to utter His counsels, but as His prophets God takes the holy among men. These can grasp more of His teaching, and we receive more than we should through other channels. By their zeal for holiness they are brought nearer unto God, and made more receptive of the teaching of the Spirit, who Himself is holy. But "men spake from God" conveys a true idea of prophecy. Even one who was not holy could feel that the power given to him was not his own, nor could he speak after his own will. "What the Lord saith unto me, that must I speak," was the confession of Balaam, though his greed for gain prompted him to the opposite. And there are many expressions in the Old Testament which bear witness to the effective operation of God's power, as when we read of the Spirit of the Lord coming mightily upon those whom He had chosen to do His bidding. And the same lesson is to be found in St. Peter's words here. "Being moved" is literally "being carried." An impulse was given to them, and a power which was above their own. This is betokened, too, when the Old Testament prophets tell how the Spirit of the Lord carried them to this place or that, where a revelation was to be imparted which they should publish in His name. Thus were they moved by the Holy Ghost, and thus were they able to speak from God.

Such is St. Peter's lesson on the nature and office of prophecy. It is an illumination to which men could not have attained by any wisdom of their own, nay could not have framed the wish to attain unto it. For it lay hid among God's mysteries. It is imparted from the holy God to holy men, as His mediators to the less spiritual in the world; it has received abundant confirmation through the incarnation of the Son of God, but yet it has many a lesson for mankind to ponder and seek to comprehend. It is their wisdom who follow its guidance and bear it with them as a lamp amid the dispensations of Providence, which still are not all clear, and amid the darkness which will often surround them while they live here. That men may be prompted to its use, God is a God that hideth Himself, yet through it He will lead those who follow its light along the road to immortality.

XXIII
THE LORD KNOWETH HOW TO DELIVER

"But there arose false prophets also among the people, as among you also there shall be false teachers, who shall privily bring in destructive heresies, denying even the Master that bought them, bringing upon themselves swift destruction. And many shall follow their lascivious doings; by reason of whom the way of the truth shall be evil spoken of. And in covetousness shall they with feigned words make merchandise of you: whose sentence now from of old lingereth not, and their destruction slumbereth not. For if God spared not angels when they sinned, but cast them down to hell, and committed them to pits of darkness, to be reserved unto judgement; and spared not the ancient world, but preserved Noah with seven others, a preacher of righteousness, when He brought a flood upon the world of the ungodly; and turning the cities of Sodom and Gomorrah into ashes condemned them with an overthrow, having made them an example unto those that should live ungodly; and delivered righteous Lot, sore distressed by the lascivious life of the wicked (for that righteous man dwelling among them, in seeing and hearing, vexed *his* righteous soul from day to day with *their* lawless deeds): the Lord knoweth how to deliver the godly out of temptation, and to keep the unrighteous under punishment unto the day of judgement." — 2 Peter ii. 1-9.

This second chapter contains much more of a direct description of the heretical teaching and practices from which the converts were in danger, and is full of warning and comfort, both alike drawn from that Old Testament prophecy to the light of which St. Peter has just been urging them to take heed. The chapter has many features and much of its language in common with the Epistle of St. Jude. But the opening of the chapter seems a suitable place to call attention to a difference of motive which is manifested in this Epistle and in that. They resemble one another greatly in the illustrations which they have in common, but St. Peter makes a twofold use of them: while showing that the ungodly will assuredly be punished, he comforts the righteous with the lesson that, be they ever so few, even as the eight who were saved at the Deluge, or as Lot, with his diminished family, at the overthrow of Sodom, the Lord knows how to deliver His servants out of trials. Of this latter side of the prophetic picture St. Jude shows us nothing. The evil-doings of the tempters must have waxed grosser in his day, and he is only concerned to preach the certainty of their condemnation. The unbelievers in the wilderness, the angels who sinned, the Cities of the Plain, the error of Balaam, and the overthrow of Korah are all cited in proof that the wicked shall not escape; but he has no word about the deliverance of those whose souls are tortured by the wicked doings of the sinners among whom it is their lot to live.

But there arose false prophets also among the people, as among you also there shall be false teachers, who shall privily bring in destructive heresies, denying even the Master that bought them, bringing upon themselves swift destruction. It is as though the Apostle would say, Be not unduly dismayed. The lamp of Old Testament prophecy shows that yours is a lot which has befallen others. As Israel of old was God's people, so the Church of Christ is now. And among them again and again false prophets arose, not only those of Baal and Asherah, not only those who served the calves at Dan and Bethel, but those who called themselves by Jehovah's name, and of whom He says to Jeremiah, "The prophets prophesy lies in My name; I sent them not, neither have I commanded them, neither spake I unto them: they prophesy unto you a false vision and divination, and a thing of nought, and the deceit of their heart" (Jer. xiv. 14). The picture is exactly repeated for these Asian Churches. False teaching had attached itself to the true, used its language, and professed to be at one with it, except in so far as it was superior. For the history of corruptions in the faith repeats itself, and—

"Wherever God erects a house of prayer,

The devil always builds a chapel there."

It is the most perilous aspect of error when it parades itself as the truest truth. Hence the name by which St. Peter calls this dangerous teaching: "destructive heresies." They beguile unstable souls to their ruin. Their exponents choose the name of Christ to call themselves by, but cast aside the doctrine of the Cross both in its discipline for their lives, and as the altar of human redemption. And the men to whom St. Peter alludes were either among the teachers, or put themselves forward to teach; and there was a danger lest their authority should be recognised. They accepted Christ, but not as He loves to be accepted. He has called Himself Lord and Master, and has paid the price which makes Him so; but by their interpretations both of His nature and His office these men in very deed renounced and deserted His service, ignored their relation as His bondservants, and in this way denied the Master that bought them. Soon they chose other masters and became the slaves of the world and the flesh. Thus they entered on the path that leads to destruction, and soon it will come upon them. They who destroyed others shall themselves be destroyed. The lords whom they serve have all their empire in this life; and when the end thereof comes, it comes all too soon, and is a dread overthrow of everything they have set store by. On their lot the lamp of prophecy sheds its light: "How suddenly do they perish and come to a fearful end."

And many shall follow their lascivious doings; by reason of whom the way of the truth shall be evil spoken of. St. Jude, who had seen the results of such teaching, says these men turned the very grace of God into lasciviousness; they perverted the teachings of the Gospel concerning the freedom which is in Christ, and their phraseology they made to have a Pauline ring about it. Did he not teach how Christ had made men free? Had they not heard from him that men should cast off trust in the bondage of the Law? In this wise they taught a doctrine of lawless self-indulgence, which they extolled as the token of entire emancipation and of a loftier nature on which the taint of sins could leave no defilement. In the blindness of their hearts, self-chosen blindness, of which they boasted as knowledge, they gave themselves over to the flesh, to work all uncleanness with greediness.

St. Peter knows that baits of this sort appeal to the natural man; that there is within the citadel of the heart a traitorous weakness which is ready to betray it to the enemy. So, with prophetic foresight, he laments, Many shall follow after them. And such sinners do not sin unto themselves: their falling away brings calamity on the whole Church of Christ. It did so then; it does so still. The faithful cannot escape from the obloquy which is due to the faithless; and the world, which cares little for Christ, will readily point to the evil lives which it sees in the renegade brethren, and draw the conclusion that in secret the rest run to the same excess of riot. Evil-speaking of this kind became abundantly common in the first Christian centuries, and furnishes the object of many Christian apologies.

And in covetousness shall they with feigned words make merchandise of you. St. Paul in writing to Timothy gives a comment which throws much light on these words. He tells of men who consent not to sound words, even the words of our Lord Jesus Christ, thus denying the Master that bought them. He speaks of them as bereft of the truth, supposing that godliness is a way of gain; and he adds, "They that desire to be rich fall into a temptation and a snare, and many foolish and hurtful lusts, such as drown men in destruction and perdition. For the love of money is a root of all kinds of evil, which some reaching after have been led astray from the faith, and have pierced themselves through with many sorrows" (1 Tim. vi. 3-10). From the first days of the Church's history we see, from the instances of Ananias and Sapphira, and of Simon, with his offer of money to the Apostles, that both among the disciples and the would-be teachers covetousness made itself very apparent. The communistic basis on which the society was constituted lent itself to the schemes of those who desired to make a gain of their Christian profession. In the time when St. Peter wrote the evil had spread. Teachers were discovering that, by a modification or adaptation of the Christian language and doctrines, they could draw after them many followers. These were the feigned words to which the Apostle alludes, and the contributions of their satisfied hearers were proving a gainful merchandise. The Gnostic teachers were of various sorts, but of all alike the language was boastful as coming of superior insight; great, swelling words they spake, having men's persons in regard because of the prospects of advantage. The evil was a sore one, and is so wherever it finds entry. And later ages have also known somewhat of its mischief. It is the wisdom of all Christian communities so to order themselves that their teachers and guides may be safe from this temptation. For such teachers do not stop at small beginnings of error, but prophesy smooth things, and close their eyes at evil; nay, in this case they seem to have encouraged sensual living, as though it were an indication of the freedom of which they boasted.

Whose sentence now from of old lingereth not, and their destruction slumbereth not. In thought the Apostle reads the book of prophecy. It is as if he said, "It is written in the prophetic word." And when the overthrow of the sinners comes to pass, those who behold it may say, "Thus is the prophecy fulfilled." The doom of such sinners is sure. They may seem to live their lives with impunity for a while, as though God's eternal law were inoperative; but the issue is certain. None such escape. God's mills grind slowly, but they grind exceeding small. And the lot of such men is destruction. Of illustrations the Apostle chooses three, applying each to a different vice of these teachers of error. These men were proud; so were the angels that sinned, but their pride was only a prelude to their fall. These men were disobedient; so were the antediluvian sinners, and would neither hearken nor turn, and so the Flood came and swept them all away. These men were sensual; so were the dwellers in the Cities of the Plain, and their overthrow remains still a memorial of God's wrath against such sinners. Verily the sentence of all such men is written from of old.

For if God spared not angels when they sinned, but cast them down to hell, and committed them to pits of darkness, to be reserved unto judgement. To each of the three instances which St. Peter adduces the reader is left to supply the unmistakable conclusion, "Neither will He spare the sinners of to-day." The sentences are all the more solemn from their incompleteness. Some have thought that the reference in this verse is to the narrative found in Gen. vi. 3; but that account is very full of difficulties, and there is no mention of a judgement upon those who offended. It seems more sound exposition to take the Apostle's words as spoken of him concerning whom Christ has told us (John viii. 44) that he was a murderer from the beginning and stood not in the truth, and of the condemnation of whose pride St. Paul speaks to Timothy (1 Tim. iii. 6). For him and for his fellow-sinners the Gospel teaches us (Matt. xxv. 41) that eternal fire was prepared, and an apostle (James ii. 19) says that "the devils believe and shudder," it must be in apprehension of a coming judgement. All that St. Peter here says is implied in these Scriptural allusions to Satan and his fall; and it is more prudent to apply to them the highly figurative language of the Apostle here, which is exactly after his manner, than to seek for fanciful interpretations of the Mosaic story. We may rest assured by the way in which these things are spoken of, though but dimly, by Christ and His Apostles, that they formed a portion of Jewish religious teaching and constituted part of the faith of St. Peter and his contemporaries, though there is but little mention of the fallen angels in the Old Testament.

And spared not the ancient world, but preserved Noah with seven others, a preacher of righteousness, when He brought a flood upon the world of the ungodly. Here the Apostle points to a consolation for the converts amid their trials. The ungodly do not escape, be their multitude ever so great. A world full of sinners is involved in one common overthrow. Nor are the righteous forgotten, though their number be but few. The lamp of prophecy sheds much light here. Amid all God's dispensations toward Israel, His faithful ones were the remnant only; but these were saved by the grace of the Lord, they were brought out from the destruction, and not forsaken, and had a promise that they should take root downward and bear fruit upward. The words in which St. Peter describes the chief person of the few saved in the Deluge appear intended to point out that feature in Noah's history which most resembled the lot of the Asian Churches. They were now, as he was of old, God's heralds in the midst of a naughty world; and to bring to their minds the thought of his long-sustained opposition and mockery could hardly fail to nerve them to stand fast. What lot could be more desperate than the Patriarch's? For a hundred and twenty years by action and by word he published his message, and it fell on deaf ears; yet God was guarding him (ἐφύλαξεν) through it all, and words could not express more complete safety than when the early record tells us, ere the Flood came, "The Lord shut him in."

And turning the cities of Sodom and Gomorrah into ashes condemned them with an overthrow, having made them an example unto those that should live ungodly. These cities stood in a land fair enough to be likened to the garden of the Lord. To Lot himself their fertile fields had been a temptation, and by yielding thereto he brought on himself a plenitude of sorrow; and the sacred record counts his deliverance rather to the faith and righteousness of Abraham than to himself. God remembered Abraham, and brought Lot out of the overthrow. One of the fairest parts of His world God condemned for the wickedness of them that inhabited it. Nature was defaced for man's sin, and still lies desolate as a perpetual homily against such ungodly living as often comes of wealth and fulness of bread. After such a state were these false teachers seeking while they made their gain of their disciples; and in the later times of which St. Jude speaks, having fostered all that was carnal within and around them, in those things which they understood naturally, there they cast themselves away.

And delivered righteous Lot, sore distressed by the lascivious life of the wicked (for that righteous man dwelling among them, in seeing and hearing, vexed his righteous soul from day to day with their lawless deeds). The thrice-named righteousness of Lot is perhaps thus set down because of the struggle which it must have been to maintain the fear of Abraham's God among such sinful surroundings. Lot was in the land of the enemy, and his deliverance is pictured as a very rescue: he was saved, yet so as by fire. He had gone down into the plain with thoughts of a life of abundance, and it may be of ease, a contrast to the wandering life which he had hitherto shared with Abraham. Instead of this he found anguish and distress of mind, which no amount of temporal prosperity could alleviate; and to this would be added self-reproach. It was of his own choice that he was dwelling among them. The Apostle paints his misery in the strongest terms. He was distressed; and of the sights and sounds on every side, and never ceasing, he made a torture to his soul. It was no mere offence to him that these things were so: it was very anguish to see men setting at defiance every law human and Divine. To behold the evils of a lascivious life waxing rampant in the midst of the Christian Churches, and countenanced by those who assumed the office of teachers, must have been an agony to the faithful akin to that with which Lot tortured himself. St. Peter would strengthen the drooping hearts of the brethren; and no greater comfort could there be found than this which he offers, taking the lamp of prophecy and shedding its rays of hope into the dark places of their lives.

The Lord knoweth how to deliver the godly out of temptation. Already he has given the lesson (i. 6) that true godliness must have its root in patience. It is a perfect trust, which rests securely on the Father's love, and willingly waits His time. The hearts of the faithful ones must have found solace in the thought which he here joins to his former teaching. The trials they endure are grievous, but "The Lord knows" is an unfailing support. The floods of ungodliness make His servants many a time afraid; but when they feel that there, as amid the raging ocean, the Lord ruleth, they are not overwhelmed. They are protected by Omnipotence; and the tiny grains of sand, which check the fierce tide, are an emblem of how out of weakness He can ordain strength. Hence there comes a knowledge to the struggling saint which makes him full of courage, whatever trials threaten. The world has its wrathful Nebuchadnezzars, whose threats at times are as a fiery furnace; but he is proof against them all who can say and feel, "The Lord knows." I am not careful nor disturbed; my God, in whom I trust, is able to deliver me, and He will deliver me. The Lord knoweth the way of the godly, and His knowledge means safety and eternal deliverance.

And to keep the unrighteous under punishment unto the day of judgement. The unrighteous—yes, over them too God keeps ward. They cannot hide themselves from Him, and through their conscience He makes life a continuous chastisement. They may seem to men to walk on heedlessly, but they have hidden tortures of which their fellows can take no count. Even the offender against human laws, who dreads that his sin will be found out, carries in his bosom a constant scourge. Fear hath torment (κόλασιν ἔχει), and this it is of which the Apostle speaks. And if the dread of man's judgement can work terror, how much sorer must their alarm be who have the fiery indignation of the wrath of God in their thoughts and stinging their soul. Such men are kept all their life long under punishment. Yet in this constant anguish we trace God's mercy: He sends it that men may turn in time. His blows on the sinful heart are meant to be remedial; and those who disregard His chastisements to the last will go away, self-condemned, self-destroyed, despisers of Divine love, to a doom prepared, not for them, but for the devil and his angels.

XXIV
"BY THEIR FRUITS YE SHALL KNOW THEM"

"But chiefly them that walk after the flesh in the lust of defilement, and despise dominion. Daring, self-willed, they tremble not to rail at dignities: whereas angels, though greater in might and power, bring not a railing judgement against them before the Lord. But these, as creatures without reason, born mere animals to be taken and destroyed, railing in matters whereof they are ignorant, shall in their destroying surely be destroyed, suffering wrong as the hire of wrong-doing; *men* that count it pleasure to revel in the daytime, spots and blemishes, revelling in their lovefeasts while they feast with you; having eyes full of adultery, and that cannot cease from sin; enticing unsteadfast souls; having a heart exercised in covetousness; children of cursing; forsaking the right way, they went astray having followed the way of Balaam the *son* of Beor, who loved the hire of wrong-doing; but he was rebuked for his own transgression: a dumb ass spake with man's voice and stayed the madness of the prophet."—2 Peter ii. 10-16.

The Apostle now pictures in the darkest colours the evil-doing and evil character of those who are bringing into the Churches their "sects of perdition," those wolves in sheep's clothing who are mixing themselves, and are likely to make havoc, among the flock of Christ. He hopes that thus the brethren, being forewarned, will also be forearmed. And not only does he describe these bold offenders: he also reiterates in many forms the certainty of their evil fate. They aim at destroying others, and shall themselves meet destruction; their wrong-doing shall bring a recompense in kind upon their own heads. They are a curse among the people, but the curse will also fall on themselves; they are agents of ruin, and shall perish in the overthrow which they are devising.

But chiefly them that walk after the flesh in the lust of defilement, and despise dominion. These chiefly—that is, above other sinners—does God keep under punishment. It cannot be otherwise, for on them His chastisements have little effect. They have entered on a road from which return is rare, neither do they take hold on the paths of life; their whole bent is for that which defileth, not only defiling them, but spreading defilement on every side. They are renegades, too, from the service of Christ; and having cast off their allegiance to Him, they make their lust their law. The verse describes the same character in two aspects: those who walk after the flesh follow no prompting but appetite, have no lord but self.

Daring, self-willed, they tremble not to rail at dignities. The Apostle passes on to describe another and more terrible manifestation of the lawlessness of these false teachers. They have so sunk themselves in the grossness of material self-indulgence that they revile and set at nought the spiritual world and the powers that exist therein. In the term "dignities" the Apostle's thoughts are of the angels, against whom these sinners scruple not to utter their blasphemies. The good angels, the messengers from heaven to earth, the ministering spirits sent forth to minister to those who shall be heirs of salvation, they are bold to deny; while concerning the evil angels, to whose temptations they have surrendered themselves, they scoff, representing their lives as free and self-chosen, and at their own disposal. The two terms "daring," "self-willed," seem to point respectively to these two forms of blasphemy. They tremble not, they dare to deny the existence of the good, and they shrink not to mock at the influence of the powers of evil. Thus in mind and thought they are as debased as in their bodies, and by their lessons they corrupt as much as by their acts.

Whereas angels, though greater in might and power, bring not a railing judgement against them before the Lord. The explanation of this passage is not without difficulty, because of the indefiniteness of the words "against them." To whom is reference here made? It can hardly be questioned that by δόξαι, "dignities," literally "glories," in the previous verse the Apostle meant angels, the dignities of the spirit-world, in contradistinction to κυριότης, "dominion," in which he before referred to those earthly authorities whom these false teachers set at nought. The verbs used in the two clauses support this view. The dominion they venture to despise, at the dignities they rail, whereas they ought to be afraid of them. Now even to the fallen angels there attaches a dignity by reason of their first estate. In the New Testament the chief of them is called by Christ Himself the "prince of this world" (John xiv. 30), and by St. Paul "the prince of the power of the air" (Eph. ii. 2); and he has a sovereignty over those who shared his rebellion and his fall. Having described the railing of the false teachers in the previous verse as directed alike against the evil angels and the good, it seems preferable here to take "against them" as applying to the evil angels. Even against them, though they must be conscious of their sin and rebellion against God, the good angels, who still abide in the presence of the Lord, bring no railing judgement, utter no reproach or upbraiding.

There may have been in St. Peter's thought that solemn scene depicted in Zech. iii., where, in the presence of the angel of the Lord, that highest angel who is Jehovah's special representative, Joshua the high-priest appears, and at his right hand Satan standing to be his adversary, and to charge him, and the nation through him, with their remissness in the work of the restoration of God's temple. There the angel of the Lord, full of mercy, as Satan was full of hate, checked the adversary's accusation, saying, "The Lord rebuke thee, Satan." The same application of the words "against them" is suggested by the apocryphal illustration in St. Jude (ver. 9), where in the contention about the body of Moses no greater rebuke is administered to the devil by the archangel Michael.

This exposition does not remove all difficulty. For as the angels in the verse appear to be spoken of as superior in might and power to these corrupt teachers, it seems natural at first sight to refer to them the indefinite expression, and to explain that the angels, though they be so exalted, bring no railing judgement before God against these teachers and their evil doings. But from what Scripture tells us of the angels, it is not easy to understand how or why they should bring such a judgement. Nowhere is such an office assigned to, or exercised by, these spiritual beings, nor are we anywhere told that the observance of the deeds of the wicked is in their province. They rejoice over one sinner that repenteth; they stand in God's presence as the representatives of spotless innocence; they are sent forth by God as His messengers of judgement and of love; but we never find them as accusers of the wicked. That office Satan has taken for his own.

But the words which the Apostle uses seem hardly to make it necessary that the comparison should be between angels and these teachers of destruction. In the passage of Zechariah which we judge to have been in St. Peter's mind when he wrote, the angel is that mightiest spirit among the angelic host who is identified in the language of the prophet with Jehovah Himself; and the angel in St. Jude's illustration is the archangel Michael. Conceiving that by "angels" St. Peter intends these chief members of the celestial powers, the sentence may be taken to mean that the most glorious beings among the angelic throng, those who are greater in might and power than the "dignities" of whom he has spoken, bring no railing judgement even against the fallen angels, whereas these men presume to blaspheme beings of an order far above themselves. Such a conception of subordination in the spirit-world as is here suggested is not foreign to New Testament thought. St. Paul speaks of the angels in heaven as representing "principality, power, might, and dominion" (Eph. i. 21); and in the same Epistle the evil angels are mentioned in like terms: "the principalities, the powers, the world-rulers of this darkness" (vi. 12). Similar language is found also in Col. i. 16. Taking this view of St. Peter's meaning, the daring and presumption of these false teachers are set in a stronger contrast. Whereas the highest angels, those who stand first among the heavenly host and dwell in the immediate presence of the Lord, though they might accuse Satan and his angels of rebellion, yet refrain; these bold transgressors among the race of men cast forth their blasphemy against the whole spiritual world.

But these, as creatures without reason, born mere animals to be taken and destroyed, railing in matters whereof they are ignorant, shall in their destroying surely be destroyed. The glory of man in creation is his reason. It is bestowed that he may freely, and not by constraint, consent unto the will of God, and also may by it discipline the body and hinder it from becoming his master. For the soul tabernacling in the flesh there is ever this peril, and by it these false teachers in the Asian Churches had been ensnared. Thus they were degraded, and were frustrating the end for which the light of reason was given. They were become like the horse and mule, which have no understanding. When the serpent tempted Eve, he set before her his own elevation through the fruit which to her was forbidden.

"I of brute human, ye of human gods,"

was his tempting speech. These men had given themselves up for a less noble bribe. The bait of sensual indulgence was offered, and their acceptance of it had brought them down to the level of creatures without reason. Their conduct and their lessons merited such a comparison, and showed how their nobler part had been warped by excess. To blaspheme against the powers of the spirit-world is conduct which can only be paralleled by that of the senseless animals, which, with utter ignorance of consequences, will rush upon objects whose strength they know not, and perish in their blind onslaught. But the beasts were born to be taken and destroyed; no higher fate was in their power. Men were meant for a nobler end, and it is only when the rein is given to appetite that they become from human brutish in their knowledge, more brutish than to know. Thus in their ignorance they rail at all loftier thought, and of their railing make a show of knowledge. Here they are more noxious than the unreasoning brutes. Their blinding lessons gain a hearing; and those who listen are drawn on by the same lust, and willingly follow after ignorance. But the work of all carries condemnation with it. Man, whose gaze was meant ever to be upward, is bowed down to earth like the beasts of the field, which are meant only for capture and destruction. On such perversion God will surely visit. They shall reap the fruit of their bold self-will, and in the time of their visitation they shall perish.

Suffering wrong as the hire of wrong-doing. The Authorised Version translates a somewhat different text (κομιούμενοι), "and shall receive the reward of wrong-doing." This is the easier sentence, and connects itself well with what precedes; but it has not the strongest support. By the text which the Revised Version has adopted (ἀδικούμενοι) the Apostle does not mean that these sinners meet a punishment which they have not deserved, and in that sense suffer wrong; but that they are themselves brought under the penalties of the wrong into which they are leading others. As the Psalmist says, their wickedness comes down on their own pate, and in the net which they hid privily is their own foot taken. They differ from Balaam, whose example St. Peter is soon about to instance. These men secure the reward they seek, larger resources to squander on their lust; yet this, their success, as they would call it, proves their overthrow.

Men that count it pleasure to revel in the daytime. They that are drunken are drunken in the night, and the same holds ordinarily of other excesses. They come not to the light because their deeds are evil. But these men have cast aside all such timorousness. They find a zest in outrage and in going beyond others, so as to add the daytime to the night for their indulgences. The sense of "luxury that lasts but for a day," that is ephemeral, and perishes in the using, is hardly to be extracted from the Greek; but with St. James (v. 5) in mind, where the verb is connected with the noun of this verse, "Ye have lived delicately on the earth and taken your pleasure," it may perhaps be allowable, as some have done, to interpret ἐν ἡμέρᾳ as signifying "the time of this present life." The men live as though life were bestowed for no other object than their revelry.

Spots and blemishes. St. Peter must have had in his thought the epithets which he applied to Christ: "a lamb without blemish and without spot" (1 Peter i. 9). Utterly alien to the spirit and life of Jesus is these men's wantonness. They belong rather to him who is described as a roaring lion, walking about to find whom he may devour.

Revelling in their lovefeasts while they feast with you. Here also the Revised Version accepts a text different from that rendered by the Authorised, which for the first clause has "sporting themselves with their own deceivings" (ἀπάταις). This refers to "the feigned words" with which they have been pictured as making a gain of the unstable souls whom they lead astray. They find a sport in their delusion, a pleasure, which is devilish, in the evil they are working. The other reading, ἀγάπαις, which is also found in Jude 12, refers to those gatherings of the faithful in the earliest period of the Church's history where the brethren by partaking in common of a simple meal gave a symbol of Christian equality and love. It may be that this in its origin was the assembling of the congregation for "the breaking of bread," but we soon find the social meal had become a distinct observance. And we know from St. Paul's letter to the Church of Corinth that disorder was introduced into these meetings, and that luxury and disparity ofttimes took the place of simplicity and equality. "In your eating," says the Apostle, "each one taketh before other his own supper, and one is hungry, and another is drunken.... When ye come together tarry one for another" (1 Cor. xi. 21). In these Asian congregations the evil had gone to a greater length. Instead of a sober assembly, where friendly converse might form a fitting accompaniment to the more solemn breaking of bread in remembrance of their Lord, these lovefeasts were converted into a revel by the luxurious additions which the false teachers took care to have supplied. The Apostle calls them *their* lovefeasts, because it was from their conduct that the gathering took its character. The members of the Church were indeed invited, but these men made themselves leaders of the meal, and turned what was meant to be a simple repast into a scene of riot and indulgence. But such excess only opens the floodgates for more.

Having eyes full of adultery, and that cannot cease from sin. These preachers of freedom from the restraints of the Law must make their evil liberty known, and so they shamelessly parade it even in the meetings of the brethren. They cast about them their licentious glances, and their lustful gaze is unchecked. Nay, they have so given it rein that now it is beyond their control. Their eyes *cannot* cease from sin. The original speaks of "eyes full of an adulteress." By this unusual expression the Apostle seems to point to the danger that such conduct would meet with a response, that the sisters in the Church would be beguiled and led to join hands with these teachers of licence. With this we may compare the language addressed to the Church of Thyatira concerning "the woman Jezebel, which calleth herself a prophetess, and teacheth and seduceth My servants to commit fornication" (Rev. ii. 20).

Enticing unstedfast souls; having a heart exercised in covetousness; children of cursing. A very pestilence must such men have been to the Churches. For there are always many to be found who are not established in the truth, though it be present with them, men whom the bait of a promised freedom, with its assumption of superiority, will always catch. There is in it a witchery worse even than that which, in another direction, had once before led the Galatians astray. Satan himself offers the temptation, and finds allies within men's hearts to help his cause. It is only by those stedfast in the faith that he can be withstood (1 Peter v. 9). They look beyond to-day, and to a brighter, purer joy than any which he can offer. So they are safe. But, alas! in the Churches such men are often but the remnant, and the trade of the beguiler makes its gain in every age. And it was for material gain these men were laying themselves out; and, that they might be perfect in their craft, they had put themselves, as it were, to school, gone through a training. As was said of Israel in old time (Jer. xxii. 17), their eyes and their heart are but for their covetousness, greed of defilement, and greed of gain. Children of cursing are they in a double sense: they are a curse to those whom they lead astray; and in spite of the popularity which for a time they will seem to enjoy, there is no blessing upon them. Their doom is foretold from of old. The lamp of God's prophecy makes it clear that such men are the children of Cain.

Forsaking the right way, they went astray, having followed the way of Balaam the son of Beor, who loved the hire of wrong-doing. It is an aggravation of wrong-doing when those who know the good willingly choose the evil. Of such men there is little hope. To wander is their choice; and as wrong paths are many, and the right but one, they become wanderers to the end. That the closing of their eyes was in these teachers a self-chosen course we see from the example which St. Peter has chosen to illustrate their character. Balaam, however he gained his knowledge and however unworthy he was to possess it, certainly knew much of Jehovah, and had been used to keep alive the knowledge of God among the heathen round about him; but his heart was not whole with God. To be known as the prophet of the Lord was a reputation which he prized, but mainly, as it seems, for the credit it gave him among his fellows. When the chance came, he would fain endeavour to serve two masters. It has been for ever true, "Ye cannot serve God and mammon"; but Balaam resolved to try. He thought by importunity to prevail with God for so much liberty of speech as would gain Balak's silver and gold. When his intention was thwarted, and his mouth was filled with blessings instead of curses, he still hankered after Balak's honours and money, and wrought for Israel by his counsel the curse which his lips were hindered from uttering.

And these teachers of licence in the name of freedom moved among the Christian Churches as though they were true brethren. They used Christian phrases in their "feigned words," yet were ready to lead their followers in a way as dissolute as that which the son of Beor suggested to the Midianites (Num. xxxi. 16) that the children of Israel might trespass against the Lord. For these men's hearts were set on the hire of wrong-doing. Yet their offence was even fouler than Balaam's, for to their lust and covetousness they added hypocrisy.

But he was rebuked for his own transgression: a dumb ass spake with man's voice and stayed the madness of the prophet. The word which St. Peter here uses for "rebuke", and which is found nowhere else in the New Testament, implies a rebuke administered by argument, a refutation such as reasonable persons will yield to. The dumb ass (St. Peter's word is literally *beast of burden*) appealed to her conduct all her life through. Was I ever wont to do this unto thee? Should I do so now without good reason? The reason was made plain at the sight of the angel. That presence made the rider bow his head and fall on his face. But what excuse was there for his lawlessness? For that is the sense which the Apostle puts on Balaam's transgression. And the word which he adds makes the rebuke more strong. It was *his own* transgression. The swerving of the dumb beast was not of herself. She would have held to the right way had it been possible, but her master's lawlessness was very madness; and he was the prophet, she the speechless brute. It has been said, *Quem Deus vult perdere prius dementat.* But the proverb is not true. The destruction is not of God's will; the madness comes of a self-chosen course of rebellion. Ever God's voice is, as it was of old, "It is thy destruction, O Israel, that thou art against Me, against thy help" (Hos. xiii. 9). The ruin is self-destruction, an infatuation which will accept no remonstrance, brook no check. For the warning voice of the dumb beast only hindered Balaam's evil project for a brief moment; and though the Divine power which loosed the tongue of the ass kept her master's in check, the maddening greed for Balak's gold was in his heart, and at all costs would be satisfied, and led him to destruction. Such is the penalty of those who willingly desert the right way through love of the hire of wrong-doing. In forsaking God, they forsake the fountain of wisdom. Then their lawlessness degrades their human endowments to the level of the brutish, and the obedient drudging of the dumb beasts of burden speaks loud—for God gives it a tongue—against the mad errors of rebellious men.

XXV
ALTOGETHER BECOME ABOMINABLE

"These are springs without water, and mists driven by a storm; for whom the blackness of darkness hath been reserved. For, uttering great swelling *words* of vanity, they entice in the lusts of the flesh, by lasciviousness, those who are just escaping from them that live in error; promising them liberty, while they themselves are bondservants of corruption; for of whom a man is overcome, of the same is he also brought into bondage. For if, after they have escaped the defilements of the world through the knowledge of the Lord and Saviour Jesus Christ, they are again entangled therein and overcome, the last state is become worse with them than the first. For it were better for them not to have known the way of righteousness, than, after knowing it, to turn back from the holy commandment delivered unto them. It has happened unto them according to the true proverb, The dog turning to his own vomit again, and the sow that had washed to wallowing in the mire."—2 Peter ii. 17-22.

The Apostle now describes these traitors to the cause of Christ under another aspect. They proffer themselves as guides and teachers. As such they should be sources of refreshment and help. But in every respect they belie the character which they have assumed. *These are springs without water.* The blessing of a spring is only known to the full in Eastern lands. Hence it is that in Bible language wells and fountains are constantly used as emblematic of happiness. When Israel is brought out of Egypt, their destination is described as "a land of fountains." Mental and spiritual blessings are pictured by this figure: "The mouth of a righteous man is a well of life" (Prov. x. 11); "The wellspring of wisdom is a flowing brook" (Prov. xviii. 4). The invitation which the prophet publishes in God's name runs, "Ho, every one that thirsteth, come ye to the waters" (Isa. lv. 1); and the gracious promise is, "With joy shall ye draw water out of the wells of salvation" (Isa. xii. 3). To those who had been accustomed to language of this sort St. Peter's words convey a picture of utter disappointment. Where men had a right to expect that they would find brightness and refreshment, where they were promised an oasis in the world's desert, there proved to be only a delusive mirage; and for this the brethren were beguiled to forsake the living waters which Christ has promised to His faithful ones. *And mists driven by a storm.* Here the same thought is put into another shape. Mists, resting above the ground, play a part like that of the watersprings beneath. They protect from scorching heat, and drop down blessing on the thirsty land. But when they are chased away by the whirlwind, they can furnish neither protection nor nourishment. And so helpless for those who followed them were these apostles of licence. Like mists they were, it is true, but only in their blinding influence. They brought with them blasts of vain doctrine, in their craftiness, after the wiles of error, and so created a desolation for those who sought unto them. We cannot help comparing this description with the ever-increasing illumination that flows from the lamp of prophecy, making the world's dark places light.

For whom the blackness of darkness hath been reserved. Yes, for these also God has a destiny in store. It is reserved, as is the incorruptible inheritance (1 Peter i. 4) which awaits His faithful ones. But it is in those pits of darkness to which the rebellious angels were committed. Yet even in the Apostle's language there shines out somewhat of God's mercy. The sinner's doom is certain, but the blow has not yet fallen; the blackness of darkness is prepared, but was not prepared for men. Only those fall into it who persist in their rebellion. For them, in the words of Christ, it will be the outer darkness, where is the weeping and the gnashing of teeth.

For, uttering great swelling words of vanity, they entice in the lusts of the flesh, by lasciviousness, those who are just escaping from them that live in error. St. Peter's words are here very aptly chosen to contrast the boastful pretensions of these corrupters with the hollowness and delusion of all they promise. St. Jude (16) tells of the great swelling words, but does not add that further touch which proclaims their emptiness; St. Paul (1 Tim. i. 6) says that such men fall to their vain and boastful talking because they have swerved from purity of heart, from a good conscience, and from faith unfeigned. From such there is nothing to be expected but falseness and unreality; they arrogate to themselves a penetration which others have not. Theirs it is to have found a deeper meaning in revelation, to have worked their way to a freedom beyond the rest, a freedom in the midst of sin, which imparts to those who attain to it a freedom to sin with impunity. Thus do they entice in the lusts of the flesh by lasciviousness. Such a liberty suits the natural man; such guides find many to follow them.

True Christian freedom, the freedom of St. Paul, calls for constant watchfulness, earnest anxiety at every step, for life is full of treacherous roads. But forethought and carefulness are lacking for the most part in those who have just escaped from the entanglements of error. "I buffet my body," was the Apostle's rule, "and bring it into bondage" (1 Cor. ix. 27). This was the discipline to free the soul. And to others he preaches in his letter to Timothy that "the grace of God hath appeared, bringing salvation to all men" (2 Tim. ii. 11). But mark the pathway which leads to this life: "Instructing us to the intent that, denying ungodliness and worldly lusts, we should live soberly, righteously, and godly in this present world." Such precepts these men mocked at. There was a nobler knowledge, they said, a higher initiation. To this they had attained; to this they beguiled their followers.

Such men are unspeakably dangerous to those who have made but little progress in spiritual life. It is only those who, like Nehemiah of old, have become firm of purpose through prayer to the God of heaven, and know the dangers that everywhere beset them, that can withstand such temptation. As he laboured amid the ruins of Jerusalem, which he was so zealous to restore, there came to him the invitation of the Samaritans, "Come, let us meet together; ... let us take counsel together" (Neh. vi.). No doubt the village in the plain of Ono, to which they asked him to come, was a pleasanter place just then than the bare hill-top of Zion, with its desolation and ruins. But his heart misgave him at the words of such counsellors. "They thought to do me mischief." And his sturdy answer to the tempters is a pattern and a lesson for all time: "I am doing a great work, so that I cannot come down." For it is always to come *down* that such counsellors invite us, not to be afraid of putting ourselves on their level. They may cloke it under the name of elevation, as these Asian tempters did. They talk of this as liberty and power, just as the archfiend himself spake to the Saviour, tempting Him to a boastful display of His trust in His Father: "Cast Thyself down." Those who fall fall in this way, by a too ready yielding to some acceptable bait; and then they find themselves, not free, but prisoners. And the weak in the faith, those who are only just escaped from error, are those from among whom the deluders seek and find their victims.

Promising them liberty, while they themselves are bondservants of corruption; for of whom a man is overcome, of the same is he also brought into bondage. Here we have two views of the same persons. First their own picture. They proclaim their superiority in lofty terms. Satan and his servants have always been liberal with promises. "Ye shall be as gods, knowing good and evil," "All these things will I give Thee, if Thou wilt fall down and worship me," are sample speeches of the arch-tempter. And these men follow their master; but, says the Apostle, they are themselves in the grossest slavery. He personifies Destruction as a power who holds them in her chains. And the idea sets sin before us in a terrible light. It begins in the single act, over which men fancy they have entire control; but the acts become a habit, and this, like a mighty, living power within men, but beyond their sway, overmasters their whole being, and drives them at its will. In the case of these men, no faculty was free; their very eyes could not cease from sin.

For if, after they have escaped the defilements of the world through the knowledge of the Lord and Saviour Jesus Christ, they are again entangled therein and overcome, the last state is become worse with them than the first. Corruptio optimi pessima is a well-known and very true dictum, and the Apostle sets these false teachers before us as a notable illustration of it. The backsliders, the renegades who desert a good cause, are sure to exhibit intense hostility to the position from which they have fallen away. They are constrained to do so that men may think they have a warrant for their conduct; and often they have an uneasy conscience, which they must try to silence by large assertion of the rectitude and wisdom of what they do. Satan himself is the great instance. The state from which by rebellion he fell was unspeakably glorious, a life in the presence of perfect holiness. Now he takes his pleasure in marring everything that is holy, in defiling God's world and filling it with pollution through the sin which he has introduced.

These Asian backsliders had tasted the good grace of God. The Apostle speaks of their knowledge of Christ as that true comprehension of His love and mercy which draws men away from the world and its allurements. They had escaped and found a camp of refuge. But to take service under Christ means to bear the cross, and to bear it patiently. Jesus puts His servants to the proof, and not all who have set their hands to the plough continue stedfast in their work till the harvest comes. They halt in the process of that growth of grace which St. Peter describes in the first chapter of this letter. In their temperance they should provide patience, endurance in well-doing. Many, however, persevere but for a little time; and the world seizes the opportunity of their doubt and hesitation, comes forward with its allurements, and captures the weak in faith. And such were these men, and their capture was fatal. They were now in the toils of a net from which there was little chance of escape; they were overcome and made very slaves. In their first efforts to walk with Christ they had been enabled to wrest themselves away from their evil life; but now they were sunk down, overpowered, and blind, with a blindness the more terrible because they had known what it was to have sight. Their last state was unspeakably worse than the first.

St. Peter has in mind the parable of his Master (Matt. xii.; Luke xi.) which was spoken prophetically of the Jewish people. There Christ tells of the evil spirit which has been cast out, but no attempt made to fill his place with a better tenant. Soon finding no rest, he returns, and beholds his former home swept, and garnished, and unoccupied. Then he goes and takes seven other spirits more wicked than himself, who enter with him and dwell there. With what solemn meaning come those words which follow the parable, "Blessed are they that hear the word of God and *keep* it!" (Luke xi. 28). To have heard, and not to have kept, indeed makes the last state worse than the first.

For it were better for them not to have known the way of righteousness, than, after knowing it, to turn back from the holy commandment delivered unto them. These words of the Apostle point out the fear and care which should possess the hearts of those whom God blesses with large opportunities: fear lest they receive them amiss and fail to value them; care lest they pervert them to a wrong use. Our Lord's own words form the mightiest homily thereon when He spake to those cities of Galilee upon whom a great light was shining as He dwelt in their midst, but He could not do His mighty works there because of their unbelief. "He came unto His own, and His own received Him not." Hence the solemn denunciations of woe upon them: "It shall be more tolerable in the judgement for Tyre and Sidon, for Sodom and Gomorrah, than for them"; "The queen of the south shall rise up in the judgement against them and condemn." And more sorrowfully still He speaks to Jerusalem: "If thou hadst known in this thy day the things that belong unto thy peace, but now they are hid from thine eyes."

Christ went away unto the Father, but He left the Apostles their commission to teach the way of righteousness as He had taught it. "Teach them," He says, "to observe all things whatsoever I have told you; and lo, I am with you always." By the ministrations of St. Paul and his fellow-labourers the feet of these Asian converts had been set in the right way. They had made a profession of faith in Christ's sacrifice, and thus had been reckoned among the righteous, among those called to be saints. But the journey unto righteousness is made by daily steps in keeping God's law; and if these be not taken, the road may lie open, the traveller may see it, but he comes no nearer to the goal. Nay, in this road there is no standing still. They who fail to press forward inevitably slide back. It was here that these false teachers had failed. The command of God checked their evil appetites and greed; and so they set it at defiance and turned aside, and taught their deluded followers that God's freedom in its highest sense meant a licence to sin.

Here one of the Apostle's words is very significant. He says, not holy commandments, but holy commandment, telling us thus that the Divine law is all comprehended in the right ordering of the heart. In principle all God's laws are one. If that inward source of all our right and wrong be kept pure, from it are the issues of life; and every action flowing from it will then have a righteous aim. Thus men lead holy lives; thus they keep

God's commandments in every relation. They do not in this life become free from offence; they stumble, because they are compassed by infirmity. But they act from a right motive; and this, and not the sum-total of results, is what the loving Father of men regards. Thus the Divine law is the law of true freedom, supplying a principle, but leaving the particular actions to develop according to the circumstances of each man's life. This is the freedom of which the Psalmist sings: "I will walk at liberty, for I seek Thy precepts" (Psalm cxix. 45); and one of our own poets extols a life so ordered by Divine law as the truest, grandest freedom:—

> "Obedience is greater than freedom. What's free?
> The vexed straw on the wind, the tossed foam on the sea;
> The great ocean itself, as it rolls and it swells,
> In the bonds of a boundless obedience dwells."

It has happened unto them according to the true proverb, The dog turning to his own vomit again, and the sow that had washed to wallowing in the mire. To describe in all its horror the abysmal depth to which these false teachers have sunk, the Apostle makes use of two proverbs, one of which he adapts from the Old Testament (Prov. xxvi. 11), while the other is one which would impress the Jewish mind with a feeling of utter abomination. The dogs of the East are the pariahs of the animal world, while everything pertaining to swine was detestable in the eyes of the Israelite. But all the loathing which attached to these outcasts of the brute creation did not suffice to portray the defilement of these teachers of lies and their apostate lives. It needed those other grosser features—the return to the disgorged meal; the greed for filth, where a temporary cleansing serves, as it were, to give a relish for fresh wallowing these traits were needed ere the full vileness of those sinners could be expressed.

Solomon spake his proverb of the fool who goes back to his folly; but of how much grosser lapse is he guilty who, having known the mercy of Christ, having tasted the Father's grace, having been illumined by the Holy Spirit, turns again to the world and its pollutions, goes back into the far country, far away from God, and chooses again for his food the husks that the swine did eat!

XXVI
AS WERE THE DAYS OF NOAH

"This is now, beloved, the second epistle that I write unto
you; and in both of them I stir up your sincere mind by
putting you in remembrance; that ye should remember the
words which were spoken before by the holy prophets, and
the commandment of the Lord and Saviour through your
apostles; knowing this first, that in the last days mockers
shall come with mockery, walking after their own lusts, and
saying, Where is the promise of His coming? for, from the
day that the fathers fell asleep, all things continue as they
were from the beginning of the creation." —2 Peter iii. 1-4.

In the previous chapter the Apostle showed how the renegade false
teachers had published among the brethren their seductive doctrine,
declaring that God's fatherly discipline was something which they need
not undergo, that the trials which He sent them might be escaped, and
the natural bent of man's heart indulged as fully as they pleased. The foul
results of such lessons both to the flock and to the teachers he also depicted
in such wise as to render them abhorrent. Now he tells of a further lesson
which these guides on the downward road added to the former. Those who
do not accept God's judgements here soon go on to deny the coming of
judgement hereafter. It could hardly be otherwise. The wish is father to the
thought as truly in matters of faith as of practice. Men whose lives are all
centred on this world must try and convince themselves, if possible, that
the day of the Lord, of which God's word speaks so often, is a delusion, and
may be cast out of their thoughts. This these men did, and it is against this
scoffing of theirs that St. Peter directs his exhortation in this chapter.

This is now, beloved, the second epistle that I write unto you. Judging from
the adverb which he uses (ἤδη, now, already), we should conclude that no
long time had elapsed between the Apostle's first letter and the second.
And by calling this the second, he shows that it is intended for the same
congregations as the former, though he has not named them in the salutation
with which the letter opens. Aforetime they had been tried by inward
questionings, and he sent them his exhortation and testimony that, spite

of all their trials, this was the true grace of God which they had received, and therein they should stand fast (1 Peter v. 12). Now the danger is from without: false doctrine and evil living as its consequence. So, though he may have written but a little while ago, he will neither spare himself, nor neglect them. For the danger is of the utmost gravity. It threatens the overthrow of all true Christian life.

And in both of them I stir up your sincere mind by putting you in remembrance. Mark how trustfully he appeals to the sincerity of the minds of the brethren, just as before (i. 12) he said they knew the things of which he was putting them in remembrance, and were established in the truth which they had received. And what he means by the "mind" we may see from 1 Peter i. 13, where he uses the same word: "Gird up the loins of your mind"—do not indulge vain, lax, and speculative opinions, as though these would forward you in your travel through the world—"be sober, and set your hope perfectly on the grace that is to be brought unto you." A mind so braced looks onward to the revelation of Jesus Christ, looks for every token of its drawing nigh. And because it is sincere, the man dare look into its inmost recesses, and by self-examination and discipline maintain its purity. He can think soberly of the Lord's coming because he is preparing for it. But he whose mind is dark, within whom the light has been turned into darkness, dare not think on these things, but with all his might endeavours to forget, ignore, and deny them. All that St. Peter thinks needful for these Asian brethren is that he should remind them. He knows that men's minds are prone to slumber, especially about the things unseen as yet; and his aim is to rouse them to thorough vigilance. But he has no new lesson to give them.

That ye should remember the words which were spoken before by the holy prophets. On few themes do the prophets dwell more earnestly than on those visitations of Jehovah which they publish as the coming of the day of the Lord. With Joel (ii. 11, 32) it is to be a time great and terrible, the prospect of which is to move men to repentance, for whosoever shall call upon the name of the Lord shall be delivered. And Israel were taught in many ways that this great day was constantly at hand. They were pointed to it by Isaiah (xiii. 6) when the overthrow of Babylon was foretold. For that nation the day of the Lord was coming as destruction from the Almighty. Jeremiah (xlvi. 10) and Ezekiel (xxx. 3) preach the same lesson, with the ruin of Egypt for their text. It is a day of vengeance, when the Lord God of hosts will avenge Him of His adversaries, a day of clouds, in which a sword shall come upon Egypt, and her foundations shall be broken down. By what they beheld around them God's people were to learn that a like day would come upon them also, upon everything that was high and lifted up against God; and for those who were unprepared another prophet (Amos v. 18) declared that it would be darkness, and not light. Before its coming, therefore, they were urged (Zeph. ii. 3) to turn to the Lord, that they might be hid in the day of His anger. For God designed by it to make Himself King of all the earth (Zech. xiv. 9), wherefore it would be great and terrible. For though Elijah should first be sent (Mal. iv. 5) to turn the hearts of the fathers to their children and the hearts of the children to their fathers, in its manifestation that day should still be like a refiner's fire to purge the evil from among the good.

Not without solemn purpose were all these words written aforetime, and the Christian preachers who felt that God was faithful were sure that such a day would come upon all the earth. How it would be manifested was for God, and not for them. Some of those who lived when St. Peter wrote beheld part of its accomplishment in the overthrow of the Holy City. But they felt—and their lesson is one for all time—that it is presumptuous in men to compute God's days, and that it is rebellious blindness not to acknowledge the coming of His day continually in the great crises of history. How many a time since St. Peter spoke has the Lord proclaimed by partial judgements the certainty of that which shall come at the last. The day of the Lord is attested when empires fall, when hordes of barbarians break in upon the civilised world that has grown careless of God, when convulsions rage like those which preceded the Reformation and which shook Europe at the French Revolution, and we may add to these the troubles which harass our own land to-day. All these things preach the same doctrine; all proclaim that verily there is a God that judgeth the earth. Not yet is the voice of prophecy silent. Oh that men would but remember how long and how surely it has been speaking!

And the commandment of the Lord and Saviour through your apostles. In connexion with the subject on which he is writing, the commandment of Jesus to which St. Peter alludes can hardly be other than that which occurs in the address of our Lord to His disciples after His last visit to the Temple: "Watch therefore, for ye know not on what day your Lord cometh; ... therefore be ready, for in an hour that ye think not the Son of man cometh" (Matt. xxiv. 42). And with the last judgement in his thoughts, we cannot fail to be struck with the frequency with which the Apostle in this letter repeats as the title of Christ "the Lord and Saviour" (i. 11; ii. 20; iii. 2, 18). This precise form occurs in no other part of the New testament. And it seems from the Apostle's use of it as though, while speaking of the certainty of the coming of the day of the Lord, he desired to give special prominence to the thought that to such as were looking for Him He would manifest Himself as the Saviour and Redeemer.

The words "your apostles" also appear to be used with design. They contain a direct acknowledgment of the mission of St. Paul as an apostle. By him more than by any other had these regions been brought to the knowledge of Christ, and we may rest confident that the gospel which he preached elsewhere he preached to them also. The lesson of watchfulness is oft repeated in his letters. To the Corinthians he writes, "Watch ye; stand fast in the faith; quit you like men; be strong" (1 Cor. xvi. 13), while, in connexion with this subject of the day of the Lord, his words to the Thessalonians are, "Ye yourselves know perfectly that the day of the Lord so cometh as a thief in the night.... But ye are not in darkness, that that day should overtake you as a thief. Let us watch and be sober" (1 Thess. v. 2-6). St. Peter's letter was to be read in those Galatian Churches whose members in past days had doubted about the apostolate of St. Paul. Its warnings would sink the deeper because enforced by the authority of him who even in his rebukes had spoken to them as his "little children" (Gal. iv. 19).

Knowing this first, that in the last days mockers shall come with mockery. St. Peter says the mockers will come; Polycarp[14] says in his day they had come. He terms them the first-born of Satan, and tells how they pervert the oracles of the Lord to their own lusts and deny that there is either resurrection or judgement. The signs of the times were not difficult to read; and the Apostle would have the brethren know what to look for, know in such wise that they should not be shaken in mind by what they saw or heard. For this the first need was Christian sobriety. Thus settled, they could ponder on the words of ancient prophecy and recall the lessons of those who had spoken to them in the name of Christ; and therewith their hearts might take comfort, and their heads be lifted up with expectation, knowing the last days were bringing their redemption nearer. The mockery of the sinners would keep no bounds. This he expresses by his emphatic words, just as largeness of blessing is described: "In blessing I will bless thee."

Walking after their own lusts, and saying, Where is the promise of His coming? They would be a law unto themselves, and so they followed an evil law. As sinners before them had said, "Our lips are our own" (Psalm xii. 4), so these men by act and word alike proclaimed, "Our lives are our own, to use as we please. We have no account to give." Thus they made themselves bondslaves to the lust of the flesh, the lust of the eye, and the pride of life, and, with these fetters heavy about them, boasted of their liberty. They strengthened themselves in their evil way by jeering at the thought of Christ's return to judgement. "We have heard of the promise," they said, "but we see no signs of its fulfilment. The angels, you say, spake of His return when He was taken away from you. Let Him make speed and hasten His coming, that we may see it. You are for ever speaking of it as sure and pointing us back to the ancient Scriptures, as though they were a warrant for what you preach. 'Where is the word of the Lord? Let it come now'" (Jer. xvii. 15).

For, from the day that the fathers fell asleep, all things continue as they were from the beginning of the creation. Here the mockers pass from the promise of Christ's return, and fall back upon the more distant records as supplying a stronger argument. "The fathers" of whom they speak cannot be the Christian preachers. Not many of them could as yet have fallen asleep in death. But the ancient prophets of the Jewish Scriptures had long ago passed away, and against them the scorners direct their shafts. "Centuries ago," they urge, "the prophetic record was closed; and its final utterance was of the day of the Lord, which has not yet come." Their word, "fell asleep" may have also been used as part of their mockery, classing the words of prophecy among baseless dreams. It may be they intended a special allusion to that one among the prophets who dates the time of the Lord's coming. Daniel (xii. 12) speaks of a waiting which shall last a thousand three hundred and five-and-thirty days. But say these scorners, "When his word was complete, he was bidden, 'Go thou thy way till the end be. For thou shalt rest, and shalt stand in thy lot at the end of the days.' He has fallen asleep, and the other fathers also. They all are at rest, and the end of the days is no nearer. The world stands fast, and will stand. It has seen no change since it was brought into existence."

Those who in faith clung to Christ could not fail, as they heard these scorners, to think of the Master's question, "When the Son of man cometh, shall He find faith in the earth?" (Luke xviii. 8), and of those other words of His which told them that the last days should be a parallel to the days of the Deluge: "As were the days of Noah, so shall be the coming of the Son of man. For as in those days which were before the flood they were eating and drinking, marrying and giving in marriage, until the day that Noah entered into the ark, and they knew not until the flood came and took them all away, so shall be the coming of the Son of man" (Matt. xxiv. 37-39). The strong earth was under the feet of those antediluvian mockers, the firmament above their heads. So in ignorance they jeered at what they would call the folly of Noah. But the Flood came, and then they knew. Yet the last days have seen, and will see, men as blind and as full of satire and scoffing as they.

XXVII
JUDGEMENT TO COME

"For this they wilfully forget, that there were heavens from
of old, and an earth compacted out of water and amidst
water, by the word of God; by which means the world that
then was, being overflowed with water, perished: but the
heavens that now are, and the earth, by the same word have
been stored up for fire, being reserved against the day of
judgement and destruction of ungodly men."—2 Peter iii.
5-7.

"The world lasts on" (διαμένει) "through all times," say the scoffers,
"just as it was at the Creation. There has been no change; there will be
none." But out of their own mouth their folly is rebuked. How can these
men speak of a creation? If there is to be no Judge, why believe that there
has been a Creator? That must be included in the general denial. *For this
they wilfully forget.* Yes, here is the reason of their conduct, the root of all the
evil. They forget because they wish to forget; they speak of the fathers, but
of set purpose ignore the history of Noah; they are casting God out of all
their thoughts: and so even to the things that are made, and by which He
testifies to all men alike His eternal power and Godhead, they close their
eyes, and refuse to read His wide-open lesson-book. And still less do they
regard all that His written word records of the world's past history and
God's discipline for men therein.

*That there were heavens from of old, and an earth compacted out of water
and amidst water, by the word of God.* They close their ears as well as their
eyes. "In the beginning God created the heavens and the earth." As the
study of nature progresses men are learning to comprehend more of the
vastness of that phrase "in the beginning," and in the light of science to
read a larger meaning into St. Peter's words, "There were heavens from
of old." But even in that generation to which the Apostle soon alludes the
unchanging character of the skies spake of duration and permanence. The
antediluvian world had run a long course; from Adam to Noah men had
beheld the sun rise and set daily in the skies, just as it rose on the morning of
the Deluge. And the mockers then living could say, and doubtless did say,

to the preacher in their midst, "These things have always been as they are, and will be so for evermore." The later scorners had their prototypes of old, who pointed to the existence of an eternal law, and wilfully forgot that law implies a lawgiver, and that He who made must have the power to unmake.

St. Peter takes their text, but reads from it a very different lesson. There were heavens from of old, yea, long before there was an earth fit for man to dwell in. This world in that old time was formless and void, and the waters covered its face like a garment. The word of the Lord went forth, and the waters were gathered together as a heap, and the depth was laid up in God's storehouses. Then the dry land appeared; then there was an earth. The streams took their appointed place down the mountain-sides and in the valleys, and rivers began to roll onward to the sea; the waters of ocean learnt their bounds, neither turned again to cover the earth. The Divine word clothed in all the glory of vegetation the hitherto barren land, making it a fit home for man, who was not yet; and the water ministered sustenance to everything that grew out of the ground. Birds, beasts, and fishes were made, and the waters were the birthplace of most of these. For God said, "Let the water bring forth abundantly the moving creature that hath life," not its own tenants only, but fowl that may fly above the earth in the open firmament of heaven. So there was an earth, not the bare ground only, but the whole wealth of vegetable and animal life; and this was all existent, compacted, supported out of water and by means of water (δι' ὕδατος). For without it nothing could have flourished. God had laid up water above the firmament and water below the earth, and by means of watery vapour refreshed and blessed everything that grew. This was the reign of God's law, and ere the Flood came men could point to it and say, "What mean you to talk of a deluge? The sand is made the bound of the sea by a perpetual decree, that it cannot pass it; the earth is set high above the waters, and has been so from old time." But that long duration did not hinder the same productive, nurturing water being turned, by the word of the Lord, into an agency of destruction.

By which means the world that then was, being overflowed with water, perished. Every word in the Apostle's sentence is meant to tell. God employed as means of overthrow the very powers which at first He ordained for blessing. His word makes things what they are. The reign of law endures until He, who is before all law and the source of all law, gives another direction to those forces which His law has always been controlling. In this way the world that then was, the world which had endured and been stedfast from the Creation to the Flood, perished. The world was full of order, full of glory. The name (κόσμος) expresses all this. Yet, for the sin of man, it repented God that He had made this glorious order; and this it was which perished. The earth was not destroyed; it only received again that covering of primeval waters which, at God's word, had retired and let the dry land appear. At the same word both earth and heaven combined to destroy the goodliness with which creation was adorned. For, on the day of the Deluge (Gen. vii. 11), all the fountains of the great deep were broken up, and the windows of heaven were opened, and the waters came again to cover the earth. They prevailed exceedingly, and all flesh died that moved upon the earth; even the fowls and the moving creatures, which had been brought forth from the teeming waters, perished, and all things were destroyed from off the earth. Thus does St. Peter lay bare the unwisdom of those who will not listen to, who are wilfully forgetful of, the parables of God's word, who close their eyes to His judgements, sent that by them men may learn righteousness.

But the heavens that now are, and the earth, by the same word have been stored up for fire. The Apostle now turns away from what the Old Testament Scriptures relate as history of the past to what the same records teach us concerning the future; and he deals partly with promise, partly with prophecy. The earth will not be destroyed again by a deluge. God hath made His covenant: "I will establish My covenant with you, neither shall all flesh be cut off any more by the waters of a flood, neither shall there any more be a flood to destroy the earth" (Gen. ix. 11). But there will be a judgement; and then not, as in the days of Noah, will the κόσμος, the beautiful order of nature, alone be destroyed, but heaven and earth alike shall be involved in the common overthrow. Here the Apostle is but the expositor of the words of psalmists and prophets of the older times. He who sang, "Of old Thou hast laid the foundation of the earth, and the heavens are the work of Thy hands," was inspired to add, "They shall perish, but Thou shalt endure; yea, all of them shall wax old like a garment: as a vesture shalt Thou change them, and they shall be changed" (Psalm cii. 25). Isaiah, the evangelist among the prophets, saw more, and connects this mighty change with the day of the Lord's vengeance: "Then shall all the host of heaven be dissolved, and the heavens shall be rolled together as a scroll" (Isa. xxxiv. 4); and in another place he foresees how "the heavens shall vanish away like smoke, and the earth shall wax old like a garment, and they that dwell therein shall die in like manner, ... for Mine arms shall judge the people" (Isa. li. 6); and yet again in more solemn wise, "The Lord will come with fire, and with His chariots like a whirlwind, to render His anger with fury and His rebuke with names of fire, for by fire and by His sword will the Lord plead with all flesh" (Isa. lxvi. 15). And this he proclaims as the preparation for "the new heavens and the new earth which He will make." Daniel also tells us of God's "throne of judgement to be set, which is like the fiery flame, and His wheels as burning fire" (Dan. vii. 9).

With such light from the lamp of prophecy, the Apostle in his exegesis proclaims the nature of the final judgement. Like other New Testament writers, he has attained, since the day of Pentecost, a deeper insight and a firmer grasp of the purport of what Moses in the Law and the prophets did write. We can see how on that very day thoughts like these which he expresses in his letter were borne in upon his mind. For not only does he apply the prophecy of Joel to the events which then struck the multitude with wonder, but he carries on the lesson further to the coming of the great and notable day of the Lord, and reminds his hearers that then God "will show wonders in heaven above and signs in the earth beneath, blood and fire and vapour of smoke, when the sun shall be turned into darkness, and the moon into blood" (Acts ii. 19). And the like illumination had been bestowed on St. Paul. For he too tells (1 Cor. iii. 13) of a day when each man's work shall be proved by fire; and more definitely he assures the Thessalonians, to whom he wrote much concerning the day of the Lord, that there will come a "revelation of the Lord Jesus from heaven with the angels of His power in flaming fire, rendering vengeance to them that know not God, and to them that obey not the gospel of our Lord Jesus Christ" (2 Thess. i. 8).

In such wise did the Apostles read the utterances of prophecy; and thus did they apply them as lessons for their own and all future times. They felt that not unto themselves, but unto us, did the prophets minister. And St. Peter does but put their message into his own words when in his bold figure he says that the heavens that now are and the earth are stored up for fire.

The Revised Version on its margin renders the last words "stored with fire." And when we reflect on the storing of the waters at the Creation, afterwards to be let forth to destroy the world which hitherto they had made fruitful and lovely, the parallelism is very suggestive. God has stored the earth within with fire, which from time to time makes its mighty presence and power for destruction known. The visitations of earthquakes may therefore well remind us that He who used the treasures of waters in the Deluge for His ministers may in like manner hereafter employ this treasury of fire.

Being reserved against the day of judgement and destruction of ungodly men. When God no longer waits for sinners to repent, then will come the judgement and destruction of the ungodly. At that day the heavens that now are and the earth shall be exchanged or transformed. God will prepare a new heaven and a new earth wherein the righteous may find a congenial home with their Lord. Here they can never be other than pilgrims and sojourners, seeking to be clothed upon with their house which is from heaven. What the destruction of the ungodly shall be we can only judge and speak of in the terms of Scripture. The language of St. Paul to the Thessalonians seems to teach us that the very advent of the Judge shall bring their penalty: "They shall suffer punishment, even eternal destruction" (the word is not the same which St. Peter uses) "from the face of the Lord and from the glory of His might" (2 Thess. i. 9), in the presence of which nothing that is defiled can dwell. So God, of His mercy, still reserves the heavens and the earth, and thus to every new generation offers His mercy, saying continually through their silent witness, in the spirit in which He spake to Israel at the close of the volume of prophecy, "I am Jehovah" — that is, the merciful and gracious, long-suffering and abundant in goodness and truth, keeping mercy for thousands, forgiving iniquity, transgression, and sin—"I change not; therefore ye sinners are not destroyed."

XXVIII
THE LORD IS NOT SLACK

"But forget not this one thing, beloved, that one day is
with the Lord as a thousand years, and a thousand years as
one day. The Lord is not slack concerning His promise, as
some count slackness; but is long-suffering to youward, not
wishing that any should perish, but that all should come to
repentance." —2 Peter iii. 8, 9.

"All things continue as they were from the from the beginning of the
creation," said the mockers. It was foolish therefore to believe in, or to think
of, a judgement to come. In the words before us the Apostle not only supplies
an answer to the scorners, but gives a precious lesson to Christians for all
time on the nature of God and His government of the world. It is but a single
thought, but when the mind of the believer has grasped its significance, he
will look out upon the world untroubled. No mockery will disturb his faith.

*But forget not this one thing, beloved, that one day is with the Lord as a
thousand years, and a thousand years as one day.* Here the Apostle quotes some
words from that psalm (xc.) which is entitled "A Prayer of Moses, the Man
of God." In it the Psalmist is contrasting God's eternity with the frailty of
man and the shortness of human life. "A thousand years in Thy sight are
but as yesterday when it is past." But St. Peter not only adopts, but adapts,
the words for his own purpose. He wants to teach the Christians in their
trials that, while what is long in man's estimation may in God's providence
be counted but little, yet through God's decree what to man appears little
may be big with mightiest consequences. He therefore first inverts the
words of the Psalmist. One day is with the Lord as a thousand years, while
a thousand years may be as one day. One day of His deluge swept a whole
generation out of the world, while His day of Pentecost remains potent in
the history of His grace for all the ages which are yet to come. Through
a mistaken literalness, men have sometimes expounded the lesson as if
Jehovah's dealings were a question of arithmetic. Nothing could be farther
from the Apostle's thought, who would have us know that of great and little
God's work makes no account. With Him there is no short or long in time.
What He does is not to be measured by the petty standards of humanity.

Men *must* take note of time, for they feel its lapse and its loss. They are ever conscious that a period is coming after which what is undone must continue undone. Again, the length of time is known to them by the recurrence of the various acts of life, and by the weariness which comes of continued labour, and by the grief of protracted waiting. These things force them to speak of short and long, but with God it is not so. For Him all time is one. He knows nothing of toil. Whatsoever He pleaseth, that doeth He in heaven and in earth, in the sea and in all deep places (Psalm cxxxv. 6). The Psalmist had attained a true conception. The whole world and all worlds were in His control, and their order the working of His eternal will. He needs no rest; He slumbereth not, nor sleepeth. To Him there is no waiting, no weariness. Hence the past, the present, and the future are for Him one unbroken now.

This is the one thing which the Apostle offers to the Christian brethren for their support and consolation against the scoffers. And the knowledge is mighty for those who grasp it. It helps them to cast themselves securely upon the almighty arms, convinced that God's working is not to be estimated according to man's days and years, but is certain in its effect. One generation passeth away, and another cometh; but death, they learn, does not take men out of the knowledge or the hand of God, be it for mercy they are reserved, or for judgement. God does not defer His action because He lacks power to perform, neither does He tarry because He is unmindful of His servants or insensible to what they endure.

Such thoughts can minister to the faithful abundant consolation, and this was the desire of the Apostle. But they raise for all time large questions which can find no answer here, questions concerning the lot of those who pass from this brief day of life into the eternal world and have not known God's will, that they might do it; questions concerning a discipline which may yet be reserved for some who have not bent themselves to it here, perhaps from want of light; questions of how far hope may extend itself beyond the veil which divides this world from the next. Such questions rise within many earnest souls, often rather for the sake of others than themselves; but God has vouchsafed us no answer, lest men should wax presumptuous.

The Lord is not slack concerning His promise, as some count slackness. Many things conspire to make the doings of men to tarry. At one time pledges are given beyond what foresight would warrant; and when the day of performance arrives, they are forced to plead that events have falsified their expectation, and they cannot do the things that they would. Again, men, with the most earnest zeal, attempt a work beyond their powers, and of necessity have to delay the fulfilment of their promises; while some are taken away untimely from the midst of their fellows, ere life has enabled them to achieve what they counted on once as certain. Want of knowledge, of time, and of power is the heritage of the sons of men; and therewith conspires not seldom a change of mind and consequent want of will. But He with whom is no variableness, the omnipotent, omniscient, eternal Lord of all, is subject to no hindrance. Whether events appear to men to linger or to be sudden, all move under the control of the same unchanging will. He is not slack, as men are slack, either to rescue the righteous or to punish the ungodly. Of this the son of Sirach spake: "The Lord will not be slack, neither will the Almighty be patient, ... till He have taken away the multitude of the proud and broken the sceptre of the unrighteous, ... till He have judged the cause of His people and made them to rejoice in His mercy" (Ecclus. xxxv. 18).

Here is a medicine for fainting souls, of whom there must have been many among these Asian Christians. And it is a solace furnished, too, by the teachings of prophecy. "The vision," says one, "is yet for an appointed time" (Hab. iii. 3). God's will has ordered when and how it shall be accomplished; all moves by His decree. "At the end it shall speak, and not lie." There is no disappointment to those who wait upon the purposes of God. "Though it tarry, wait for it," even though the waiting may last beyond this life, "because it will surely come; it will not tarry. The just shall live by his faith."

The order of the words in the original (ὁ κύριος τῆς ἐπαγγελίας) and the unwonted construction of the verb, of which no other example is forthcoming, have suggested to some to render thus: "The Lord of the promise is not slack." Even so the words give a powerful sense. God, who makes the promise to men, is supreme over all on which its faithfulness depends, supreme both as Maker and Fulfiller of His word. He sees and controls the end from the beginning. Blessed are all they that put their trust in Him.

But is long-suffering to youward. The Authorised Version heads "to usward". And some have thought it more in accord with the Apostle's manner and humility to include himself with the brethren. The other reading is better supported, and none will doubt on that account St. Peter's sense of God's long-suffering towards himself. The term which he here employs to describe the Divine character implies the holding back of wrath. God might justly punish, but He stays His blow. Men have sinned, and still sin; but His love prevails above His anger. The word is formed by the LXX. translators to render one expression in that passage (Exod. xxxiv. 6) where God proclaims unto Moses the attributes by which He would be known unto men. Through all the list mercy is the dominant feature. Term upon term seems devised to magnify the tenderness of Jehovah towards His people, though at last, if the continual offers of mercy are despised, He "will by no means clear the guilty." No other language furnishes such a word, for no other people had such a knowledge of the God of all grace.

Not wishing that any should perish, but that all should come to repentance. We are wont to connect statements like this with the gracious messages of the New Testament. Yet some saints of earlier time felt all that St. Peter here teaches. The writer of Ecclesiasticus has some striking words. He is connecting God's mercy with the shortness of man's life, and his language anticipates in the main this teaching of the Apostle: "The number of a man's days at the most are a hundred years. As a drop of water unto the sea, so are a thousand years to the days of eternity. Therefore is God patient with them, and poureth forth His mercy upon them. The mercy of man is toward his neighbour, but the mercy of God is upon all flesh; He reproveth, and nurtureth, and teacheth, and bringeth again as a shepherd his flock" (Ecclus. xviii. 9-14). In such wise had some who waited for the consolation of Israel grasped God's promises by anticipation, seeing them afar off and being persuaded of them. Such men owned themselves, equally with the Apostle, to be strangers and pilgrims, and sought for that inheritance which Christ sent him to preach.

The word "wishing" (βουλόμενος) implies deliberate consent. This God does not give to the death of any sinner. If any perish, it is not because God so desired or designed. But some will ask, "Why, then, should any perish?" St. Peter in this sentence, full of grace, supplies the answer. They continue in sin, and repent not. Even offers of mercy are of no avail. But why does not the Almighty Father drive them to repentance by His judgements? Because He has made His children free, and asks from them a willing service. They are to *come* to repentance. The invitation is full and free. Christ says, "Come unto Me, all ye that labour." Nay, God makes at times a less demand: "Look unto Me and be ye saved, all ye ends of the earth." Could words breathe more of mercy? To come, to look—that is the sole demand. God bestows all besides. Let men but manifest a desire, and His grace is poured forth. He wisheth not that any should perish.

And Christ, too, when He speaks of the gifts of the Holy Spirit, has the same lesson. The Father, the Son, and the Holy Ghost all conspire to further the work of man's salvation. "All things," said our Lord, "whatsoever the Father hath, are Mine. Therefore said I, He shall take of Mine, and shall show" (R.V. declare) "it unto you." But the eye to see what He shows, the ear to hear His declarations—these He asks from men. He willeth that they should *come* to repentance, and through that gate should come to Him.

XXIX
"WHAT MANNER OF PERSONS OUGHT YE TO BE?"

"But the day of the Lord will come as a thief; in the which the heavens shall pass away with a great noise, and the elements shall be dissolved with fervent heat, and the earth and the works that are therein shall be burned up. Seeing that these things are thus all to be dissolved, what manner of persons ought ye to be in *all* holy living and godliness, looking for and earnestly desiring the coming of the day of God, by reason of which the heavens being on fire shall be dissolved, and the elements shall melt with fervent heat? But, according to His promise, we look for new heavens and a new earth, wherein dwelleth righteousness." — 2 Peter iii. 10-13.

The Apostle, ever earnest to put the brethren in mind of the things they had heard or read, never fails to follow his own precept. His thoughts perpetually go back to the words of Jesus, of which the passage before us is but one example out of many. "If the master of the house had known in what hour the thief was coming, he would have watched" (Luke xii. 39). So spake Christ to the disciples when urging them to be like unto servants that look for the coming of their lord. To the Master's parable St. Peter now gives its application: *But the day of the Lord will come as a thief.* He means first to mark the unexpected advent, which steals upon men when they least think of it. Sinners will have lulled themselves into security, and the thought farthest from their minds will be the all-important preparation. St. Paul uses the same figure in speaking of the same subject (1 Thess. v. 2), from which passage the words "in the night" have found their way into the text of St. Peter, to which, as the Revised Version indicates, they do not belong. And in the Epistle to the Hebrews the Apostle has defined the preparation which, joined with patience, should keep men in readiness for the certain advent: "Exhorting one another, and so much the more as ye see the day approaching" (Heb. x. 25).

St. Peter passes on to tell of the terrors which shall attend on that day. Here also he has in mind the words of his Master, who, after a prophecy of the destruction of Jerusalem, spake of that greater coming of the Son of man of which the overthrow of the Holy City was to be but a partial type: "There shall be signs in sun and moon and stars, and upon the earth distress of nations, in perplexity for the roaring of the sea and the billows, men fainting for fear and for expectation of the things that are coming on the world, for the powers of the heavens shall be shaken" (Luke xxi. 25; Matt. xxiv. 29). With the Lord's language for his warrant, he paints, largely in the words of the prophets of old, the things which shall befall the world in that great and notable day: *In the which the heavens shall pass away with a great noise, and the elements shall be dissolved with fervent heat, and the earth and the works that are therein shall be burned up.* Isaiah had used like words of old: "All the host of heaven shall be dissolved, and the heavens shall be rolled together as a scroll" (Isa. xxxiv. 4); and in another place he speaks (xxiv. 19) of the earth as utterly broken, clean dissolved, moved exceedingly; Micah has to proclaim the coming of the Lord, and he pictures it thus: "The mountains shall be molten under Him, and the valleys shall be cleft as wax before the fire" (Micah i. 4); and Nahum, describing the day of the Lord which he foresaw was coming upon Nineveh, says, "The mountains quake at Him, and the hills melt; and the earth is upheaved at His presence, yea the world and all that dwell therein." It is St. Peter's, by the light of the words of Jesus, to read their full purport into these prophetic messages, and to teach those upon whom the ends of the ages are come that all these things will have their consummation in that coming of the Lord which shall be the close of these latter days.

When thus considered his description contains many striking details. "The heavens will pass away." Christ Himself had so spoken, not of heaven only, but of the earth also. His word was the same which Peter employs, but He used it in the same sentence thus: "My word will not pass away" (Matt. xxiv. 35). That is the one thing to which we may trust. All else will be destroyed or changed. Only those who are in Christ will be fit for the new order. For them old things are passed away; behold, they are become new (2 Cor. v. 17). They have been purified by the fire of the Holy Spirit, and so can abide the day of Christ's coming.

To describe the dread process he has a striking word, which, like so many of the Apostle's expressions, is used nowhere else in the New Testament: "With a great noise" (ῥοιζηδόν). It is applied to many sounds of terror: to the hurtling of weapons as they fly through the air; to the sound of a lash as it is brought down for the blow; to the rushing of waters; to the hissing of serpents. He has chosen it as if by it he would unite many horrors in one.

Then the thought of nature's dissolution. All that was bound together at the Creation, and then received a law of cohesion which sustained it thenceforth, will be cast loose, the compacted world dissolved. These things have been thought of as emblems of stability. God hath made the round world so fast that it cannot be moved (Psalm civ. 5), but He who made can also unmake. How foolish then must they be who bound their thoughts and aims by what the world can give, making themselves thereby of the earth, earthy, and so sure to fail when that is destroyed. And what are those works that are in the earth of which the Apostle speaks? Do the words mean no more than "the world and all that therein is," a phrase so common in Scripture? At first sight it appears so. But some most ancient manuscripts, instead of "shall be burned up," read "shall be discovered." Of this the Revised Version takes note on its margin. From this reading the mind goes to the words of the Preacher, "God shall bring every work into judgement, with every hidden thing, whether it be good or whether it be evil" (Eccles. xii. 14). The sense is thus bound closer with the coming of the day of the Lord.

Seeing that these things are thus all to be dissolved, what manner of persons ought ye to be in all holy living and godliness? The Apostle says more than "are to be dissolved." His word signifies "are being dissolved." The event is so sure, and the interests involved so weighty, that he speaks of it as present, that thus he may more forcibly urge his lesson of preparation. "What manner of persons ought ye to be?" Christ had supplied the answer, and so St. Peter gives none: "Let your loins be girded about, and your lamps burning, and ye yourselves like unto men looking for their lord" (Luke xii. 25). The figures imply readiness for any service, most of all, to an Eastern mind, readiness to set forth on a journey. Such should ever be the attitude of those who are but sojourners and pilgrims. And by his words the Apostle intimates how this preparedness should enter into every relation of the Christian life. The translation says, "in *all* holy living and godliness"; but in the Greek there is no word for *all*. Literally the words are "in holy conversations and godlinesses." In English we could not use words thus. Hence the device of the translators to come as near to the sense as is possible. But if we carry with us the thought contained in these plural words, we see how St. Peter teaches by them that in our daily life and work as well as in our religious exercises we should be ever watchful, ever ready. Our life with men and with God should be stamped as "Holiness unto the Lord." By such a walk we shall keep ourselves apart from sinners, and be helped thus far to keep away from sin. And the godliness of which he speaks springs, as he has already taught (i. 6) in this Epistle, from a patient waiting on the Lord. Thus the whole attitude of the Christian becomes one of wakeful readiness. He is of those of whom it is said, "Blessed are those servants whom their lord when he cometh shall find watching."

Looking for and earnestly desiring the coming of the day of God, by reason of which the heavens being on fire shall be dissolved, and the elements shall melt with fervent heat. The question of the mockers, "Where is the promise of His coming?" will not disturb those whose lives are thus made ready. That coming fills their every thought, moulds every desire, controls and chastens every action. For not only do they look for it: they long for it, and earnestly desire it. For to be with Christ is far better. Hence they hear of the melting elements and the fires of heaven without alarm. With them it is as with the Hebrew children in the days of Nebuchadnezzar. The fires which others dread, and by reason of which the heavens dissolve and the elements melt, will have no power over them save to loose their bonds, to free them from the burden of the flesh, to further that change from the natural to the spiritual which St. Paul teaches we must all undergo; while with them there will be the Son of God. And thus they will attain to their desire, and become partakers of the Divine nature.

But the translation "earnestly desiring" by no means exhausts the significance and solemnity of St. Peter's word. The Authorised Version rendered it "hasting unto the coming of the day of God"; but the word "unto" is not in the Greek, though the verb means "hastening." The word is found in the LXX. of Isa. xvi. 5, where the Authorised Version translates the Hebrew by "hasting righteousness" and the Revised by "swift to do righteousness." But though a king, as in that passage, may be said to hasten righteousness by being swift to do it, is there any sense in which men could be said to hasten the coming of the day of God? It seems as though Christ intended to set such an aim before His servants. Before He was crucified He spake that prophetic promise, "I, if I be lifted up, will draw all men unto Me." When He had been lifted up on the cross and as a testimony to His Godhead, lifted up from the grave, He gave His commission to the Apostles: "Go ye therefore and make disciples of all the nations.... Lo, I am with you alway, even unto the end of the world." He promised His Spirit also to be their Guide into all truth.

Thus were they sent to be heralds of and labourers for his kingdom; and one of them has testified to the abundance of the aid bestowed: "I can do all things through Christ that giveth me power." But he who thus spake could say to his converts, "Be ye imitators of me, even as I also am of Christ" (1 Cor. xi. 1). In this way men can lift up Christ; in this way can they draw men to Him. And to do this by examples of holy living and godliness is the work which He has committed to His Church, to let the light of Christian lives shine before men in such wise that they may be won for Him. And when we see His kingdom's slow advance, St. Peter's question is turned into a reproach, "What manner of men ought ye to be?"

But, according to His promise, we look for new heavens and a new earth, wherein dwelleth righteousness. All creation was marred at the Fall. It groaneth and travaileth until now in pain along with the sons of men. It was made subject unto vanity, but that was by reason of God, who made it thus subject in hope that it shall be delivered, along with man, from the bondage of corruption. And that victory was promised from the first. The seed of the woman shall not always be the spoil of the serpent. The world was in many ways kept alive to this thought. A race was promised from whom all nations should be blessed. God established a kingdom to represent His rule in the world, and at length Isaiah was inspired to tell of new heavens and a new earth (Isa. lxv. 17). He too foresaw that this was for a reign of righteousness, that it pointed to a time when the wickedness of the wicked had come to an end: "The sun shall be no more thy light by day, neither the moon by night; for the Lord shall be thy everlasting light, and as for thy people, they shall all be righteous." And Christ while on earth endorsed the prophetic word: "I go to prepare a place for you. I will come again and receive you unto Myself, that where I am, there shall My servant be."

Hence St. Peter says, "According to His promise we look forward." And by using the same he identifies the new heavens and the new earth with the coming of the day of God. The believer heeds no more the mockers who ask, "Where is the promise of His coming?" He can look and lift up his head, assured that his redemption draweth nigh. For his expectation has been fostered through a life of holy conversation and godliness, and the assurance of the day of God is firm, for the kingdom of God is set up within him.

And the consolation of the promise consists largely in the thought that in the new creation righteousness will dwell, will make its home. First, there will be Christ the righteous, who is also our righteousness; and all the hindrances and stumbling-blocks of this life will be removed. Here the sojourners and pilgrims abide for the time amid many foes and countless perils; then they will be delivered even from their own frailties. As their home is new-created, so they shall become new creatures. So their thought, their prayer, their struggle, is ever, *Sursum corda*; and day by day they are bound less to earth and realise more of heaven.

> "The distant landscape draws not nigh
>
> For all our gazing, but the soul
>
> That upward looks may still descry
>
> Nearer each day the brightening goal."

XXX
"BE YE STEDFAST, UNMOVABLE."

"Wherefore, beloved, seeing that ye look for these things, give diligence that ye may be found in peace, without spot and blameless in His sight. And account that the long-suffering of our Lord is salvation; even as our beloved brother Paul also, according to the wisdom given to him, wrote unto you; as also in all *his* epistles, speaking in them of these things; wherein are some things hard to be understood, which the ignorant and unstedfast wrest, as *they do* also the other Scriptures, unto their own destruction. Ye therefore, beloved, knowing *these things* beforehand, beware lest, being carried away with the error of the wicked, ye fall from your own stedfastness. But grow in the grace and knowledge of our Lord and Saviour Jesus Christ. To Him *be* the glory both now and for ever. Amen." —2 Peter iii. 14-18.

In these solemn closing words the Apostle sums up his exhortations and warnings. His admonition is of a twofold character. First, he urges the brethren to strive after stedfastness, but to beware of sinking into a careless security which may make them an easy prey to false guides. "Stand fast," he would say, "and be ever watchful against falling." Then, let your Christian life be one of steady, constant, temperate progress; let it imitate God's works in nature, which wax, man sees not how or when, by drawing constantly from the hidden sources which minister life and increase. Let believers seek thus that in their lives there may grow from God's seed of faith first the blade, then the ear, then the full corn in the ear, to yield some thirty, some sixty, some a hundredfold, to the praise and glory of the Lord of the harvest.

Wherefore, beloved, seeing that ye look for these things, give diligence that ye may be found in peace, without spot and blameless in His sight. The whole passage runs over with Christian affection; a very working out it is in a believer's life of Christ's teaching, "By this shall all men know that ye are My disciples, if ye love one another." Love to the brethren, love to his fellow-apostle, breathes in every line of these final sentences. Beloved are the Churches, beloved his fellow-labourer. And he is never weary of repeating that word "looking for," which marks the true attitude of the Christian pilgrim: Seeing that ye look for the coming of the day of God. Before he had said, We look for it; now he brings the lesson nearer home to every one of them: Ye are looking for these things. Be ye therefore ready. Give diligence that ye may be found in peace by Christ when He appears.

Peace is the bond which clasps together the brotherhood of Christ. But things which need a bond are prone to break asunder, and St. Paul marks the care which is needed in this matter by using the same word (σπουδάζοντες) which St. Peter employs here. And his list of the virtues which make for peace shows how much anxiety is needed: "With all lowliness and meekness, with long-suffering forbearing one another in love, *giving diligence* to keep the unity of the Spirit in the bond of peace" (Eph. iv. 2). Such are the graces to be fostered by those who look for the Lord's coming. The Hebrew knew no nobler word to use for blessing than "Peace be with you." Christ at His parting says to His disciples, "My peace I leave with you; My peace I give unto you." It embraces reconciliation with God and union with the brethren; it is a treasure worthy of all striving for, and when attained it passeth all understanding.

They who are looking for Christ will strive to become like Him. Christ came down from heaven and assumed humanity that His brethren might take courage for this lofty aim. The Apostle (1 Peter i. 19) has spoken of Him as a lamb without spot and blemish, and this ideal purity he now sets before the brethren. For he knows that to strive after it will sunder them from the corruptions of those false teachers whom he has called "spots and blemishes" (ii. 13) in the Christian society. Instead of denying the Master that bought them, they will be hearkening constantly for His voice. Thus will they become clean through the word which He speaks unto them (John xv. 3). For His voice is ever helpful; and abiding in Him, they will bring forth much fruit.

And account that the long-suffering of our Lord is salvation. The mockers had made the delay of God's day the subject of their scoffing. "It tarries," said they, "because it is never coming." Their speech was, in fact, a challenge: "If it is to come, let it come now." The Christian is of another mind. His heart is full of thankfulness for the mercy which allows time for that diligence which his preparation demands. St. Paul expresses this feeling concerning God's dealings with himself: "For this cause I obtained mercy, that in me as chief might Jesus Christ show forth all His long-suffering, for an example of them which should hereafter believe on Him unto eternal life" (1 Tim. i. 16). And the opportunity thus granted him that Apostle used to the full; yet ever mindful was he not only from whom was the mercy, but also from whom came the power which was with him in his diligence: "I laboured more abundantly than they all, yet not I, but the grace of God which was with me." And in another place (Phil. i. 22), though he longs to be released from life and to be with Christ, he recognises that there may be a Divine purpose in delaying *that* day of God also, that to live in the flesh may be the fruit of his labour; and if this be so, he is content.

For the believer thinks not only of his own salvation and his own opportunities. The Christian's faith is not selfish. He beholds how large a part of the world is not yet subject unto Christ, and owns in the delay of the day of the Lord a wealth of abundant grace, offering salvation still to all who will accept it.

Even as our beloved brother Paul also, according to the wisdom given to him, wrote unto you. Some, who have restricted the allusion of St. Peter here to the "long-suffering" of God, have thought that the Epistle to the Romans is intended. That letter is the only one in which St. Paul speaks generally on this subject. In ii. 4 he asks, "Despisest thou the riches of God's goodness, and forbearance, and long-suffering, not knowing that the goodness of God leadeth thee to repentance?" and, again, asks another question: "What if God, willing to show His wrath and to make His power known, endured with much long-suffering vessels of wrath fitted unto destruction, and that He might make known the riches of His glory upon vessels of mercy?" (ix. 22). Others, considering the great subject of the day of God to be specially present to St. Peter's mind, have found parallels in the two epistles to the Thessalonians. It has also been pointed out that Silvanus was with St. Paul when these letters were written, and that through him (1 Peter v. 12) their import might have been brought to the knowledge of the Asiatic congregations. But we know too little of the intercommunication of the Churches of Europe and Asia to arrive at a conclusion, while the definite statement "wrote unto you" seems certainly to refer to some letter addressed to the Churches of Asia. Among these, beside the Galatians, were the Ephesians and the Colossians. Reference has already been made to the way in which St. Paul speaks in his first epistle to Timothy of the long-suffering of God towards himself. Would the letter to the bishop of Ephesus be held too personal for its contents in some form to be imparted to the whole Church? Then in the Ephesian epistle such a passage as ii. 4-7 may well have been in St. Peter's thoughts: "God, being rich in mercy, ... quickened us together with Christ, ... that in the ages to come He might show the exceeding riches of His grace in kindness towards us in Jesus Christ," or Col. i. 19, 20: "It was the good pleasure of the Father that in Him should all the fulness dwell, and through Him to reconcile all things unto Himself, having made peace through the blood of His cross." But there is no reason from St. Peter's words to assume that he is referring to an extant epistle. He may have known of a letter to the brethren in Asia of which we have no trace. Of one thing we may be sure: that his words had a definite sense for those to whom they were written.

But his reference to St. Paul has much interest for other reasons. Among these brethren there would be current many memories of the great Apostle to whose labour the formation of these Churches was chiefly due. His name would for them add weight to St. Peter's admonitions. The mention of the wisdom Divinely given to him would remind the Galatians at least how foolish had been their doubts and waverings in bygone days. While, as they knew how one apostle had withstood the other when he saw that he was to be blamed, such words as these from St. Peter would come with double force. Most of all, while the teachers of error were perverting St. Paul's language for an occasion to the flesh, it was good that the Churches should be reminded that he ever taught men to strive after lives without spot and blemish and had given no licence to the excesses for which his words were offered as a warrant.

As also in all his epistles, speaking in them of these things. From this it appears that it is the whole drift of St. Peter's letter, its warnings as well as its counsels, which is in harmony with the words of St. Paul. But we need not assume that St. Peter's readers were acquainted with all the fellow-Apostle's writings. He is telling them what his own experience has proved.

Wherein are some things hard to be understood, which the ignorant and unstedfast wrest, as they do also the other Scriptures, unto their own destruction. This passage is noteworthy as the only place in the New Testament in which the writings of the Apostles are regarded as ranking with the Scriptures of the old covenant. Everywhere else "Scripture" means the Old Testament. Yet, as the Apostles were passing away, it must have begun to be felt that a time was coming when great authority would attach to their words, as of persons who had seen the Lord. St. Peter has just spoken of the wisdom which was given to St. Paul. That wisdom came from the same source as the illumination of the prophets; and it is not unnatural, after such an allusion, that his writings should be classed with those of old time. Both were subjected to the same treatment. So perversely had the Old Testament been read that when He came of whom it spake—came to those who held the volume in their hands, and who regarded it with much show of reverence—He was not recognised. His people had blinded their eyes. Just so was it faring with that "freedom" of which St. Paul had said so much to the Galatian Church. Wrested from its true meaning, it was put forward as if it gave warranty and encouragement for the life of the libertine.

That many things in the writings of St. Paul are difficult to comprehend is beyond question. He more than any of the New Testament writers works out the principles of Christ's teaching in their consequences. He deals most fully with the great questions which circle round the doctrine of redemption; with election and justification; with the casting off of God's ancient people and the certainty of their restoration; with the objects of faith, the things hoped for, but as yet unseen; with the resurrection of the body and the changes which shall pass upon it; and with the nature of the life to come. He of all men realised to the full the length, and breadth, and depth, and height of the love of God, and spake in his letters of much which passeth knowledge.

But in St. Peter's word (δυσνόητα) "hard to be understood" there appears to be the thought that men's difficulties arise in part because they look on these subjects as studies for the intellect (νοῦς) alone, and fail for this reason to attain to the best knowledge which is given to man. It is of God's order that for the lessons which come from Him He also imparts the power of true discernment. Those who approach the study of Christian truth as a cold intellectual exercise, in the comprehension of which heart and soul bear no part, will go away empty, and as dark almost as they come.

The "wresting" of which St. Peter here speaks may come either of the misuse of single terms, just as the apostles of licence put a wrong sense, for their own ends, on St. Paul's "liberty," or it may be the effect of severing a lesson from its occasion and its context. Such perversion also happened to St. Paul's doctrine. To those who, like the Galatians, had been drawn back to an undue estimate of the legal ordinances of Judaism, the Apostle, as a corrective, had exalted faith far above outward observances; and there soon arose those who under his language sheltered themselves in a dissolute Antinomianism. The same befell in later days when Agricola and the Solifidians perverted Luther's teaching of justification by faith. And when such misleading guides find hearers who are "ignorant and unstedfast," the false lessons, which always have the frailties of humanity to back them, gain many adherents. To the thoughtless such teaching is seductive, and is unsuspected because it puts on a semblance of affinity with truth. Hence grow those ruptures of the Christian body, those heresies which lead to destruction (ii. 1).

Ye therefore, beloved, knowing these things beforehand, beware lest, being carried away with the error of the wicked, ye fall from your own stedfastness. In the first chapter the Apostle has already (ver. 12) addressed the converts as those who knew the things of which he wrote and needed only to be put in mind, who were established in the truth, and not to be classed with the ignorant and unstedfast. Yet for all there is need of watchfulness. The lies which are abroad clothe themselves in the garb of truth, wresting the Scriptures. "Therefore," says he, "guard yourselves" (φυλάσσεσθε). The word is not only a notice against dangers from without, but an admonition to watchfulness within. The wandering of the lawless may beguile; to many it has attractions. But if they join that company and follow with them, the end will be a shipwreck of the whole Christian life. The verb (ἐκπίπτειν) is that which we find (Acts xxvii. 26, 29) in the description of the wreck at Melita, when the sailors feared lest they should be cast ashore on rocky ground. It is against a moral peril of even more terrible character that St. Peter warns the Churches; and the contrast is most instructive which is pictured in the two words by which he defines error and stedfastness. The former (πλάνη) betokens a ceaseless wandering, a life without a plan, a voyage without rudder or compass, every stage made in doubt, uncertainty, and peril; the other word (στηρυγμὸς) tells of firmness, fixity, and strength, and comes fitly into the exhortation of that Apostle whose charge was, "When thou art converted, strengthen" (στήριξον) "thy brethren" (Luke xxii. 32). "This stedfastness," he says, "is now your own" (ἰδίου); "barter it not away for any illusions of wayward error."

But grow in the grace and knowledge of our Lord and Saviour Jesus Christ. As if to attest his own stedfastness; he ends as he had begun. "Grace unto you and peace be multiplied," was the opening greeting of his first letter, to which in his second he adds, "through the knowledge of God and of Jesus our Lord." But there is great significance in the way in which St. Peter's words hang together in this verse. The structure of the sentence shows that he intends to say not only that grace is the gift of Jesus Christ, but that from Him comes also all knowledge that is worthy of the name, a lesson most fitting and most necessary in those days, when teachers, who claimed to be possessors of a special higher knowledge, were denying Jesus altogether both as Master and as Judge. "Root yourselves in Christ," is the apostolic charge; "seek His help; walk by His light. Thus only can your power increase; thus only can your way be safe."

To Him be the glory both now and for ever. Amen. This is the end of the Apostles labour: that Christ may be glorified in His servants; that they may know Him here as the Way, the Truth, and the Life, hereafter as the High-priest of His people, but deigning to become the First-born among many brethren. For those who find Him here and there also eternity will be too short to show forth all His praise.

FOOTNOTES:

[1] 2 Cor. i. 3, xi. 31; Eph. i. 3, with which may be compared Rom. xvi. 6.

[2] The better reading, looking back to the ἡμᾶς of ver. 3, appears to be εἰς ἡμᾶς, and it is well supported.

[3] Ἐι δέον ἐστί—if need be, as need there is.

[4] παρακύψαι is the word employed to describe the stooping of the disciples and Mary that they might look into the grave of Jesus (Luke xxiv. 12; John xx. 5, 11).

[5] This would appeal with force to the hearts of those who were of the dispersion. Therein they would behold a picture of what all earthly life is as compared with the home to come.

[6] Hermas, Mand. ii. 2.

[7] Παρὰ θεῷ ἐκλεκτόν speaks of Christ in His glory, in that place where the reward of the faithful is kept in store. Cf. the words of Matt. vi. 1.

[8] For illustration of what is here said, Matt. xxi. 16 may be compared with Psalm viii. 2, Acts xv. 15-17 with Amos ix. 11, 12, and Eph. iv. 8 with Psalm lxviii. 18; and the list might be largely increased.

[9] Hence the New Testament writers quote from the LXX. in a very large proportion. The writer of the Epistle to the Hebrews quotes nothing else.

[10] The LXX. translators use the word θέλωθέλω very frequently to translate such expressions as "to delight in," "to have pleasure in." Cf. Deut. xxi. 14; 1 Sam. xviii. 22; 1 Kings x. 9.

[11] It marks the time of this change of opinion that in the first form of the English Articles (the forty-two of 1553) the text 1 Peter iii. 19 was given as evidence for the descent into hell in Article III., but in the later form (the thirty-nine of 1563) the allusion to St. Peter's words was omitted. No doubt the divines of that time wished to do away with all that might be used to countenance the doctrine of purgatory.

[12] *Apol.* i. 65.

[13] *Ep. ad Magn. 8.*

[14] *Ad Phil.* vii.